Bruce W Munro

Groans And Grins of One Who Survived

Bruce W Munro

Groans And Grins of One Who Survived

ISBN/EAN: 9783744725071

Printed in Europe, USA, Canada, Australia, Japan

Cover: Foto ©ninafisch / pixelio.de

More available books at **www.hansebooks.com**

Groans and Grins

OF

ONE WHO SURVIVED.

BY

BRUCE MUNRO.

TORONTO:
PUBLISHED BY WARWICK & SONS.
1889.

THIS VOLUME IS NOT
RESPECTFULLY DEDICATED TO
ANY POTENTATE, DOMESTIC OR FOREIGN,
NOR TO ANY COLD, CYNICAL, AND UNSYMPATHETIC
AUTHOR, DICTATOR, OR REVIEWER,
NOR YET TO THE SHADE OF ANY IMMORTAL.
BRIEFLY,
IT IS NOT DEDICATED AT ALL.

PREFACE.

I MIGHT begin with a hackneyed phrase, or with a highly original one. I shall do neither, but shall simply try to be brief and pointed. Preface-writing is a fine art, anyway, in which one naturally wishes to show off his talents to the best advantage and startle the reader into the belief that he has picked up the work of a genius ; while the aim of the desultory sketches, etc., of this volume is rather to catch the reader *en deshabille*, figuratively speaking, when he is in a humor to lay aside the stereotyped conventionalities of the pains-taking author, and enjoy a frolic with some whimsical characters who often break the rules of etiquette and throw grammar to the bow-wows. Not that these sketches were all written at odd times, in an easy, indifferent, off-hand way, when laid up with the quinsy or thawing out frozen anatomy on a cold day, and not minded to lose any golden minutes. By no means ; they were written deliberately and soberly, when I should often have been reading the newspapers ; and as the printer will bear witness (if he isn't already a victim to softening of the brain), the MS. is scarred with frequent and annoying erasures.

A little more regard for future reputation and a little less queasy compunction about destroying the wishy-washy effusions of boyhood would no doubt have prompted the cutting out of the bulk of the book—including this so-called preface. But while the great majority of us lay claim to having common sense, few of us can judiciously exercise it ; and it is a question, after all, whether any one but a weather-prophet could determine just how much of the book was originally written before my wisdom teeth were cut, and how much after the dentist pried them out as superfluous. I shall be quite satisfied if the results be these : First, if the verdict of the general reader be that the stories are amusing in spots, and that the writer must certainly have his lucid intervals. Second, if any boy, on the perusal of this compilation (it is worthy of no better name), be led into the way of writing alleged funny things, and thus developing the latent humor there is in every masculine personality.

But it is so easy to ask impossibilities. For instance, it would be pleasant to have this volume judged by some of its cat and dog stories; whereas the unkind reader will be just peevish enough to prejudge it by the twaddle on the fifteenth page.

An inquisitive young lady of sixty well-preserved years (I generally respect age, and do so, even in this case, because it is hypothetical) asked what had been survived, or whether the title of the book were a misnomer. I gravely suggested ship-wreck, the Inquisition, and worse evils, but seeing her incredulous smile, truthfully said that I had once entertained the idea of calling it "A Maiden's Inheritance; or, A Hero to the Rescue; or, The Witch's Curse; or, Buried 'Neath the Blasted Pine." This would have been a good all-round title, that would admirably fill the bill and serve in lieu of a frontispiece; but consideration for the reader caused me to forbear. Besides, it would not be fair to delude any guileless youth into the belief that he had got hold of an interesting dime novel. The question, however, is so easily answered that it is not expedient to argue it further; and the truth is, it has not been survived; it is liable at any time to checkmate me.

While in a former volume I was continually prodding the reader under the fifth rib with an alpenstock to keep him from falling asleep, in this the reader is left severely alone, or but guardedly taken into my confidence. It is regretable, though, that some of the best things buried in these GROANS AND GRINS are apparently meaningless passages and obscure allusions to individuals and incidents. These, of course, I do not condescend to clear up; in fact, the ethics of novel-writing would forbid it, even were I so disposed.

It may be added that this preface is really an impromptu effort, written without premeditation or malice aforethought. Let it go at that. The chances are that the indifferent reader will never look at it, anyway. I have written prefaces before, and ought to know what I am talking about.

BRUCE MUNRO.

CONTENTS.

	PAGE.
PROEM	1
My First Proposal	3
Groans of the First Frenzy Period	15
To Margarita	16
The Month of May	17
Some Village Characters	19
Our Visit to the Country	25
How I Loved and Lost My Nelly	31
How I Loved and Lost My Janet	37
Hart Gilbert Palmer	43
To My Old Dog, Nero	58
An Meine Verlorene Liebste	60
The Scarce and Bitter Fruit of the Summer of 1884	60
The Canadian Climate	61
Lottie	64
Hard Luck	87
The Railwayman's Trials	91
An Experienced Traveler	98
The Folder Fiend	102
A Severe Test	109
The Long-Suffering Tramp	112
Rejected	115
The Hardships of a Brave Man's Life	117
How the Hatchet Came to be Buried	131
Verse for the Twenty-ninth of May	143
What Augustus Wrote in Lucy's Album	143
Sing Me a Song of the Old Days	144
Give Back to Me My Diamond Rings	145
Her Majesty's Customs	146
A Disillusioned Innocent	152
The Little Lone House	155
Such is Life	168

	PAGE.
How a Coolness arose between Bill and Nero	169
A Quiet Evening at Home	178
Discouraging a Journalist:	
I. As a Mute, Inglorious Milton	186
II. As an Unfledged Humorist	196
To Mignonne	203
Hiram's Oath	205
Vain Triumph	246
The Young Violinist	250
Mammon	261
Time, the Healer	261
Things Begin to Get Interesting	262
Signs of Spring	270
Our New Girl	272
A Missing Testimonial	281
Another Valued Testimonial	285
An Interview with the Prophets	289
To the First Organ-Grinder of the Season	292
Judith's Dilemma	294
City Life *vs.* Country Life	313
Could I But Know!	325
Lucy and the Fortune-Teller	327
How He Quit Smoking	337
"C'est pour Toujours, Nelly"	341
Her Story and His Story	342
Nancy Ann's Elopement	350
A Trip to Washington	363

PROEM.

As in dreams the old delusions,
The old faces, the fond mem'ries,
Are revived, and the old heart-break,
That in sleep is oft rebellious,
With o'ermastering vehemence,
Bursts the mighty Past's locked portals—

MY FIRST PROPOSAL.

A MOST UNSATISFACTORY LOVE-STORY.

I FELL desperately in love with Mary Blakely. I was young, only nineteen, and she was younger, only sixteen. She was beautiful,—at least, my passion for her told me she was,—amiable, sprightly, and altogether bewitching. Further, she was poor, and so was I.

Oh, how I loved that girl! I could set my mind on nothing, accomplish nothing, for thinking of her. I seemed to know intuitively when she was coming, and on going to the window would see her pass; but she seemed to be near me always.

I resolved that she should be my wife; I resolved further to become a great man. To that end, I would write a wonderful love-story, which should be the admiration of the rest of the nineteenth and the whole of the twentieth, twenty-first, twenty-second, and twenty-third centuries. By that time my wonderful love-story would have become a hoary antiquity, like Shakspeare's dramas; and, as in the case of Shakspeare, there would then be grave, fussy, and spectacled littérateurs to comment on my Mary, my book, and me.

I wrote slowly, laboriously, and solemnly; and as my story grew and grew, I loved Mary more and more. Of course she was the heroine, and of course I took care to make this so plain that she could not fail to recognize herself. How pleased she would be, how honored she would feel, to find herself some day the heroine of the most popular novel of the decade; and when the world-renowned writer of this novel should ask her to be his wife, how quickly would a brilliant wedding ensue!

Did she love me? As I loved her, she must love me. On such an argument I laid the foundations of my air-castle. I seldom saw her, except to say "good-day," and I could not determine to a certainty whether I had won her entire love or not. But I trusted I had; I tried hard to persuade myself I had. At all events, as soon as my book should be published, the road to her heart would be open. And with this I must be content till the day of my triumph should come.

One day I could not forbear telling her about my book adding that I meant to send it to Boston for publication. I hadn't the courage to tell her that she was the heroine of the book, but I hinted at it darkly by saying I thought she would like to read it, because there were certain persons in it that she would know.

I often had cause to be furiously jealous—at least, I fancied I had cause. Didn't she go to school, and didn't every boy in school fall in love with her? Of course they did—how could they help it? Most of the boys were a year or so younger than she, it is true; but what of that? Didn't women marry men younger than themselves 365 days out of the year? And besides, was not the head master—though as ugly as a schoolboy's caricature of the rascal who "tells on" him—an unmarried man? Again, did she not get a letter every week or so? The address on these letters was written in a hand decidedly feminine; but what of that? That was a mere ruse between Mary and some mustached lover. (I, alas! had met with nothing but disappointment in my endeavors to cultivate a mustache.) In fact, it seemed to me that everybody was in love with her, and that she was in love with everybody. And yet, she was to be my wife!

One day, the brightest day in my calendar, she said to me, "Haven't you been well lately, Weston? I haven't seen you for nearly a week."

From that time I began to rebuild my air-castle on a better foundation. It is to be remarked, also, that although she received a letter that very day in the feminine handwriting, I refused to believe in the existence of a mustached lover.

But I am wandering from my starting-point. I did not often see my Mary, but when I did she always said "good-day" very courteously, and always accepted the apples I gave her. I have said that I was poor. I had no money to buy little trinkets and knick-knacks for her—I had not money even to buy her caramels. But my brain was pretty active at that period, and writing my wonderful book kept my ingenuity always in play. (What with writing, fancying a lover in every shadow about her path, plotting to circumvent visionary rivals, and trying to guess her thoughts, I all but ruined my imaginative powers.) One day I gave her a Union Pacific railway map; another day, some home-made popped corn; still another day, a little treasure of a pop-gun—not for herself, but for her little brother. I had painstakingly fashioned this pop-gun myself, and covered it with kisses. She would not be able to detect any trace of these fond kisses, to be sure—in fact, I doubted whether she would ever know anything about them; but the gun would necessarily pass through her hands, and if she should happen to kiss it—!

My uncle supplied me with pens to write my book, and I took occasion to supply her.

At all this the reader may smile contemptuously. Very good; I expect him to smile; a year before I myself should have smiled aloud.

Mary accepted all these things; but what did she do for me? She gave me no popped corn; no railway "folders;" nothing whatever. But she lent me, unsolicited,—except through broad hints,—a French book.

Toward the end of May she seemed to grow weary of me. The "good day, Weston," was very distant sometimes; and when I yanked the forty-fifth apple out of my coat-pocket, and began, "Here is," she cut me short with an "oh, never mind," and passed on. My imagination was very active as, sleepless and feverish, I wore out the night following that dreadful day. I distinctly read a dozen letters addressed to her, each one being an offer of marriage. I vividly saw her married over and over again, but I was not once the bridegroom. My powerful imagination pointed out that the "mustached lover" was my most formidable rival; that he was twenty-one; that he was an accomplished gentleman; that he was the heir of a noble estate; that he would eventually marry Mary. My imagination went further; it told me that Hubert (that was his name, for Mary often said she liked the name of Hubert) was utterly unworthy of her; that her married life with him would be thorny; that in the end he would desert her; that I should then find and snatch her from her misery; that she would simply say to me, with such a piteous look, "Oh, Weston, forgive me!" and then shudderingly die. At this culmination of horrors, I fell sound asleep.

But worse than this was in store for me. I saw two or three of the youths of the village escort her home from church, in a timid and rustic manner that should have made me laugh. But if they had more courage than I, how could I laugh? It was *their* privilege to do all the laughing. Worse and worse! I saw her go for a boat-ride with a young curate and two young ladies of her own age. Of course the dashing clerical planned the boat-ride for *her*; the other two were but figure-heads, nonentities, who had probably shoved themselves in, uninvited and undesired. Of course the young hero was desperately in love with her; of course he was dying to marry her.

Now, I had no boat; I wouldn't borrow one—for I was a blunderhead at rowing, anyway.

I will not harrow up my feelings by attempting to describe the agonies I endured. In my desperation I resolved to lay my heart, and hand, and unfinished love-story at her feet the first opportunity. I had intended to wait till I could lay my story printed, and through it the world, before her; but now I could endure suspense no longer; I must know my fate at once.

I did not encounter Mary again for nearly a week. She seemed rather pleased to see me, and I said huskily, " I have not seen you for some time, Mary. I—I—"

" No," she said slowly, and was slowly moving on.

I meant to propose then; but we were on the street; she seemed to be in a hurry. Of course I could not propose, on the street, under these circumstances; no one, surely, could expect it of me. So that opportunity slipped past. But, making a superhuman effort, I said, "Shall you be at home this evening? I should like to have an interview with you."

Her face showed a little surprise, and, it may be, pleasure. Did she suspect? I think she did.

"Yes, I expect to be in," she replied.

And so we went our different ways.

The battle had now begun. Had I the courage, and, above all, the self-command, to go on to victory—or defeat? I devoutly hoped so; but I was so dazed that I had no clear idea of anything.

Very early that evening I put in my appearance. But early as it was, Mary was ready to receive me. Further, even to my unpractised eyes, she seemed to have taken special pains with her toilet.

Surely, she expected an offer of marriage! This so unnerved me that I could hardly frame what the garmmarians call a simple sentence. Then Mrs. Blakely came into the room for a moment, and greeted me with marked politeness. My boyish verdancy prompted me to conclude that she had been told something, and expected me to propose.

Now, all this should have encouraged me, for if it meant anything, it meant that they regarded me with favor. But my head was dizzy, and I felt deathly sick.

Mary's mother discreetly withdrew, and we were alone.

"How are you getting along at school, Mary?" I faltered.

"Oh, very well," she said gaily; "but I'm rather tired of school."

"How are your plants thriving?" was my next question. "I see they are gracing the windows."

"Oh, they're coming on finely," she replied, stepping to the window and re-arranging some of the flower-pots.

I had never been in her house before, and it was somewhat embarrassing for both of us. But she was busying herself with the flowers, while I had nothing— not even my hat. How I wished that a gentle kitten or a pet dog would stray into the room, that I might pick it up and fondle it! I believed I could pluck up courage to propose if only my hands were occupied. What big and clumsy hands they were, to be sure; and, yes, there was an ugly ink-stain on the index finger of my right hand.

Apparently I thought I had not yet exhausted school topics, and I said, " How are you getting along with your French, Mary ? "

" I'm translating Souvestre now," she answered.

" Did you ever take up Latin again ? " I asked.

These idiotic questions must have been highly entertaining to her. But she answered pleasantly, " No, not since we came to this place. It is only the boys that study Latin here now, and of course I didn't wish to take it up with them," shooting me an arch look.

" No, of course not! " I replied hastily.

Now, if ever, I should have had the courage to ask the vital question. But I had not.

Soon I inquired, " How do you like 'We and Our Neighbors' ? "—a book I had lent her.

" I like it pretty well," she answered, a little wearily.

Then ensued a solemn and oppressive silence.

" Mary," I said at length, " I—I thought you had taken a dislike to me lately."

This was the nearest approach to a proposal that I had yet dared to venture on, and I trembled as I spoke.

"Why, no, Weston!" she said, coming back from the window. "What made you think that? I always liked you, Weston."

At this my nineteen-year-old heart beat furiously; a dimness impaired my vision; everything in the room went spinning around in the craziest manner imaginable. It was happiness enough to be able to call her Mary and to be called Weston in return; but it was thrilling and delirious joy to hear her say that she always liked me.

With an effort I recovered myself. But instead of popping the question, as I should have done if I wished her to be my wife, I—answered the question she had asked! "Oh, I suppose I was grum," I said.

Another painful pause.

In sheer desperation I blurted out, "I'll speak to you about it again in about six months,—six or seven months,—good night, Mary;" caught up my hat, and tore out of the house.

Notwithstanding my agitation I perceived that Mary looked annoyed, and her "good night" was cold and formal.

Only those who have passed through the ordeal can form a just conception of my feelings. As I strode away I heaped the most scurrilous epithets upon myself—and yet I was happy; for had she not said emphatically, "I always liked you, Weston"? If I could but have had the moral courage, she might now be my promised wife. But she loved me; of course she did; why else had she spoken in that way, so unhesitatingly?

Did I believe in "Hubert"? Certainly not; "Hubert" was but a myth. As for the youths who dared to escort —or rather shadow—her home from church—. Pshaw!

The good-for-nothing fellows loved her, perhaps, (how could they help it?) and she, perhaps, liked them, in a sisterly way, (what of that?) but she *loved* me. As for the young curate—Well, he might be her uncle, for all I knew, or her cousin—no, cousins often marry. Granted even that he was a rival, had I not stolen a march on him? Mary loved me, even as I loved her; and the clerical candidate was playing a losing game.

So I could afford to pity the young clergyman, for he seemed a man who would take a disappointment very hard. Poor fellow! Yes, I could pity him with all my heart—but, at the same time, I could narrowly watch over my own interests.

Why had I said, "I'll speak about it again in about six months"? Such a thought had never occurred to me before—in fact, it must have been the spell of some presentiment that had constrained me to speak in that way. Yes, clearly it was destined that in six months' time there would be a great change wrought in my life. There would then be a period, an epoch, a—a—something startling. Certainly; I could sum up the matter in a few words: Six months later, my book would be before the world; I should be hailed as a second Dickens—perhaps it would even be said that I eclipsed Dickens; and, best of all, Mary would be my promised wife, for I should then have no hesitation in boldly asking the dreadful question. And it might be that my young friend in holy orders should perform the marriage ceremony for us just six months from that date!

But, awful thought! why had I subjoined, "six or seven months"? What was the significance of that addendum? Was there to be some hitch in the presentiment? Was some unforeseen calamity to threaten me at the expiration of six months, or of seven months? No; no. The interpretation clearly was, that everything depended upon my own exertions; I must make the most of my opportunities.

"Good evening," smote my ear.

With a start I awakened out of my reverie, and, behold! my clerical rival! He was going the way I had come, and I had come from Mary's! Where was he going but to Mary's!

My diseased imagination, like a mighty engine too forcibly set in motion, began to play with a destructive velocity that could not be restrained.

I lost track of the young man, but retraced my steps to Mary's. I came in sight of the place just in time to see some one going backwards down the slat walk leading to the gate, talking to—Mary!

My elaborate and beautiful air-castle came toppling about my ears with a crash that was startling.

They were laughing and talking merrily. Who was it? the curate, or "Hubert," once more resuscitated?

I never knew; for the figure on the walk abruptly took leave of Mary, and glided away at a lively pace. The door slammed to; I looked up; Mary had disappeared in the house.

Then I remembered her cold "good night" and her look of scorn as I took leave of her, and I again heaped abuse on my head. "She will think," I reflected, "that I entrapped her into saying what she did. What does it all signify? In reality, nothing! What a downright fool I am! I *will* have a definite answer! I *will* know my fate! I will ask her, now, to be my wife—*I swear it!*"

Without waiting for my resolution to waver, I dashed up the walk and the door-steps, and sounded a peal that made my ears tingle. Mrs. Blakely came running to the door in the liveliest alarm.

"Is it fire?" she gasped.

"Is Mary in?" I asked, and brushed past her into the hall.

Then Mrs. Blakely recovered her composure, and ushered me into the parlor, where Mary was. As the door opened, Mary, who knew me by my voice, sat down at the piano and began playing softly.

"An air that Hubert loves," I groaned. But my resolution was still firm.

Seeing a rug in disorder, I leaned over it and spread it out smooth and straight. "Mary," I said, in so sharp a tone that she started, turned, and faced me, "if I—should become—a famous fellow, will you marry me?"

A rosy hue overspread her face, she nervously turned to her piano, played idly on three notes, and said tremulously, "Oh, Weston! You mustn't talk that way!"

"Oh, I'm in earnest," I declared.

A long and painful silence. Mary, with her face turned from me, pretended to be deeply interested in monotonously thumping away on those three notes.

What had possessed me to say "fellow"? How commonplace it sounded, and how it must have grated on Mary's sensitive ear. If only I could have written it, how polished and precise it would have been!

I broke the silence, saying, "I don't want any promise, Mary; I only want to know what you think."

But the poor girl still harped away at nothing. "I wish you hadn't said anything about it," she at length said peevishly.

I waited a moment longer, expecting her to stop that hateful tum-tumming and say something. But she did not. Perhaps she was waiting for me to exclaim passionately, as the orthodox lover would have done, "I love you!" But I did not.

I should have urged my suit, and received a definite answer. Instead of this I mournfully said, "Very well, Mary," and went hopeless away, leaving her to her sonata of three notes and her own meditations.

And so ended my first proposal. Who among us is a hero on that momentous occasion? For my further extenuation, let me urge it upon the indulgent reader to bear in mind the fact that I was only nineteen.

For my reader's sake, I wish I could wind up by saying that Mary looks over my shoulder as I write these last words, and gives me a wifely kiss. Alas, no! Both Mary and I are still unmarried; but the "great gulf" problem is here, and such a consummation of my idyllic dream will hardly be realized.

GROANS EVOKED

DURING THE PERIOD OF THE FIRST FRENZY.

Les Soupirs d'un Jouvenceau.

COULD IT BE SO!

Si elle etait assisse auprès de mon oreiller,
Si ses cheveux ondoyaient autour de ma tête,
Si sa voix parlait à moi,
Si ses yeux me regardaient,
Si ses lèvres baisaient les miennes,
Si mes mains tenaient les siennes,
    Que je serais heureux !
    Que je serais heureux !
Que je serais heureux, m'amour ! m'amie !

Marguèrite, mignonne, ma bonne, ma chère, m'amie,
Si je pouvais te chercher aujourd'hui,
Si je pouvais baiser tes joues si douces,
Si je savais que tu pensasses à Bruce.

Et je songe que tu es proche moi, ô ma mignonne,
Songe que tes petites mains sont mises dans les miennes ;
Songe tes baisers brûlent sur mes joues et lèvres,
Pendant que ta voix dit, "m'amour, j'y suis."

And I dreamed that thou wast with me, oh my darling,
Dreamed thy little hands lay lovingly in mine ;
Dreamed thy kisses burned upon my lips and forehead,
Whilst thy voice did murmer softly, " I am thine,"

TO MARGARITA.

Sweetheart, I love your winsome face,
Your soft, dark eyes, your witching grace,
   Your artless ways, your heart sincere,
   Your many charms, which all endear.
   My jealous heart can have no fear,
If in your love it have a place.

You have bewitched me with your smiles,
Your laughing voice, that swift beguiles,
   Your pouting lips, that coy invite
   A bold attempt from frenzied wight
   Castilian sonnets to indite—
Though I would draw my sword the whiles.

Carissima, I love you well,
I love you more than verse can tell.
   Wed with me ; do not say me nay ;
   Turn not my joy into dismay ;
   Wed with me on this happy day,
And glad will ring our marriage-bell.

Belovèd, say you'll be my own,
My wife, ere yet this day has flown.
   Your sparkling eyes shall know no tears,
   Your sun-lit locks will mock the years,
   E'en Time can bring naught but which cheers ;
Your fame I'll spread from zone to zone.

Not for a span of time, soon fled,
Not for this life alone we'll wed ;
   When this world's sunshine disappears,
   Together in the brighter spheres,
   Throughout eternal, tranquil years,
Our spirit life may still be led,

THE MONTH OF MAY.

WHEN May comes, the small boy first begins to think seriously of trading off his marbles for fish-hooks, and from fish-hooks his thoughts revert to long-tailed kites. Before May is half over he yearns to build a dam and launch a raft.

The small boy is not content to go fishing where it is dry and wholesome, but seeks out the dampest marsh he can find. Every night he comes home a good deal too late for supper, with his pants tucked in his long-legged boots, to hide the alluvial deposits streaked on them; his hands in his pockets, to hide the mud stains and the lacerations of his patent fish-hooks; and his hat, his new straw hat—what of that? Alas! the evil-smelling marsh water has played sad havoc with the small boy's new hat, and he has followed the dictates of prudence, and left it in the woodshed. He sits down to the supper table with a light heart, and clears it of everything save the dishes and the mustard. He had caught an amazing number of fish, of course; so many, in fact, that he couldn't count them all—couldn't begin to do it. But some of them were too small to bring home; some of them he lost; some of them *got away;* and some of them were bull-frogs, every time. Anyway—and he lays marked and exultant emphasis on this—anyway, he had a " splendid time."

Those who stroll about the city find the drug store windows full of patent cough medicines, and spring anti-febriles, and awful satires on the man who died a wretched death because he would not invest a paltry dollar in a bottle of spring medicine. Remembering how they have exposed themselves to the May sunshine, they hurry into the drug store and glance at this medicine and at that, feeling all the time that they will share the suicidal miser's fate if they do not dose with spring medicine at once; and they invest a paltry dollar—perhaps three or four paltry dollars—in Eau de Cologne and other perfumes, and saunter out into the street with a light heart.

There is a beauty in the fields, and the woods, and the apple orchards, that tempts human nature to while away the time out in the meadows and the woodlands, to study botany, and to envy tinkers and tramps. The sun may be like a fiery furnace, but under the trees it is cool and delightful. The woods are always cool; but in the pent-up city the stone pavement is so intensely hot that it frizzles, and scorches, and burns everything that passes over it—except the naked foot of the friendless hoodlum.

"In the spring the young man's fancy turns lightly to thoughts of love," and in May he decorates himself with a new watch-chain and a new cane, and finds out where cream caramels retail at the most reasonable price. And on Sunday afternoons the highways and the bye-ways are full of top buggies, and the top buggies are full of lovers, and the parlors of the farmhouses are suggestive of protracted Sunday evening courtships. And the country maiden, as well as the city maiden, discards last year's fashions, and parasols, and earrings, and appears in raiment and off-settings of the most enchanting and dazzling newness; and the Niagara hackman, reflecting on all these things, chuckles a sordid chuckle, for he knows that twenty-four hours after the marriage of these lovers, they will be at the Falls, and at his mercy.

SOME VILLAGE CHARACTERS.

OUR village does not lie under the shadow of an historic mountain, nor is it laved by the waters of a sparkling river. Alas, no! It is bounded by millponds, pasture-grounds, and cross-roads. But its streets are named; its site is shown on all the more ambitious railway maps; it gets the daily papers before they are two days old; and it can boast (but does not) of having given to the world a champion dog catcher, a combination corn-doctor and horse-trainer, an unsuccessful mind-reader, an insanity expert, a Mormon missionary, and a courteous lady book-agent.

Our village is inhabited—inhabited by human beings; boys and dogs; cows and porkers; sheep and mosquitoes; and certain insects that troubled Egypt during the fourth plague. It has many buildings—churches, "commercial houses" (in truth, some of them were houses once, and may be again), hotels, dwelling-houses, ramshackle sheds, a big school, and more hotels.

On sauntering out into the streets of our village, we immediately see a figure ahead of us. We do not pass this figure, because no one was ever known to pass it. It is the old woman in black, who is always lugging about a market-basket, and always just ahead of you. Next, we discern the town-clerk's time-worn dog, trudging leisurely along in the imperfect shade afforded by the "splendid" new stores on Waddell's block, on his way to the shambles, to wrangle with other hungry dogs for a paltry bone, of which, ten to one, he will be despoiled by the postmaster's over-fed bull-dog, which we shall meet presently.

It is a proud day for our villagers when a son of the soil hauls a load of hemlock in from the back-woods, and gazes, with rapturous admiration, at our beautiful new stores. There is, in fact, but one prouder day in the whole year for them. That is every Fair-day, when the Sweedish photographer and watch-maker draws his camero (as he calls it) and his other apparatus conspicuously down opposite that pile; presses a dozen little orphan boys into his service, causes them to lift, and strain, and groan, and whisper slang (?), and finally gets his apparatus into what was the right position only to find that old Sol, like time, waits for no man, and that it will have to be shifted. But at last everything is arranged to suit the magnate; and, after sending one little boy to get him a drink of water (?), and another all the way back to his "gallery," on some mysterious errand, and two or three to every shop within sight, to announce that operations are about to commence, he deliberately takes off his coat, which he consigns to some adult bystander for safe keeping, gives his "camero" a final hitch, and takes a picture of those stores. Although his name and dual employment are emblazoned on his belongings in ornamental gilt letters, the villagers do not seem to think that he is advertizing himself, but patrioticly buy his pictures, and have them framed by the cabinet-maker and sign-painter.

But we have wandered. Pretty soon we confront the man who appears to be always stepping out of the corner hotel. He is not a handsome fellow, not the sort of personage the editor's heiress would select to elope with;

but he is the undisputed owner of the most unamiable rat terrier within the town limits. This rat terrier is an ancient—a venerable—canine, but it has none of the milk of human kindness in its gaunt frame. Poor Hero! He has caused more boys' pants to be prefaced with big patches, and stopped short the course of more sizable stones, than any of his congeners.

Soon we catch sight of a middle-aged man and woman passing the compliments of the day as they meet each other. Judging by appearances, one would fancy they must be lovers, though they are rather elderly to indulge in the tender passion. On making inquiries it is learned that presumably they *are* lovers—for they have been engaged these eighteen years.

Here is Sam Weller's Hotel. Lounging under the shade of a horse-chestnut tree is a remarkable individual, of a youthful and jaunty appearance. His coat is off, but it is hanging close by, spread out so that all its gorgeousness may be seen to the best advantage. A pair of seven-dollar boots protects his feet; a seven-dollar hat is carefully balanced on his artisticly cropped head; a seven-dollar meerschaum is dangling between the second and the third finger of his left hand; a seven-dollar gold watch-chain, freighted with not a few seven-dollar trinkets of ample dimensions, fetches a tortuous course across his natty vest, and disappears in his vest pocket; a seven-dollar diamond ring causes the fourth member of his right hand to stick out and point jeeringly at a boy shying stones at a stray feline. Who is this great man? is asked, with bated breath. It may be the proprietor of the hotel; but no, it—it must be one of Thomas Nast's political corruptionists from the Capital. "I never before," says a stranger, "saw a man who looks so like the English lord of the *Bow Bells.*"

Curiosity is great, but it is soon gratified. A man who is evidently no respecter of persons comes swinging along the street, and seeks to insult the seven-dollar phenomenon with these opprobrious words:

"Hello, Jim! I want to get my hair cut."

We expect to see the noble lord start to his feet in a burst of awful anger. We expect to see, perhaps, a tragedy. We do not wish to be impanelled on a coroner's jury, but we resolve to see how this grandee will resent an insult. Perhaps he will think the clown beneath contempt, we reason, and go on peacefully pointing his finger—

"All right, Tom," he says, with alacrity, and away they go, and turn into a "hair-cutting parlor" round the corner.

* * * * * *
* * * * * * *

Pretty soon we encounter the postmaster's dog. It is a powerful brute, with a deceptive smile on its mouth, a deceptive wag about its tail. It will bite a shoemaker, an errand-boy, an errandless boy, a boy with ragged clothes on, a boy without any clothes on at all, an organ-grinder, a doctor, a schoolboy (or half a dozen schoolboys), a man with a cane, a man without a cane, an invalid with three or four canes, or a brass jewelry peddler. It will bite one and all of these, without remorse; but it will not bite man, or boy, or scarecrow, carrying a gun, or anything in the shape of a gun. And wherefore? Because in puppyhood it was shot twice. But the canine is doomed; sooner or later it will die by violence. So say the schoolmaster, the consumptive wood-sawyer, the butcher's boy, and all the hoodlums of the village. So, it is doomed. But perhaps "sooner or later," like to-morrow, will never come. It is not the dog, but the dog's master, that is respected and feared. Perhaps the votes cast at the last election may influence the destiny of this canine autocrat.

A little farther on we come up with a meek-eyed urchin, of the negativest of negative temperaments, who tremblingly gasps out "yes, ma'am", "no, ma'am," to everybody, of whatsoever sex or dignity. No matter what you ask him, he doesn't know, or he doesn't remember, or he isn't sure, or he forgets. Once he clean forgot himself, and said he didn't think he was sick.

The people of our village are so cultured that nothing could induce them to say anything they think vulgar. On the hottest day in July, when the mercury is boiling and respiration almost suspended, they meet one another and say, gaspingly, "Isn't it awfully warm?" The more genteel among them—that is, those who have plodded through the first sixty-seven pages of some one's grammar, and hammered the idea into their head that the suffix "ful" is an adjective, but that "fully" is an adverb, and that adverbs and *warm* (whatever that may be in grammar) are in some mysterious manner connected—say "awfully warm;" but those whose education has been neglected, shock the refined ears of the genteely educated ones by saying "awful warm."

Marry, after hearing this "isn't it awful (or awfully) warm?" asked by perspiring mortals on every side for days together, how refreshing it is to hear the gamins sing out to one another, "It's hot, ain't it, Bill!"

According to our villagers, though, "hot" is a word fit only for cooks, vagabonds, and scientists, "cold" is orthodox, and expressive merely of chilliness. About the middle of September, when the equinoctial is brewing, and small boys begin reluctantly to leave off "swimming" in the creek, the genteel ones say, "It's cold to-day, isn't it?"

If the villagers would drop their scandalous gossiping leave off reading their idle village weekly newspapers, and devote a little of their wearisome leisure to the acquisition of just a modicum of Bostonian—or even Leadvillian—culture, it would be well for them and for their posterity. As to awful and awfully, why, existence would be a burden if the use of these two words were forbidden them. Why, they would not be able to manifest their ideas at all.

"The good die young," and the kindly-disposed inhabitants of this hypothetical village are so unobtrusive that the stranger is not likely to notice them—although they largely outnumber the others.

The moral of this fragmentary sketch seems to be that while some inoffensive people are so thin-skinned that they are sensitive to the least prick from any spluttering little old Gillott pen, that may have long since spluttered out all its venom, others again are so much like a pachyderm in their nature that they will bob up sulkily smiling, even when sandbagged by a crack from a muleteer's rude bludgeon.

OUR VISIT TO THE COUNTRY.

ONE joyous day in May I decided that it would be very pleasant to go down to the old home in the country and pass the summer there. What could be so delightful as a picket hen-house, a vagabond sheep-dog, an honest cordwood stove, and a roomy frame house, built by an architect who had never studied architecture or trigonometry? Three miles from the post-office, five miles from the Erie railway, and one hundred and fifty miles from the nearest large city—what more could a mortal ask who simply wished to forget, for a few months, that the world moves, and that Ireland longs to join in the procession.

Such were the arguments I used to persuade my wife, Fanny, much against her will, to pack up and go down into the country. I had my way, and we went.

The old house had been vacant nearly a year, and consequently needed airing. The doors would all open easily enough, but, as Fanny said, they wouldn't shut again without putting forth great effort. I tried hard to persuade her that by leaving them all wide open, such a state of affairs would result in a net gain to us of seven full golden hours in the course of every five years.

A spavined horse and a mild-mannered cow were procured and installed in the cowstable, and a most substantial buggy was borrowed from a man who had owed my father ten dollars. I felt that nothing more could be desired to make home happy, but my wife insisted on having a cat. Scarcely a day passed but an adult cat, touring the country incognito, would wander into our premises, partake of liquid refreshment from the milk pans, and then good-humoredly resume its Knight-errantry. I tried to persuade Fanny to take up with some one of these Bohemian cats, but the adventurous spirit was too strongly developed in them, and besides, she preferred a feline of domestic, and not of cosmopolitan tastes.

At the end of two brief weeks our cow, infused with the spirit of the age, boycotted us, refused absolutely to give any more milk; and I engaged a warty-fingered boy (not necessarily because he was afflicted with warty fingers, but because it was difficult to find a well-developed boy not so afflicted) to bring us milk daily. He always came before we were up, and generally hung about till dinner-time—not because he sympathised with us in our loneliness, but because such was his idea of etiquette. From him Fanny got a kitten, and our household was now complete.

We were three miles from the post-office, as was mentioned above, and the mail-carrier, on his route past our place once a day to an inlying village, left our letters, etc. It was odd how eagerly I would watch for him, considering that I had come to this place to get away from the world. The carrier had an easy, graceful way, acquired from dexterous practice, of tossing mail matter into the ditch, and of cracking our sheep-dog's ears with his whip. But as he drew a salary of TWO HUNDRED DOLLARS A YEAR from the Government for carrying Uncle Sam's mails, he was the autocrat of the road and everyone meekly yielded to his imperious ways.

Our house stood almost on the road—or rather, on a crose-road, and we were hailed night and day by stalwart tramps. At night I bade them follow the telegraph poles, and during the day mechanically directed them to Chicago, New York, Vermont, Ireland, and the Black Hills. Right over the way from our house stood a large open shed, appertaining to a disused chapel close by, thus making our corner quite conspicuous. I always had my suspicions that a tramp occasionally put up over night in this shed, but never hinted it to Fanny, knowing it would dispel all the charm of country life for her.

One evening as I sat in the open doorway a gaunt and shadowy figure emerged from this shed, sidled over to me, and humbly asked permission to stay there all night. I told him that the shed didn't come under my "jurisdiction," but belonged absolutely to the public, and was free to the public. "As you," I continued, "are a public man—presumably a publican and a sinner—you are perfectly at liberty to occupy the shed." All this sounded magnanimous on my part, and the stranger gravely thanked me, and as gravely informed me that he was a Division Superintendent of the mines along the J. M. & I. railroad, on his way east to arrange for a shipment of new plant. I said I was very happy to make his acquaintance, and I loaded him up with cold victuals enough to win over the farmers' dogs for the next thirty-six hours, and fifty cents to help pay the freightage on his shipment of plant. Then he cordially invited me to visit him some time at his beautiful home in Louisville, or to come and pass a fortnight with him on his ranch in Texas. I always *could* make friends; I presume I have twenty-five standing invitations to put in a week or a month at gentlemen's ranches in Texas, Colorado, California, British Columbia, La Plata, New South Wales, and Cape Colony.

Coming in from a swing in the hammock, Fanny overheard the latter part of our conversation, and at once took alarm—in fact, she was frightened almost to death. In vain I assured her that the Division Superintendent was a patriarchal-appearing man; that his right hand hung in a sling; that he could see well out of only one eye; and that the only visible weapon he carried was a heavy brass ring, worn on the index finger of his left hand.

But my wife was morally certain that the Division Superintendent proposed to draw his supply of plant from our premises, and she insisted that everything out of doors should be brought in and locked up. Accordingly I brought into the kitchen ten croquet hoops, fifteen yards of clothes line, a willow bird-cage, a buck-basket full of oyster and peach cans, a fragment of a horse-shoe, our dog's dinner plate, and likewise some of his best beef-bones, a saw-horse, and a basswood bench. I furbished and reloaded my seven-shooter, and slept with it under my pillow; but Fanny, with the sheep-dog, sat up all night long, with the lamp on a low chair, and blankets hung over the windows, reading the History of Alonzo and Melissa. The next morning the Division Superintendent was gone, and so were a pair of pullets and the padlock of the hen-house door. Fanny was right, but I would never acknowledge it.

About this time we were alarmed one night by the most demoniacal—or rather supernatural—cries from the chapel near us. I pretended to be simply mystified as to the cause of the "phenomenon," but Fanny showed more nerve than I did. The next day it was discovered that her kitten had made a mysterious disappearance. A strange dog had chased it under the chapel, and the poor creature had got into so tight a place that it could not get out again. At the risk of my neck I rescued it, of course; and the ghost was laid.

We had often noticed bees flying in and out of cracks in the outside of the house, but paid no attention to it till, too late, we found that the whole frame-work of the house was literally infested with bees, wasps, and hornets. We were almost besieged by them; there was not a square yard of "clapboard" but had its stronghold of the buzzing pests. They soon had such a footing established at the back door that it was no longer safe to come in that way; so we bolted the door on the inside, and notified such of our neighbors as were back-door callers. I believe it afforded Fanny no little cold-blooded amusement to see a tramp march boldly up to this door, and knock, ostensibly to inquire the way. The first knock not being answered, he would pound vigorously on the door, and a detachment of hornets, fully a hundred strong, would sally out of their ambush and haughtily demand the pass-word. Not being acquainted with the pass-word, the tramp would answer back in forcible and even treasonable language. (It was in this way that I picked up the expressive phrase "get out," in every modern tongue.) The hornets would invariably resent any impolite insinuations or undignified gestures, being constitutionally averse to impulsive human kind. If the tramp happened to be of a naturally shiftless character, and had left the gate open behind him, he could generally make a break for the highway, when he would keep straight on till he began to feel thirsty; but if he had carefully shut the gate on coming in—! But why recall these harrowing scenes? Suffice it to say that none of these unfortunates ever dropped me an invitation to go to Texas, but always a hearty invitation to try a climate still more genial. Taking pity on suffering humanity, we hung a placard over the door, solemnly warning all and sundry to keep away from it. This scarcely mended the matter. Unfortunately, this rear door could be distinctly seen from the road, and passers-by who could not plainly decipher my chirography, imagined that the place was to let, or else that a wayside tavern had been opened, and we were pestered almost to death from 6 a.m to 11 p.m.

Without giving official notice a colony of hectoring and barbarian wasps one day jumped a claim over the front door,—our only remaining out-let, except by way of the cellar,—and this brought matters to a crisis. They were very jealous of their rights, and when Fanny proposed that we should vacate in their favor and return to the city, I promptly replied that my sole object in life was to please her, and that I was calmly waiting till she should have had enough of country life.

HOW I LOVED AND LOST MY NELLY.

> He had no breath, no being, but in hers ;
> She was his voice ; he did not speak to her,
> But trembled on her words.
> —BYRON.

To My Silent Love,

These Rugged Lines are Religiously Dedicated.

    In my youth I loved a maiden,
Loved a laughing, blue-eyed maiden,
Who was very fair to look on ;
Of a quiet disposition ;
5   Even temper ; candid ; loving.
    As I loved her, so she loved me ;
And though we were both but children,
She but fourteen, I but sixteen,
Yet our hearts were knit together
10   In a firmer bond of union
Than is oft rehearsed in story.
    All my thoughts were of my sweetheart ;
All my plans to her confided ;
All her pleasures were my pleasures.
15   And at school I sat and watched her,
With my open books before me ;
But my thoughts were of the future,
Of the day when I should proudly
Lead her up before the altar ;
20   And my pref'rence was so open
That the master and my schoolmates
Came to see it, came to know it ;

Called me bridegroom, called me husband,
Jeered me, watched me, and alarmed me
25 Lest they should estrange my Nelly.
But my faithful little sweetheart
Only laughed at all their sallies,
Only bade them to our marriage.
   How I loved my little sweetheart
30 In those happy days of boyhood!
   But there came a rude awak'ning
When her father, Nelly's father,
Heard the rumor of our courtship.
   He was sad, and stern, and haughty,
35 And it grieved him and incensed him
That his child, his darling Nelly,
At her age should choose a lover,
Should receive one as a lover,
Who lacked fortune, fame, and honor,—
40 For my father once in anger
Had shot down a fellow-mortal;
And he harshly did enjoin her,
Under pain of close immurement,
To forget that I existed;
45 And made ev'ry preparation
For a sojourn in the Old World.
   On the eve of their departure
I received a tear-dimmed letter
From my darling little sweetheart.
50 "Faithful unto death," was written;
"We must wait my father's pleasure,
We must wait in hope and patience.—
Just one glimpse as we are leaving."
   As their train drew off that evening
55 I was standing close beside it;
And she whom I loved so madly
Leaned her head out of the carriage,
Waved a kiss, and dropped a packet.
Her farewell salute returning,
60 I took up the precious packet;

And my idol, my belovèd,
In a moment was borne from me.
"Just one glimpse," it was, too surely!
In the packet were her picture,
65 Her gold ring, her opal locket,
With her name, and date, the legend,
"As a souvenir of the old days."
Thus I parted from my Nelly,
In the golden days of August,
70 When the world was rare with beauty,
And all Nature bright with sunshine;
Hardest parting, strangest courtship,
Ever blighting two fond lovers.
All my dreams were of my loved one,
75 All my life was very lonely,
All my days passed very sadly.
As the days passed, so the years passed,
Slowly, wearily, and sadly,
And I chafed at the long parting.
80 But at last there came a message
From my absent, loving Nelly,
Breathing still her fond devotion,
Bidding me to hope on ever,
As true love must be rewarded.
85 "Send no answer," she concluded,
"For it would be intercepted."
If with me the time passed slowly,
If for me the days were lonely,
If for me the burden heavy,
90 How much more so for my Nelly!
The mementoes she had left me,
The assurance she still loved me,
Cheered me, in my deepest sorrow,
Fired my heart with hope and courage;
95 And the merry laugh of schoolboys,
And the joyous song of wild birds,
And the shrieking of express trains
As they dashed through midnight blackness,

(2)

And the crash along the sea-shore,
100 And the vivid flash of lightning,
And the moon through mountain passes,
Seemed to whisper, seemed to tell me:
"Days of happiness and sunshine
Will come to you in the future."
105 But sometimes there came a murmur,
Came a Voice from unknown darkness,
Mocking ever came it to me:
"'Tis a false hope that you cherish,
'Tis a phantom you are chasing."
110 Oft I sought relief in travel,
Oft I followed Nelly's footsteps,
But, alas! not once I saw her.
Still my restless, troubled spirit
Urged me aimlessly to wander,
115 Urged me on, a worse than outcast.
Changing scenery, Old World splendors,
Could not cure my rooted sorrow,
Brought my anguished heart no solace.
To wipe out the old dishonor,
120 To remove her father's hatred,
And secure his full approval
Of a marriage with his daughter,
I sought fame, and wealth, and honors,
Worked with dauntless resolution,
125 Waited, pondered, brooded, trusted,
Built air-castles, nursed my sorrows.
When I next heard of my Nelly
News came to me she was married,
Forced unwilling by her father
130 Into marriage with a marquis.
As a thunderbolt all-blasting,
As a whirlpool all-engulfing,
So these tidings fell upon me.
What to me were fame and fortune?
135 What to me were empty honors?
What to me that light was breaking?

I had lost my darling Nelly.
    This last sorrow overtook me
In the days of drear November,
140 When the chilling rains of heaven
Blurred the landscape, marred all Nature;
When the birds, with drooping feathers,
Tripped about in groups of twenties,
Eager to begin their journey
145 To the sunshine of the Southland.
    On that fatal day the storm-gods
Seemed to rise in pain and fury;
All the skies were black and angry,
All the air was full of threat'nings,
150 All dumb creatures were uneasy,
All things showed a coming tempest.
    All my passions glowed within me
Like a mutinous volcano;
And unable to control them
155 I rushed forth to meet the tempest.
And the bleak and naked meadows,
And the leafless trees of woodlands,
And the boiling mountain torrents,
Seemed attuned to my own sorrows,
160 Seemed in sympathy to greet me.
    I could hear the awful tempest
Roaring in the distant forest
Like a monster in his torment;
While the trees moaned and the brutes moaned,
165 As I hurried headlong onward.
    I had but one thought to guide me,
That I must reach some endeared place,
Reach a sacred haunt of old days,
Where I first had seen my Nelly,
170 There to wait the tempest's fury.
    With this single thought to guide me
I betook me to the streamlet
Which we two had crossed together
Daily as we loitered schoolward.

175 And the alders by the streamlet,
Fanned by zephyrs of the summer,
Lashed by whirlwinds of November,
Seemed to beckon, seemed to call me,
Cried in tones severe, yet pleading,
180 Tones impetuous, yet plaintive,
As a caged bird's mournful singing:
" 'Twas a vain chase after triumph ;
'Twas too much you sought in this world ;
It was Heaven on earth you asked for."
185   Ghostly figures shape before me ;
Ghostly eyes look on me sadly ;
Ghostly fingers mutely beckon ;
And the spirit Voice hoarse whispers :
" Life for you is but a mock'ry,
190 Death the sole release you long for."
    " Oh, my God ! " I cry in anguish,
" I have borne my heavy burdens,
I have wrestled with my sorrow,
Till my strength is all gone from me,
195 Hear my prayer, oh, let me perish ! "
    And the merciful Creator,
With Divine commiseration
For my mis'ry and my weakness,
Loosens and dissolves the tenure
200 Of this earthly life He gave me.
I am dying—all is over.

HOW I LOVED AND LOST MY JANET.

A Burlesque Version of how Things would have Turned Out.

    And why that early love was crost,
    Thou know'st the best—I feel the most:
    But few that dwell beneath the sun
    Have loved so long, and loved but one.
                      —Byron.

To My Evil Genius,
These Rustic Lines are Sardonically Dedicated.

     In my youth I loved a maiden,
  Loved a giggling, cross-eyed maiden,
  Who was homely as a wild cat;
  Of a giddy disposition;
5 Gusty temper; gushing; spooney.
     As I loved her, so she loved me;
  And though we were both but goslings,
  She but fourteen, I but sixteen,
  Yet our hearts were knit together
10 In a firmer bond of union
  Than a three-ply, homemade carpet.
     All our plums I gave my sweetheart;
  All my gum with her divided;
  All her melons were my melons.
15 And at school I sat and watched her,
  With my idle knife before me;
  But my thoughts were of the future,
  Of the day when I should fiercely
  Dicker with Niagara hackmen.
20 And my spooning was so open
  That the master and my schoolmates
  Came to see it, came to know it;

Called me sapgog, called me Janet,
"Charivaried" me, and alarmed me
25 Lest they should cut off my melons.
But my grinning little sweetheart
Only snickered at their sallies,
Only bade them mind their business.
How I loved my little sweetheart
30 In those oatmeal days of dad's clothes !*
But there came a birchen whaling
When her father, Janet's father,
Heard the rumor of our mooning.
He was glum, and bald, and big-eared,
35 And it rattled him and "riled" him
That his child, his squint-eyed Janet,
At her age should choose her own beau,
Should receive one as her lover
Who lacked gumption and his liking,—
40 For my father once in anger
Had upset the old man's scarecrows ;
And he harshly did enjoin her,
Under pain of no more earrings,
To forget that I existed ;
45 And made ev'ry preparation
For a sponge on his relations.
On the eve of their departure
I received a pie-stained letter
From my hungry little sweetheart.
50 "Now, old slouch, good-bye," was scribbled ;
"We must wait till paw's relations
Tire of keeping two such eaters.—
Just one peek as we are leaving."
As their train jerked off that evening
55 I was standing close beside it ;
And she whom I loved so daftly
Craned her head out of the carriage,

---

*This seems somewhat obscure. The meaning is : when the hero lived principally on oatmeal porridge, and strutted about in his father's rejected raiment. —B. W. M.

HOW I LOVED AND LOST MY JANET.

      Made wry faces, shied a packet.
      Her farewell salute returning,
60   I secured the well-aimed packet;
      And the old "accommodation"
      Slowly rumbled off my idol.
      "Just one peek," it was, too surely!
         In the packet were her thimble,
65   Her bead ring, her pet dog's collar,
      With her name, and date, the legend,
      " You can swop these for some fish-hooks."
         Thus I parted from my Janet,
      In the torrid heat of dog-days,
70   When the roads were rank with tired tramps,
      And all Nature with mosquitos;
      Quickest parting, crudest courtship,
      Ever teasing two green lovers.
         All my dreams were how to manage
75   To secure another sweetheart;
      All my days passed hoeing turnips.
      As the days passed, so the hours passed,
      Torrid, leisurely, and dusty,
      And I chafed at so much hoeing.
80   But at last there came a message
      From my absent, squint-eyed Janet,
      Breathing still her breath of spruce gum,
      Bidding me look out for two things:
      She had found some one to spark her,
84½ And her pa was getting homesick.
85   "Send no answer," she concluded,
      "For you cannot pay the postage."
         If with me time would spin onward,
      If in spite of all men's efforts
      Headstrong Time *would* reel off days' lengths,
90   Why not also with my Janet?
         The mementoes she had left me,
      The assurance she still liked me,
      Cheered me when my chores were hardest,
      Fired my heart to fight the red-skins;

95 And the merry laugh of jackdaws,
    And the joyous song of ravens,
    And the chuckling of Vermont tramps
    As they roamed about on freight trains,
    And the crash of breaking soup-plates,
100 And the vivid flash of lanterns,
    And the moonbeams on the wood-pile,
    Seemed to whisper, seemed to tell me:
    "Days of house-cleaning and cold ham
    Will come to you in the future."
105   But sometimes there came a war-whoop,
    Came a sneer from gaunt mosquitos,
    Mocking ever came it to me:
    "'Tis dyspepsy that you cherish,
    'Tis a mince-pie you are chasing."
110   Oft I sought relief in fishing,
    Oft I ran away a-shooting,
    When, alas! my father trounced me,
    Still my shiftless, flighty spirit
    Urged me all day long to shirk work,
115 Urged me off, a sorry Nimrod.
        Scrawny mud-hens, big fish-stories,
    Could not soothe my parent's anger,
    Brought my blistered palms no respite.
        To cut out my unknown rival,
120 To bring 'round her huffish father,
    And secure his full approval
    Of a courtship with his daughter,
    I learnt fiddling, grew side whiskers,
    Wore an actor's gaudy necktie,
125 Wore big slouch hats for head-pieces,
    And assumed a cowboy's hauteur.
        When I next heard of my Janet
    News came she had caught the measles,
    Forced unwilling by her father
130 To go dunning where it rampaged.
        As a school-bell which all fun spoils,
    As a wasp's sting on a dog's nose,

So these tidings fell upon me.
What to me were fiddling parties,
135 What to me were stolen apples,
What were sombreros and "siders,"
If my Janet had the measles?
This last sorrow overtook me
In the days of damp November,
140 When the chilling rains of autumn
Made lagoons along the way-side;
When the birds, with empty paunches,
Tripped about in search of fish-worms,
Eager to begin their journey
145 To the pickings of the Southland.
On that fatal day the storm-gods
Seemed to rise with aching stomachs;
All the skies looked blue and sulky,
All the air was full of Jack-frost,
150 All fat turkeys were uneasy,
All things showed Thanksgiving coming.
All my passions glowed within me
Like a smouldering firecracker;
And unable to control them
155 I rushed forth to try the weather.
And the damp and soggy meadows,
And the dripping trees of woodlands,
And the marrow-chilling north-wind,
Seemed disposed to bring on tooth-aches,
160 Seemed the weather to give hoarse colds.
I could hear the village youngsters
Yelling in the neighb'ring valleys,
Where they builded dams and bridges;
While their dogs barked, and their coughs barked,
165 As they builded, shouted, waded.
I had but one thought to guide me,
That I must reach some retired place,
Reach a likely haunt of squirrels,—
For the winter nights were coming,—
170 There to bag a few more beech-nuts.

With this prudent thought to guide me
I betook me towards the streamlet
Which we two had crossed together
Noontime on a rail-and-board raft.
175 And the scrub trees by the streamlet,
Climbed by urchins in the summer,
Climbed by scart cats at all seasons,
Seemed to beckon, seemed to call me,
Cried in tones untuned, yet jeering,
180 Tones lugubrious, yet noisy,
As a small boy's ten-cent trumpet:
"'Twas a vain chase to pay house rent."
Then the hail began to patter,
And I wandered towards the youngsters,
185 And I shied a stone among them
—And I hied me headlong homeward!

HART GILBERT PALMER

Revisits His Native Place in the Role of a Great Man.

The Story as Frankly Told to His Friends.

"Yes, it was five years since I had shaken the dust of Center Hill off my feet, and in those five years I had become generally known from Bangor to Bungay; for, besides my strike in the San Juan country, I had contrived, in various ways, to lug myself into notoriety. In the first place, I had named and built two mining towns; I had built a railroad; I had written two or three wild, frontier, two-volume books, which people read for the same unfathomable reason that they take patent medicine for old age. In a general way, I had struck it rich all around. Above all, I had put out a gaudy railroad Guide Book! As with all authors, monopolists, and western millionaires, I was universally known by the name of 'Palmer.'

"It was an historical fact that I was notorious—in a word, a marked man. I one day imagined that the simple folk I had been brought up amongst would mistake notoriety for fame, and I determined to revisit my old home to enjoy it.

"It was early in beautiful June, therefore, that I set out to revisit my native place, the obscure little Pennsylvanian village known as Center Hill. I was perfectly well aware that my fame had penetrated to this remote hamlet—in fact, at the outset of my career, I had taken care to apprise them of my triumphs; and curiosity or envy, and above all, their weekly papers, had kept them cognizant of all my brilliant exploits. But for four long years I had had no intercourse with the Center Hillites, which, I well knew, was the bitterest way I could take to revenge myself on them for the studied neglect they had shown me when I lived among them. (I may here remark parenthetically that the news of the goodly fortune my father had unexpectedly bequeathed me shortly after the appearance of my first book, was common gossip everywhere, and contributed, more than anything else, to raise my estimation in the minds of the money-loving people at C. There were many wild rumors afloat about me then, and those credulous villagers believed my fortune a princely one.)

"I again repeat that I visited my native village; and the advent of a man known to fame, a reputed millionaire, and a returned *native*, all in one pompous individual, created a great furore. The newspapers had warned them of my coming, and a dark crowd of people (for it was at night) swarmed about the depot platform, crowding one another, and whispering, 'Yes, that's him; that's him; I wonder if he will know *me*.'

"So, 'him' wasn't welcomed by a brass band, as 'him' had half expected to be. I didn't stop to know many of them, except a few important personages who thrust themselves directly in my way, and a few modest friends who kept in the background, but rode up to the hotel and went to bed. The next day was Saturday, which I spent indoors, writing letters and giving my apartments a ship-shape appearance.

"Sunday evening I went to church, bright and early, to the Episcopal church, as had been my wont aforetime. The church was better filled than of old, I noticed; and also that a goodly number of Methodists and Presbyterians seemed to have been converted from their old-time belief. When I came to leave that church after the services were over, I found the doorway absolutely blocked with young ladies. (At least, some of them were young, and some of them had passed for young five years before.) I struggled past them and slunk off, feeling, somehow, that I had grossly insulted a great many very respectable people. What were my feelings when I reasoned out that that goodly congregation had assembled to see which young lady I should pilot safe home from church! Such is fame—and fortune! It seemed to be taken for granted that as I was still a bachelor I had returned for the express purpose of marrying some one of the incomparable spinsters of Center Hill. This should have occurred to me, being a man of the world. Who would have thought me such an innocent?

"That week the campaign was opened and a reign of terror was inaugurated. I was invited here and there and everywhere; to socials, fishing-parties (and there were no fish to be caught), garden parties, picnics (and it was early for picnics, too, in that primitive place), and I know not what. I was hounded to death to contribute to undeserving charities; when, in my own heart, I saw plainly that they should appeal to the shop-keepers, the baker, and the livery-stable man; for all these did such a business as they had never done before: in fish-hooks; canned picnic meats; bread and buns and confectionery; livery outfits; brand-new market-baskets; paint and putty and wall-paper; and coal-oil; and strawberries; and æsthetic note paper and envelopes; and bewitching summer garments; and brass ornaments for hats; and boots and gloves and parasols and lace collars, that were all painful in there newness.

"I happened to mention that I intended to select a few characters for a novel I contemplated writing. I always was unlucky, anyhow; but in saying that I deliberately laid myself open to all sorts of unpleasantnesses. After I had unwittingly given offence to one young lady, she took occasion to remark that for *her* part she never *did* see anything really good in my writings; and that my book 'The Commandery Lode' was perfectly ridiculous, and not to be compared with a *New York Weekly* romance of that name. This was said 'behind my back,' it is true; but so very close behind my back that it required no mental effort, no practiced ear, to overhear it. However, I had survived other criticisms, and I bore up under that.

"One week after my arrival I was at a social gathering at a house whose doors were forbidden me in my obscure and lonely youth. I went under protest, but with the grim resolve of bagging some valuable notes that might be filed away for future use. During the course of the evening a youth whom I had always liked as a boy gravely asked me if I knew what the *Princeburg Review* had to say about me. 'Yes,' chimed in a score of eager young voices, 'and the *Center Hill Reporter*, and the *Princeburg Age*, and the *Dragonsburg Defender*. Oh, but of course you *do* know,' they added confidently. Center Hill had so improved in five years that it now had an exponent of its own. The Princeburg papers were old sheets, of some pretentiousness and very much complacency, that were always fighting each other like quarrelsome dogs. No, I was not aware, I said, that any of these papers had anything special to say about me. Straightway the heir of that house darted out of the room, and soon came back with an armful of newspapers, and began looking for the numbers that contained those blood-curdling remarks about myself. I instantly perceived that by taking prompt and vigorous measures I could throw cold water, so to speak, on his design, and impress my greatness upon every member of that assemblage. So I begged him not to put himself to so much trouble on my account, for I never could spare either time or patience to get at the pith and marrow of what local papers have to say. The poor boy's countenance fell; but the water wasn't cold enough, it seems, for he fumbled among those *Reviews, Reporters, Ages*, and what not, more excitedly than ever. Then the young lady who never could see any good points in my books, for *her* part, observed, *sotto voce*, 'There are some things anything but complimentary in them.' But any further remarks from her were drowned by a chorus of voices saying,—well, saying what amounted to this: The papers gave an account of my early struggles; of how I was respected and beloved by my old and true friends in all that section; of how I always made friends right and left; of *how greatly I was regarded in my youth, when* COMPARATIVELY *obscure*; of my colossal wealth to-day; of my flowing style; and so on, *ad nauseam*. (I notice my present auditors smile; I wish they could have seen *me* smile then.) Now, why should I want to wade through such stuff and nonsense as that? I had soared to such a pinnacle of glory that the maunderings of country—or rather village—newspapers had neither an inspiriting nor yet a depresing effect on me. I was perfectly well aware that little local journals have a trick of lauding well-known people, with a view to furthering their own ends. I was aware that all this cheap flattery would, if I suffered myself to be influenced by it, lead up to a demand for an article from my pen—just a slight, hasty sketch would do; almost anything. I was aware, also, that if I turned a deaf ear to these noisy nuisances, or that if I pleaded that I didn't bring any pen with me, their praises would give place to defamations, and that they would spill venom on me without mercy.

"But I hadn't traveled fifteen hundred miles to wade through the columns of their local weeklies. So I said, 'My dear boy, be it for good or for evil, my reputation is established—for this season, anyway. Please do not bore us to-night with any cullings from those oracular weeklies. I thank you for your well-meant kindness, I am sure. There are people who try to make my life a burden by mailing me influential newspapers with marked items about myself; but I generally burn them at once, without even preserving the valuable receipts they contain on domestic and other affairs. I am proud to be able to say, however, that it is ten years since any person had troubled me with either a penny valentine or a local weekly paper. It is not often I make a speech, but I'm afraid this is one, and I hope you will forgive me for it.'

"Now, that boy was well brought up; exceedingly well. He needed no further remonstrances from me, but hied him away with his budget of weeklies. I am sorry he didn't appear again that evening; very sorry. His mamma should have vented her anger on me, and not on him; for I must say that I had been grossly impolite—abusive, even. I reasoned at the time that all officious attention to me would at once cease; that I should be regarded as no better than a bear, and so left severely alone. I was wrong; wearied as I had become of their attentions, this did not shake them off. They seemed determined, rather, to force me into reading their weeklies. I found them in my room; thrust on me wherever I went; foisted on me through the post-office. But I steadily refused to read them, and so obstinate an indifference to the voice of their oracles must have puzzled them.

"On the 24th of June a circus was first advertized as coming to Dragonsburg and Princeburg; and the weeklies, having another lion to tackle, in a great measure dropped me. Likewise the villagers didn't persecute me to read their papers any more, but went on with their picnics. By George! they almost picnicked me to death! I have been troubled with indigestion ever since.

"I may here mention that the first day I went out into the street I was surprised to find that every family had either a boy, a horse, a dog, or a cat, that was afflicted with the name of Gilbert. Some of the boys, and very many of the cats and dogs, were called Hart—because it is shorter, I suppose. Palmer, I found, was a favorite name for their trotters. Not a few baby girls, it seems, were christened Gilbertina. All this rather pleased me, I must admit—till I found there were two foundlings baptized, or rather named, Hart Gilbert Palmer. To an honest man with a clear conscience, this was simply annoying; but when I reflected that it was the only opportunity the citizens had to bestow my name in full on one individual, and that they had improved it on two occasions, I was mollified. Still, it sometimes vexed me, and even startled me, till I became accustomed to it, to hear my various harsh names harshly bandied about the street—particularly when the gamins would yell, 'Gilbert 'll wallop your dog'; or 'Hart's got the mange;' or 'Palmer ain't the nag he used to be.'

"All this time the match-making mammas were making my life a burden. I must confess my sympathies were entirely with those lonely spinsters who, having no one to chaperon them, entered the lists, and gamely fought single-handed against those well-equipped mammas for the possession of my coveted gold.

"The Fourth of July drew near, and I determined to play a trick on the villagers that should amuse me for years to come. There were to be great local 'doings' on this day, of course; and the villagers planned to make a spectacle of me as an orator, etc. But I told them, six days beforehand, that I purposed to do my celebrating in private, away out in the country. This announcement alone whetted their curiosity. Then I visited the village tailor and out-fitter. The incessant picnics and fishing-parties had told severely on my wearing apparel; and why should I not 'patronize home industry,' as the tailor's sign read? I directed him to make me a suit, of his very best material, and to have it finished and delivered to me, without fail, by July 3rd. With great care I selected a silk hat, and, after cautioning him for the fifth or sixth time to have my suit finished by the 3rd, left his shop. Several idlers had dropped in while I was giving my instructions, and taken careful notes. I was not surprised at this. In fact, I had bargained on it; for a great many curious and gossipy people made it a business to dog me about, and watch my every movement. They took a special pride in supplying all the latest and raciest gossip about other people's affairs; and they knew that if they lagged behind in this particular, their reputation as newsmongers would be endangered.

"Next I went into various other shops, and ordered gimcrackery with a lavishness that was phenomenal: a riding-whip, a pair of lady's gauntlets, a gorgeous parasol, a box of Malaga grapes, a few pounds of confectionery, and I know not what. All these were to be sent to me, *without fail*, before the 4th. I perceived that the on-lookers noted all my purchases, and that the shop-keepers marvelled; and I chuckled.

"I suffered twenty-four hours to pass before I again appeared on the street; and as I had anticipated, a good many able-bodied people were waiting and watching for me. After taking a few steps I turned squarely about, and seeing that I was followed, I paused, as if irresolute. I feigned anxiety to avoid them by turning up one by-street and down another; and by doubling on them repeatedly I contrived to bring up at my destination, the village livery-stables, apparently unobserved. I say, apparently unobserved, for they perceived my efforts to escape observation, and considerately pretended to let me elude them; but I knew I was watched, all the time. The village now believed that I wished to keep my plans and movements a secret, and I felicitated myself on my amazing shrewdness in hoodwinking everybody so completely. I told the proprietor of the livery that I wanted a good horse—in fact, the best one he had—for the 4th.

He showed me such an animal, and I examined it critically, remarked that it seemed good for a twenty-mile run, and tendered him an eagle. He protested that was too much; but I told him it was my affair how much I paid, and that I would have given a handful of them but I would have secured the horse. Then he, in his turn, became curious, but he was crafty and disguised it. I remarked incidentally that I hoped the roads wouldn't be dusty; then added carelessly that I supposed the old private short cut to the Ochiltree's was still open, and that it was the pleasantest and quietest road I knew. I had now sufficiently piqued the man's curiosity, and after charging him to send me the horse at eight o'clock sharp on the morning of the 4th, I went back to the hotel, noticing that I had been tracked to the livery-stable.

"Let me here explain that the name of Ochiltree was an unknown name in all that county and in all that region. I had taken particular pains to consult documentary evidence, and assure myself of this fact.

"All this was four or five days before the Fourth. I wanted the thing generally known, and I also wanted to give the villagers plenty of time to make any changes in their programme for the day that they might think expedient.

"On the 1st of July I formally told most of my friends that I should leave for the Pacific coast on the great and glorious Fourth, by the night train; but that I should take my departure from a neighboring town, and that probably they would see the last of me on the 3rd inst. Several of them begged me to stay over for the circus, on which auspicious day, it would appear, they hoped to work me up to a proposal. The greatest uncertainty prevailed as to whom I should propose; but a proposal, to any person, would relieve the general anxiety.

"The news of my openly announced departure on the 4th threw the village into a ferment. There was more excitement than a local election would have caused. But who was this Ochiltree? Where did he live? Was it *his* daughter that I was to elope with, or whose? When had I made the unknown's acquaintance, anyway? In my neglected youth, probably, when no one had bothered to watch me. On the 3rd I formally bade my honest friends good-bye. A few asked me pointed questions about my proposed jaunt on the morrow, but the great majority maintained a dignified silence on that subject.

"The eve of July the Fourth came punctually on time. At the eleventh hour I sent a note to the livery-stable, saying I must have the horse at half-past seven instead of eight—which was a wise move on my part. Then I packed my trunk, carefully putting away in it all the feminine finery I had bought, and which had been delivered to me promptly that day at noon.

"At 7.30 a.m., July the Fourth, I sprang on my horse and rode away to the west. This highway led to no important point, as I very well knew, unless one followed it for some fifty miles. I rode out of the village at a smart pace, and at once perceived that my utmost anticipations were to be realized. But as I noticed what was going on about me, my heart smote me at the thought of spoiling the holiday of so many guileless people. The village was rising as one man to pursue me! I verily believe there was not a Hart, a Gilbert, or a Palmer, in all that region, sound, or blind, or spavined, or foundered, that was not pressed into service. It was indeed lucky for me that I was off half an hour before they expected me. '"A stern chase is a long chase,"' I said to myself, 'but this time it will be a woeful way longer for them than for me!'

"On they came, amid clouds of dust. It was well that I had provided myself with a riding-whip, for I needed it sorely. I had not ridden far when I saw a horseman stationed by the roadside, waiting calmly. Soon another, and another. I wheeled down a dirt road and galloped on. Lo, there, also, were horsemen!

"This was beginning to get interesting! These sentinel horsemen would be able to put the pursuers on my track at every turn. The pursuers, however, kept so far in the back-ground that I could hardly suspect, as yet, that they were actually following me. Evidently these meddlesome villagers knew what they were about, and meant business.

"'I will show them, however,' I muttered, 'that they are no match for a man who knows the world as I do.' So I inquired of each horseman, as I encountered him, the lay of the land and of the different roads, and left each one with a wrong impression as to the road I should take. I made sharp turns, and took my course over half-a-dozen roads, giving sentinels and wayfarers, each and all, a false notion of my route. All this, I argued, would confuse my pursuers and scatter them over the country in every direction, thus giving me an opportunity to escape.

"Three miles from the town I found there were no more sentinels posted. Apparently it was thought that once fairly started on my track it would be an easy matter to keep me in view. But, had these scouts been placed to the east, the north, and the south, as closely as I found them along my route? I flattered myself that that it must be so, but never made bold to probe the matter.

"Now, I mused, these searchers after knowledge will study the geography of this tract of country more thoroughly to-day than they have ever studied it before since their fourteenth year; it will give them an outing, and their holiday won't be entirely lost.

"After passing the last sentry I fetched a detour, and threw the pursuers completely off the scent. I glimpsed a party of them once as I rode along, and that one fleeting view puffed me up with pride, and amply recouped me for the gold I had squandered for that day's sport. It always does a man good to find that he is not without regard in his native place, and that his schemes are successful. And surely I had found this, to my satisfaction!

"Now I was free to journey whither I pleased; and after a good half-hour's ride I brought up at a substantial farm-house, barely seven miles from Center Hill, as the crow flies. Here lived an oldtime schoolfellow of mine, whom I had not seen for years. He was overjoyed at the meeting, and we spent the rest of the day happily together, recalling scenes of our boyhood days. If I *did* talk to his sister as much as I did to him, I don't suppose it is anybody's affair but hers and mine; and if I *did* make over my box of grapes (which I had found great trouble in bringing along) to a still smaller sister,— one whom I had never seen,—I was only treating her as well as (or rather better than) I had been treated myself in days gone by, when I was blessed with a charming elder sister of my own. But it is an irrelevancy to make any mention of such things at all in this narration. I had notified Will that he might look for me on the forenoon of the Fourth; but they ought not to have expected me to do justice to the extraordinary dinner they prepared for me. As I have said several times, the picnickers ruined my appetite.

"During the course of the afternoon three different squads of searchers passed the old farm-house, and I quaked inwardly, fearing that I had been run to earth, after all. But they all passed on. Then the entire force of village hoodlums and gamins, who served as a rear-guard, filed past, fully one hundred strong. *Their* holiday was not utterly a blank, I am glad to say, for they were freely popping off the joyous fire-cracker as they scattered along.

"The enemy were on the right trail, certainly; but they did not find me out. However, I confided in Will and his sister, and obtained their promise to keep the affair a secret.

"About six o'clock, seeing no enemies in sight, I mounted my horse and rode into town, thinking to deepen the mystery and astonish the villagers afresh. I did not find quite so deserted a place as I had fondly imagined I should. There were still enough able-bodied people left behind to have defended Center Hill against any evil-disposed tramps that might have come in by freight train. But the villagers were paralyzed to see me back, at that hour. The time they had arbitrarily fixed, it seems, for my earliest possible return—in case I should return—was ten o'clock.

"I was mean enough to tantalize them all still further.

I ate my supper and left on the eight o'clock train for Dragonsburg, a town twelve miles to the north-west. I had my trunk checked for this point, too. I don't know whether I was followed, or not; but I left my native town—perhaps forever—a prey to the most appalling speculations and doubts about myself. I changed cars at Dragonsburg, and left on the midnight train for Chicago.

"It is a question if any one individual ever brought about so many blasted hopes, and demoralized air-castles, and ruinous baker's bills, as I did by my outrageous behavior at Center Hill. Perhaps they try to console themselves with the thought that my unknown sweetheart must have given me the mitten.

"I never had the temerity to make inquiries and find out whether those poor, misguided people still go on inflicting my various names on the rising generation of men and brutes. But I presume they don't; I presume they heartily wish they had never known me or heard of me.

"Good George! I have talked myself hoarse, and my listeners fast asleep!"

"Not *all*. But what about the gloves, parasol, and other feminine luxuries?"

"That is an entirely irrelevant question. Still, as you must have inferred the significance of my visit to Will, and as I am feeling pretty good-natured, I will tell you: I have succeeded in working off most of those knick-knacks on my feminine relatives. Some of them, however, will keep!—Good night!"

TO MY OLD DOG, NERO.

Not dog and master we, but friends,
    (Nor were ever sweethearts more fond)
And naught *our* fellowship offends,
    Nor can jealousy break the bond.
My dog and I are lovers twain,
Without the lover's madd'ning pain.

His joyous bark delights my heart
    As we wander adown the stream ;
My dog and I are ne'er apart,
    And our life is a long day-dream.
We little reck how this world wags,
Nor ever find one hour that drags.

And when sometimes with gun we rove,
    Nor bold eagles that live in air,
Nor beast nor bird found in the grove,
    Than ourselves are more free from care ;
Though well we know, my dog and I,
That this old world oft gets awry.

The grand old sun, in his day's race,
    May be hidden by sullen clouds,
And never show his honest face
    To the hurried and restless crowds.
Such haps fret not my dog and me,
We view the world so scornfully.

The crackling fire within burns bright,
    And my heart is quite free from care ;
Though fondest hopes were put to flight
    By a sweetheart as false as fair,
I know my good old dog is true,
And Nero knows I love him, too.

I have no mind to be content
    With a pipe or a demijohn ;
Nor have I reason to lament
    The old love who has come and gone—
Yet in my dog I have a friend
Whose steadfast love but death can end.

The wind may roar, the black rain fall,
    And the night may be dull and sad,
Nor friend nor foe may chance to call,
    To complain, or to make us glad ;
But what care we, my dog and I,
How this old world may laugh or sigh.

GROANS THAT FOUND UTTERANCE

AFTER THE FALL OF THE SECOND BABYLON.

AN MEINE VERLORENE LIEBSTE.

WITH cruel drag eight weary years
Have come and gone, I know not how.
    My boyish dreams were wide of truth,
    My heart is not the heart of youth;
    Yet the old love still glows within,
    Yours the one smile that I would win.
To Destiny at last I bow,
And yield vain hopes to saddest fears.

THE SCARCE AND BITTER FRUIT

OF THE SUMMER OF 1884.

WOULD to God, oh! would to Heaven,
That these days and nights of torment
Might give place to just one moment
Of that happiness of old days
Which I knew ere yet I ventured
To write books and dream of * * * *;
Which I knew ere either sweetheart—
Either * * * * * of my boyhood,
Or yet * * * * of my manhood—
Had wrung my fond heart with anguish
And veiled all my life with darkness
That will haunt me to my death-bed.

THE CANADIAN CLIMATE.

IF the attempt had been made in Canada to establish our present system of seasons, and the allotment of 365¼ days to the year, the work would have proved a superhuman one, and would have resulted in the complete demoralization of every mathematician and astronomer undertaking it. Instead of the orderly system now prevailing, it would have been left a disputed question whether winter should begin on the 17th day of November, or thirteen days before Christmas; whether winter, once inaugurated, should cover a period of one hundred and twenty-seven days and nights, or discount eleven and a half days to the credit of spring. There would have arisen a far-reaching schism as to whether dog-days begin on the 29th of June, or on the 41st of August; and the more ardent supporters of one faction would have written abstruce text-books to prove by inductive logic that dog-days begin theoretically on the first-mentioned date, while the equally enthusiastic supporters of the other faction would have proved by deductive logic, the fashions regulating bathing costumes, and the hypothetical history of all exhumed mastodons, that it is *ultra vires* and high treason to maintain that dog-days ever did or ever could begin on any other date than the 41st of August, at 2 o'clock p. m. The faction of the "great unwashed" would have split off from these latter, holding that, in the fitness of things, dog-days come in with the advent of the dog-catcher, feeze off and on indefinitely, co-existent with his career, and finally leave us abruptly just ten days after the sea-serpent appears at Newport and the first tramp-loaded freight train starts for Texas. The heated disputes occasioned by all this uncertainty would have led to the rise and fall of republics, the dynamiting of Cæsars, the conversion and extermination of the cow-boy of Arizona, the premature discovery of revolvers, of Ignatius Donnelly's Key, of messenger-boys, of divorce lawyers, of subscription books, of bogus testimonials, and of mind-reading.

Then again the greatest discrepancy would have prevailed among scientists and coal-dealers in trying to strike an average temperature for January and March; and the English emigrant would have debated so long the important question whether a shilling thermometer would be likely to stand the wear and tear of a Canadian winter, or whether it would be advisable for him to arm himself with an instrument warranted to wrestle with April days in January and all-congealing cold in May, that finally he would have taken ship for South Africa and have shared the fate of the tender antelope and the juicy missionary.

If a Rip Van Winkle should awaken in our midst he could only approximately fix the season and the month. But there are in Canada four special and immortal days on which Rip Van could always and infallibly fix not only the month, but the exact day of the month. The first in order is the 20th of February, on which date the grimy gamin celebrates the initial game of marbles of the season. (The peaceable, respectable, and less warm-blooded public-school boy plays his first game from four to seven days later, and so is less to be depended on in fixing a date.) The second date is that of the 3rd of

April, on which auspicious day the first patriotic Canadian tramp and the first impetuous robin revisit the land of their birth. Both are a trifle previous in their calculations; both suffer considerably from cold feet; but they are too proud to acknowledge their mistake by any retrograde movement. Our next epochal date is the 29th of May, when the small boy—irrespective of the condition of the weather, the impurity of the water, his own temperament, his susceptibility to the quinsy, or the social position of his grandfather—takes his first "swim" in the creek. On appointed holidays the small boy may or he may not point the vivacious fire-cracker at the hired man; he may or he may not gorge himself with stuffed turkey on Thanksgiving-day, and so cease to be tormented with Dr. Bugbear's pills and other worthy remedies that he has so often dutifully choked down— but he will go in swimming on the 29th of May, or the heavens will fall. And now we come to the red-letter day of the Canadian calendar: the glorious 10th of June, in the afternoon of which day the United States circus poster makes its annual appearance on the board fences and dead walls of all inhabitable places in the land.

On any one of these dates an almanac need not be referred to in Canada by any one who has eyes to see and ears to hear; at any other time an almanac is as vital a necessity as a chart at sea. The promiscuous distribution of gaudy patent medicine almanacs in Canada is all that has saved the country and the climate from the established fate of the chestnut bell and the prospective fate of the traveling doctor.

LOTTIE.

HANS REINGOLD and Lottie Kennedy were betrothed lovers. The day of their marriage was appointed, but it was still far in the future. Lottie's people were poor, and Hans was not rich, so they were content to wait till there should be a fair prospect of their having at least a small portion of this world's goods.

Hans was the chemical expert for a large manufacturing firm in Philadelphia, and so was necessarily away from home and from Lottie the greater part of the time. It was a hard life, being called from one State to another at a moment's notice, and the work was often exhaustive; but Hans took all that as a matter of course, and tried to make the best of it.

One Christmas day, when Hans was home, Lottie received a pressing invitation from a rich but niggardly old uncle in Albany to come and pay him a long visit. In fact, the letter ran, she was to stay till she should be heartily sick of the place and of her uncle. The letter wound up with a vaguely-worded intimation that if Lottie's visit should be entirely satisfactory to all parties concerned, she would have cause to thank her stars that she came. According to Mrs. Kennedy's interpretation, this meant that if the old man was pleased with Lottie, he would make her his heiress.

With such inducements as these, Lottie quickly decided on making the visit immediately. There would be a little preparation to be made in the matter of two or three dresses and as many hats. As for gloves, etc., it was left to the uncle's generosity to supply such things.

Mrs. Kennedy, with a depth of sagacity that proved her to be a woman of no ordinary discernment, had Lottie's new garments made very plain and of cheap material. Thus the old miser, her uncle, would perceive that Lottie was poor, but not ashamed to wear plain clothing; and thus one step towards gaining his favor would have been taken. Lottie could safely be left to do the rest.

The lovers saw each other for the last time on New Year's day. They did not expect to be parted very long, but the parting was sad, especially for Hans, who must return to his employment; while Lottie would be away, with new people, new scenes, and new duties to occupy her attention.

"You will not forget me, Lottie?" said Hans. "You will not allow that selfish uncle of yours to browbeat you into a marriage with some favorite of his?"

"No, Hans; I will prove true to you."

"Promise me, Lottie, solemnly, that you will never let your heart——"

"Don't bring on the heroics, Hans," Lottie said, with a laugh.

"Promise, Lottie," Hans persisted.

"I promise, then; sincerely—from my heart of heart."

"And I will trust you, Lottie, implicitly. Lottie, suppose that we have a watch-word, a shibboleth, between us; something by means of which, in case danger should menace one of us, the other could be secretly informed of it."

"Oh, now, Hans, when this is our last day together, don't let us fritter away the time in trying to be romantic."

But Hans knew Lottie better than she thought. "Very

(3)

well," he said; "you are right enough; it would be only foolishness."

There was a pause. Lottie waited impatiently for Hans to explain what he meant by a watch-word. But as he showed no disposition to do so, she finally said, musingly: "Well, it might be well enough, Hans; at any rate, it wouldn't do any harm. What is your idea, Hans?"

"Oh, nothing; only, as I shall be traveling about continually, an item in one of the great journals that has an extensive circulation would reach me, wherever I might be, when a letter might hang fire. So, if you should ever be desperately in need of a friend, a few words, neatly put, in the personal column of one of the New York papers, would cause me to fly to you on the wings of the wind."

"Now, Hans, that figure is effective, but it isn't original with you; it seems to me I've heard it very often before."

"Yes, of course, Lottie; it is all a piece of foolishness."

Again Lottie was obliged to ask Hans what he meant.

"Let us word it in this way, and then either of us could insert it: 'The talk on New Year's was not foolishness, after all. Come.' Then sign it 'Lottie,' or 'Hans,' as the case might be."

"Now, Hans, you put it that way on purpose to tease me! Why not put it in this way: 'Lottie, you may come on the wings of the wind. Hans'? Of course, if *I* should insert it, I would reverse the names."

"Now you are teasing me! But, yes, that is a decided improvement. Now, we must agree not to make use of our watch-word unless the need should be urgent, the case imperative."

" Yes, yes ; I understand, without the 'case imperative.' I think you have been in the imperative case enough to-day—or rather, in the imperative mood."

"That's right, Lottie ; you always contrive to lug in something so that you can tack on an addendum containing the words, 'grammatically speaking,'" Hans replied, somewhat gruffly.

" Well, the caution is needless, anyway ; *I* will never insert any such personal," flashed back Lottie.

Then they kissed, and asked each other's forgiveness, and cried a little,—at least Lottie did,—and declared that nothing should ever part them. Lottie presently referred again to the watch-word, and they decided on *The New York World*, which both read, as the newspaper in which to insert the personal in case of fancied need.

Hans took the train for Philadelphia, to receive his instructions from the head of the firm ; and the next day Lottie left home for her uncle's, to make a visit of indefinite length.

Lottie's life at her uncle's big stone house was quiet enough, though not unpleasant; but she felt that it was a life which would soon become painfully monotonous. The middle-aged house-keeper was methodical and precise to an extreme, as well as dictatorial and unamiable, always keeping a sharp look-out that Lottie should not intermeddle in household affairs. The rich old uncle was crotchety and peevish—in a word, a bearish old fellow, as cross-grained as the typical step-father. He wished Lottie to be always busy, either reading musty histories, or keeping his library in prim order, or cutting out clippings from scientific journals, or reading the politics of the day to him, or answering his business letters, or knitting woollen stockings for the newsboys—the only thing he ever did to contribute to the necessities of the poor.

It is no wonder that Lottie wearied of this and longed to return home, where, after performing her toilet in the morning, she was free to spend the rest of the day lolling on a lounge and reading Miss Braddon's interminable novels.

"If this sort of thing goes on much longer," she wrote her mother, "I shall contrive to offend his seigneurship mortally, and get packed off home *in the identical garments I had when I came.* (I have purposely made these two lines emphatic.) There is no other way to get away; for whenever I hint at going home, he puts on a martyr-like air, and asks me if I am tired of my poor, forlorn old uncle, if I realize how much he is doing for me, and if I bear in mind what he said in his letter of invitation. Then he accuses me of being ungrateful, and giddy, and shallow-pated, and narrow-minded, and unduly biased, and surcharged with self-esteem, and irrational, and unpractical; and says I am a stumbling-block in my own pathway. I wasn't brought up to have such epithets and metaphors heaped upon me, and I won't stand it."

To Hans she wrote that she hadn't found an opportunity to read a novel since she left home; "and then,' she said, "I could find time to read only one during Christmas week, and that a stupid one; for, what with saffron-faced dressmakers and the excitement and bustle of packing my trunk, and your endless and often inopportune visits, my time was wholly taken up, so that I was even deprived of needful sleep. As for uncle's Napoleons, and his Charles V.'s, and his Cæsars, and his Pharaohs, and his Egyptologies, and his entomologies, and his Unhappy Stuarts—why, I have as profound a hatred for them all as I had for my first stupid, gawky beau."

Hans wrote regularly and lovingly to Lottie, and she never failed to write to him whenever he could tell her exactly where and when a letter would reach him.

But once he went to the office in Toledo, fully expecting to find a letter from Lottie. No, there was no letter, and he had specially requested her to write to him there at such a date. This was very strange.

His business detained him in Toledo twenty-four hours, and he appeared at the post-office after every mail from the east was due. All in vain.

"Poor Lottie! Poor little girl!" he murmured. "She would never wilfully miss writing to me; I know her too well for that. But what can have happened? Has that old ogre, with his romantic Roman notions about the fitness of——Romantic? *The New York World!* Oh, Lottie! Lottie! I hope all is well!"

Poor Hans had been driven so hard since New Year's that he had not found time to read the *World* or anything else. His only day of rest was Sunday, when he read and re-read his letters from home, and dozed in his room at the hotel.

Five minutes thereafter he was reading this among the personals of a late number of the *World*:

"Hans, notwithstanding the foolish talk on New Year's day, Lottie wishes you to come on the wings of the wind. Never mind business; the 'case' is 'imperative.'"

"Oh, Lottie! Lottie! what is the matter?" Hans murmured. "Dear girl; I knew something serious must have happened, or she would have written. She has remembered our watch-word, and she has availed herself of it. It is not just as we agreed it should be; but I suppose Lottie wanted to make it very pointed and imperative. Oh, I hope she is well! This really reads as if nothing very serious is wrong—can it be a joke? No; it is just Lottie's way; I remember she worked off a pun when her pet kitten died, and she would have risked her life to save that kitten; and how she cried afterwards! I know Lottie; I know something awful must be wrong. My route leads towards home, and I will go that far and then telegraph my employers, and go on to Lottie, if I lose my situation and all my prospects in life. When my love appeals to me so strongly, it is enough; I will go."

Hans left Toledo an hour later for Cleveland. Here he stopped to telegraph to his employers. Hurrying along towards the business centre of the city, to do his last stroke of business and send his telegram, he met with an accident that might have proved fatal. A coupé rattled around a corner as he was crossing a street; the horses struck him; he fell helpless; and the rear wheel passed over his right leg below the knee, breaking it.

A crowd of sympathizing people and of grinning hoodlums gathered about the helpless and unconscious man, lifted him tenderly into a cab, and had him taken direct to the hospital. A surgeon promptly set the broken limb and prescribed a soothing draught for him; and then, poor fellow, he was left alone to his sufferings, which internal injuries intensified.

"This is a pretty state of affairs," moaned Hans, when he recovered consciousness and ability to think coherently.

"The rescue is now virtually at an end. Poor Lottie! If she had only written to let me know what is wrong! But if she could have done so, she would have. Poor little girl! Anxious as I am about her, I cannot even guess what may have happened. Where is she now? Oh, why didn't I at least telegraph to ask what was wrong? But I thought it better not to do so. Why, I didn't even get my telegram sent to the firm, and when they miss me, they will not know what has become of me! Will any one know? In fact, I am the same as buried, till I can send a telegram; and those who miss me may think I have been murdered. No, this accident will come out in the Cleveland papers—probably, in other papers. But will they see it? My first duty is clearly to apprise my friends and the firm of my misfortune."

Hans gave directions to wire his employers immediately, but hesitated about sending any word to Lottie.

"As I cannot help her, why should I add to her distress? If I should telegraph, 'Laid up in the hospital with a broken leg,' what would she be benefited? She would only be uneasy about me, and think me in a worse condition than I really am. But on the other hand, if I send no message, she will still expect me, and wait confidently for me to come. It will be at least five weeks before I can leave the hospital, and that would be too late. Of course; didn't the personal say, 'the case is imperative'? Something must be done; but what? If only I could know what is the matter!"

The next day Hans had hit upon an expedient.

"It may be foolish, or even wrong, in me," he reflected; "but it is a last resource, and I will hazard it. Charley always was a loyal friend to me, always ready to lend me his assistance. If anybody can grasp the situation and bring Lottie out of her difficulties, whatever they may be, it is Charley. Brave, good-natured, heedless, indolent, rollicking Charley! When we were all boys together, he was our policeman, detective, judge, hangman, and outlaw; and he always played his part creditably. I always told him that some day kings would read his name, and he always said they shouldn't, if he could help it—he'd rather be the hero of a novel. It will do him good to leave his guns and his dogs for a while, and be detective in earnest."

This would be a fitting time to pause and mourn over Hans' imprudence, speak vaguely and darkly about the future, and hint of a day when Hans would rue this action, though the mischief would then be irreparable. But the story-teller who feels obliged to have recourse to such tricks is either antiquated, or else he does not rate his own abilities as a story-teller very highly. Besides, the inference, or moral, to be drawn from the story of "LOTTIE" lies deeper than all this.

Hans despatched a telegram to the wilds of Michigan, where Charles Worthington, his sometime schoolfellow, was idling away the summer. To insure its being effective, Hans made his message rather startling. It ran:—

"Charley: broken my leg; come first train; awful revelations; mysteries; new employment for you; for the sake of other days, come! Hans Reingold."

The 1.10 a.m. train brought a tall, fat, jolly-looking fellow, with military mustache and profuse curls, accompanied by a huge dog, that proudly wore a collar on which was the legend, Meine Fangzähne sind Blitzschnell und Teufelscharf. The man was Charley; and to complete his costume he wore a fantastic cap, turban, or head-piece of some sort, which looked as if it had often been in the dog's mouth.

"Fifteen years ago I warned you of this," was the new-comer's greeting, as he grasped Hans' feverish hand and shook it with a heartiness that elicited a groan of pain from the sufferer and a word of caution from the doctor.

"Charley, old fellow, your very presence is medicine!" Hans ejaculated.

"Rather violent medicine, I should say," laughed Charley. "Too big a dose would cause dissolution."

"How have you been all this time? How have you amused yourself?"

"Happier than the poets picture peasants and dairy-maids; as well as if I had lived on patent medicine; as idle as a 'landed proprietor.'"

"But what have you been doing?"

"I have been an Indian. Do you mean to say that Indians are not happy, and well, and idle?"

"I suppose you mean you have been camping out?"

"Exactly; I have been camping out—only, I have had no camp, no hut, no brush-house, no dug-out, no adobe—nothing—not even a schoolboy's play-house!"

"Was it pleasant?"

"Yes, very—when I was asleep, and unmindful of Nature's living wonders."

"What are you driving at now, Charley?"

"Well, Hans, if you have an illustrated natural history handy, I will look up the reptile and insect department, and show you."

"If you wish to have a private talk, gentlemen," said the surgeon, "I will leave you. But remember, Mr. Reingold, no excitement."

"Well, old fellow," said Charley, as soon as the surgeon had withdrawn, "what was the racket when you sent me such a telegram? Was the pain so intense that you were delirious? or was it a freak of nightmare? You never were an adept at schoolboyish tricks, and you are too old to begin now."

"No, Charley; this is a serious affair."

"'Affair'? That means a duel, I believe. A rival, I presume? Well, I will do my best for you; but I am opposed to duels on high moral principles. Poor fellow! poor broken-legged Hans! Got embroiled, I suppose; then challenged; then broke your leg; then had the assurance to send for me to vindicate your honor! Some scoundrels would at once right about for the 'happy hunting grounds' again—but *I* will stay and fight it out."

"You read too many novels, Charley. Why, you will be a romancer yourself, if you keep on as hopefully as you have begun."

"See here, you haven't told me anything about yourself, your accident, yet. Not another word till I know just how this happened, and how you bore it, and how it will affect your finances—that is, your business prospects. I have come prepared, in case you stand in need of any dross."

"Thank you, Charley; you are more thoughtful than I supposed. But I have plenty of money to tide me over this."

Then Hans talked constantly for half an hour, telling the story of the accident; of Lottie's visit to her uncle;

of the agreement, made half in jest, half in earnest, to insert a curiously-worded personal in the *World* in case of difficulty; of the appearance of such a personal; of the non-arrival of a letter from Lottie; and of his determination to send for Charles.

"Well," yawned Charles, "this tale reminds me forcibly of Simple Simon and his doings. Now, Hans, don't accuse me of turning romancer, for you are drifting into something worse."

"I'm sorry, Charley," said Hans quaveringly.

"'Pon my word, I forgot you are sick! Forgive me, Hans; I didn't mean anything; I never do. Yes, I will play the knight-errant; I will sally forth, like Don Quixote; besiege the castle of her captor; decapitate the dragons and gorgons; and convoy her back to you. Then I will, if you please, humbly eat a slice of wedding cake, and hunt my way back to Michigan, uncivilization, and the realities of modern times.—But seriously, Hans, I can tell you what the game is at Albany."

"*You* can? Tell me, then!"

"Miss Kennedy has forgotten that the first of April has passed; or she is homesick; or she has fallen in love with on oil-painting of some ancient worthy—perhaps, Juan de Soto."

"Oh, Worthington! How provoking you are! If my leg were better, I would pommel you like a mule."

"That's good, Hans! Now you talk rationally."

"Well, will you go?"

"On the first train in the morning."

Then the two old friends got along amicably for a few minutes longer. Hans gave Charles the address of Lottie's uncle and of her parents; and so they parted.

But very early in the morning Charles looked in for a last good-by and for Hans' final instructions.

Slowly the days passed for poor Hans—one—two—three. He did not improve so rapidly as he should have done, owing to his uneasiness about Lottie. But on the third day a letter came from Charles, to the effect that he had reached Albany, and found Lottie and her mother safe and well, at the uncle's home. The uncle was dead, and Lottie was his sole heiress, the mistress of some tens of thousands. That was all; Lottie had been so "worried" (that was the word) at the time of her uncle's death that she had not been able to write. As for the advertisement, or personal, that was merely a ruse to bring Hans home and surprise him with the news of Lottie's good fortune.

The next day Hans received a letter from Lottie herself.

"You would have done better had you written or telegraphed," she wrote. "I had prepared a fine surprise for you; and how pleased we should all have been. You see, dear Hans, the 'personal' was a mistaken idea, a 'piece of foolishness,' after all. I am sorry if I have been blamable for your accident, Hans. I suppose I should not have called you away from your business; only I knew you could well afford to give it up, and set up for yourself in something lucrative and respectable, with a large capital. Get well as fast as you can, and I will write as often as may be; but I have a great deal to attend to now.

"P. S. I am so glad you sent Mr. Worthington, Hans; he is so droll and polite. It has turned out quite like a romance, hasn't it? Just fancy! My bank account alone is fifty thousand! Sometimes I feel sorry for poor old uncle, for he was good at heart, after all; and how much he must have thought of me! It is too bad for you to be suffering all alone away off there in Cleveland, and I wish you would get well and come home. You can't realize how rich I am until you do come. What a hurly-burly there would have been if you had come straight home and made the glad discovery!

"Your own Lottie."

This was not a cheering letter, and it did not strike poor Hans as being sincere. Evidently Lottie was so engrossed with her bright prospects that she scarcely gave a thought to him. She wrote to him from a sense of duty; but what was he in her eyes but a poor traveller, while she was an heiress. And then, why should she be so interested in Mr. Worthington? And what should detain Mr. Worthington there longer? Why did he not come back and spend a few days in Cleveland with his old friend, and then retire to his fishing-grounds in Michigan?

Clearly, there was cause for uneasiness. Hans fretted about it a great deal, and wished, with all his heart, that he had not sent Charles on such a mission. But surely, when the novelty of things had worn off, Lottie would remember her promise and return to her old true love. How he longed to recover, that he might go down to Albany and see Lottie face to face.

Almost every day thereafter a short letter came from Charles. These letters, though short, were sincere, and overflowing with good-humor. Detailed accounts were soon given of Lottie's inheritance, her rapturous delight, her thoughts, and her air-castles; and the letters always wound up with kind wishes for Hans and hopes that he would soon join them. Sometimes Charles would say that he purposed leaving for Cleveland the next day; but the next day always brought a letter offering some pretext for not coming, and setting another date when he would surely come.

"Charley is still loyal to me," Hans mused; "such a friend as he is will not turn traitor in a day, nor yet a month. But *why* does he linger on and on? Well, when I get about again I will not let them know it, but will make a descent on them at unawares! Poor Lottie! her riches have turned her head. She will naturally take a liking for Charles—especially at such a time as this."

One bright day some four weeks after the accident Charles Worthington unexpectedly put in his appearance at the hospital.

He greeted Hans hilariously, and declared that in a week he would be able to leave the hospital for Albany.

"Charles," said Hans feverishly, "what of Lottie? Tell me the naked, unpalatable truth."

"What? Why, she is the delightedest girl in the Empire State! She is so full of life that she can hardly contain herself. Just think, from indigence to wealth, at a single bound! The plan is, to have you quit the buisness you are engaged in—"

"For something lucrative and respectable," Hans broke in bitterly.

"What do you mean by that?"

"She wrote me those very words, Charley."

"You wrong her, Hans. She wishes you to set up in some aristocratic business, with her own money as capital; for, after your marriage, her money is to be yours."

"Did she say that?" demanded Hans.

"'Those very words,' Hans, before I had known her half an hour."

"Ah! half an hour! Charley, do you believe she loves me now?"

"Why, of course she does; she is fretting about you all the time. Your imprisonment in this institution has warped your ideas and generally demoralized you."

"Why have you stayed there so long?" asked Hans.

"Well, my quarters at the hotel were pleasant, and I am just as contented at Albany, if comfortably quartered, as any other place. I have stayed there, Hans, because I was too lazy to go away."

"Well, what do you think of her, Charley?"

"That's a hard question to answer, old fellow. To tell the truth, I am sometimes jealous of you; I—I wish as bewitching a woman were my promised wife. I—I can't say enough in her praise."

Charles had certain business of his own to attend to down in Tennessee; and the next day he bade Hans good-bye, saying that when they met again it would probably be at Mrs. Kennedy's, where all were to hold a grand re-union.

Eight days afterwards, Hans, not fully recovered, but able to travel, left the hospital for home and Mrs. Kennedy's, without sending word to either Lottie or Charles.

As he drove up to the old home he saw Lottie and Charles lounging on the veranda steps. Charles had but just arrived from the South, having come *via* Washington.

Charles greeted the invalid with effusion, but Lottie was distant, if not indifferent. Was she not pleased to see him return?

"Hans, you old truant," said Charles, "you look like a spectre, and I dare say you feel like one. But come; there is going to be a wedding here, and you must get well in time for it."

"Whose wedding?" Hans asked sulkily.

"Why, yours, of course;" Charles replied unconcernedly.

Hans looked quickly and eagerly at Lottie. She did not smile approval—she did not even smile at all. Had she ceased to love him entirely? It seemed so like it that Hans grew faint and sick at heart, and began to realize that his love-dream was over.

Mrs. Kennedy's polite greeting confirmed his fears, and Hans experienced the utter wretchedness that only discarded lovers can experience.

"Let us have some music," Charles said presently; and sitting down at Lottie's new grand piano, he called to Hans: "This is, so to speak, my own composition. At any rate, it is entirely original with me; but as to whether you will like it, or approve of it, I don't venture to say. I *do* know it makes me solid with children and simpletons."

Then, with the solemnity of a mountebank, he rattled off the air of "Yankee Doodle," accompanying it with the words of Tennyson's "Brook." The effect was ridiculous; even Hans, secretly to his own chagrin, was obliged to laugh. Charles was so delighted with his performance that he then sang the words of "Yankee Doodle" to the music of "The Brook."

"Now, then," he said, "I think it is about time for the lovers to shut out intruders and have a few minutes to themselves. Come, Mrs. Kennedy."

Hans and Lottie were alone.

"Lottie," said Hans reproachfully, "you do not love me any longer. I know it."

"Why, Hans, what do you mean? How do you know it?"

"Do you remember the promise you gave me on New Year's day?"

"Well, what of it?" Lottie asked petulantly.

"Only this: In your heart you have not been true to that promise, and you cannot deny it."

"If you could know how how delighted I was—delighted for *your* sake, Hans, more than for my own—when my uncle's will was read, you would not reproach me in this way."

"Were you, Lottie?"

"Yes, Hans, I was; and I put the personal in the *World* to bring you home quickly, so that I might spring the good news on you before you could possibly hear it otherwise."

"If you had only written me oftener when I was laid up! But, oh, Lottie! do you love me still?"

No answer.

"I see it all, Lottie," said Hans sadly. "Your fortune did not turn your head all at once; you loved me, probably, till I sent *him!*"

"Then why did you send him? If you couldn't come yourself, why didn't you say so, and not send a deputy?"

"You have fallen in love with Worthington, Lottie, and left me to my fate. Deny it, if you dare!"

"I do not deny it, then!" Lottie retorted fiercely.

"So, you admit it! Oh Lottie! Lottie! you loved me once!"

"Whose fault is it? Why did you send him here? But, Hans, I tried to be true to you; I tried long and bravely."

"You did? But it was all in vain. Well, if it is to be, consider our engagement at an end. I suppose you are already promised to him," bitterly. "Canting hypocrites!"

"How dare you call your life-long friend a hypocrite!" Lottie cried indignantly. "As to being engaged," she added coldly, "you are entirely mistaken."

"Oh, then he has not proposed?" Hans asked sarcasticly.

"Your friend is too strictly honorable to do such a thing."

"Exactly;" returned Hans. "But," mockingly, "how came you to know that my honorable friend loves you?"

Lottie made no answer whatever, and Hans continued: "Perhaps you are most woefully mistaken in Charles Worthington, Miss Kennedy, for he is not a marrying man. In conclusion, let me observe that I do not wish to be invited to your wedding, if it should ever take place. One word more: I advise you, in case he proposes, to test his love—to put it to a crucial test. Good-by."

He steadied himself with a chair, and held out his trembling hand for a last farewell.

"Good-by, then, and thank you for your advice," said Lottie curtly, ignoring the outstretched hand. Then, drawing off her engagement ring, she tossed it to Hans, saying, "It is yours, Mr. Reingold; I do not wish to deprive you of your property."

Stung to the quick, Hans dropped it and retorted, "I have other property, and I refuse to touch it. Should I ever have occasion to need another engagement ring, Miss Kennedy, I will procure a new one, for this has surely served its turn."

The words were cutting, as Hans intended them to be.

"Very well, then," Lottie said loftily.

Hans hesitated a moment, and then said humbly, "Won't you shake hands with me, Lottie? It—it is better for us to part on friendly terms."

"Yes, Hans;" said Lottie, softening. "I—I am sorry, Hans; I really am."

So they shook hands, and parted, never to meet again.

It is quite unnecessary to follow Hans further. It is sufficient to say that he recovered health and strength; that on again seeking employment with the Philadelphia firm, he was warmly welcomed (which he hardly deserved); and that time eventually healed his grief.

Lottie did not hesitate to make it known that her engagement with Hans was broken; and that very evening Mr. Charles Worthington made a formal offer of marriage.

At first Lottie was coy, but soon said "yes."

"Poor Hans was so practical and matter-of-fact," she said. "You and I are far better suited to each other, Charles; don't you think so?"

"You prefer a lazy, good-for-nothing, smoking, easy-tempered fellow like me to poor Hans! Really, now, that doesn't speak well for your judgment of humanity!" Charles replied jokingly.

"Yes, I do; and any sensible woman would agree with me."

"Poor Hans! I should never have known you if it had not been for his accident—unless I had been invited to your and his wedding. It is really too bad, Lottie, about him. Madly as I love you, I would never have come between you. If I had thought you loved each other as at first, I should have bidden you all farewell in a day or so, and have gone away as he has done. But for the last two weeks I have suspected that you could never think of him as your husband, though I never gave either you or him cause to know it. I determined to let matters take their course; and it is well that I have done so. I don't feel quite easy in this matter, Lottie; but I don't feel altogether guilty."

"If anybody is in the wrong, Charles, it is myself," replied Lottie.

Then the two new-made lovers looked each other intently in the eyes, each one thinking how noble was the other.

Preparations for the wedding went on gaily. One day Lottie came to Charles with an open newspaper in her hand, saying the one word "Read!"

Charles nonchalantly took the paper and read that the —Bank had suspended payment. This was the bank in which the old uncle's money had been left; but the Kennedys, on its coming into Lottie's possession, had withdrawn it and deposited it in another. This, so far as Lottie knew, was unknown out of her own family; and remembering Hans' words about a love test, she had resolved to seize this opportunity to test the strength of her new lover's affection—not that she doubted its sincerity, but by way of a pretty experiment.

"So," said Charles, when he had read the item, "according to this, you are sharked out of your inheritance, eh? Well, never mind, darling; I have enough of my own for us all. It is not so much as yours; but it will be enough. But what a good thing, Lottie, that poor Hans didn't get things in shape to set up in buisness with that captial to draw on. Why, it would have resulted in the pecuniary ruin of you all! How strangely events have worked that you and I should be united!"

"And you love me the same as ever?" cried Lottie. "Oh, Charles! this is only a stratagem; my money was secured in another bank long ago."

"I suspected your little game, Lottie," said Charles, with provoking coolness. "You see, I've read a great many novels; and in about one in forty the heroine, being an heiress, resorts to some such artifice to try her lover's faith. So, bearing this in mind, and observing the studied concern in your manner, I wasn't fooled a particle. See?"

"You wicked, cruel man!" laughed Lottie. "I believe you don't love me a bit! My test wasn't any real test at all. Hans told me to test your love for me; and just for fun, I did. But I'll never let you read any more novels as long as I live!"

"Hans said that, did he? Poor Hans! He was blinded by jealousy. But then he had never known me in love; and a man in love is not to be judged as a man who is not."

Charles and Lottie were married, and live happily together.

As for Hans, the other day Lottie received a copy of the *New York World* containing a marked marriage notice. The bridegroom's name was Hans Reingold and the bride's that of a charming society belle. As Hans was a man who would marry for love only, Lottie and Charles reasonably conclude that all is well with him.

For all that, Lottie felt sore at heart when she read the little paragraph in the *World* and realized that Hans *had* found occasion to need another engagement ring. A wedding ring, as well! Lottie was not free from the little perversities of her sex.

HARD LUCK.

SHE and her cousin Molly were up stairs setting forward the buttons on a pair of new boots when she heard a smart, imperative knock on the hall door. She thought it might be Joe, although he didn't usually knock exactly in that way, and she ran down stairs to open the door herself.

No, it wasn't Joe, at all; but a stalwart individual with yellow hair and yellow teeth, clinging for dear life to a battered gripsack. He was an itinerant peddler, and she knew it before he had time to ask if she wanted to look at some good jewelry.

She surmised that he hadn't wrestled with the world long enough to have had much experience of its ways, so she determined not to shut the door haughtily in his face, but to give him a little bit of experience to ruminate on and profit by.

In answer to his half-formed inquiry she said, " Oh yes; certainly I shall; please walk right in." Then she called up to her cousin Molly, who was the most outrageously mischievous girl in her native town, and always ready for a spree:

" Molly, can you come down a minute, please? Here's a gentleman with a *beautiful* assortment of jewelry."

Molly rushed down stairs without even stopping to look in the glass, and smiled radiantly on the smirking peddler, who had struck an awkward and unrestful attitude.

With a gracious bow he plumped his treasure-case down on a newly-varnished stand in the hallway, flung it open, and began to haul out gorgeous-looking jewelry.

"Oh! Oh! How much is that?" as he lingeringly drew a heavy yellow chain out of his gripsack.

"This is a superfine article," he began, "and exceedingly val—"

"Oh, yes; we know all about that;" said the young lady of the house, who had admitted him; "but what is the price?"

"Well, it's worth twenty-five dollars, every day in the week, but seeing it's you, young lady, I'd let it go at a sacrifice."

"You would! Well, how much?"

"Say, twen—eighteen dollars."

"Oh, but I'm just awfully sorry we can't take it," Molly said, and sighed.

"Say, fifteen."

"Too much."

"See here! Seeing it's you, say, twelve."

"I'm afraid not; not to-day."

"Say, ten-fifty."

The two young ladies seemed to be making up their mind to accept this liberal offer, but still hesitated.

"Say, eight dollars—six-twenty-five—four-seventy-five—three-fifty—two-seventy-five."

This was too much for the young lady who had opened the door, and she expressed hearty laughter.

"See here, madam," he said, yanking out a whopping big locket, "see here, how much do you suppose that's worth? One hundred dollars! *One hundred dollars, every day in the week!*"

"You don't mean to say so!" cried Molly. "But I suppose you'd sell it for ten cents, any day in the week, and throw in a stick of gum."

His face showed he was afflicted with St. Vitus' dance, and that a little too much excitement was liable to bring it on suddenly. But he recovered himself and drew out another locket, that was unparalleled in its gorgeousness, and whispered hoarsely : " There, madam, how much do you take that to be worth ? I gave fifty dollars for that, in hard cash—fifty dollars."

"And I dare say you would sell it for fifty cents in cash, and a piece of apple pie 'in kind,'" said Molly.

"Some folks don't know diamonds from button rings," the peddler remarked, with fiendish sarcasm; and he crowded his valuables promiscuously into his valise, and started to go.

"Oh, don't be in such a hurry. We haven't seen your diamonds yet," said Molly. "Are they invaluable, too?"

"No, nor your button rings," said the young lady of the house. "I presume you carry a large and varied stock."

"My diamonds are worth a hanged sight more money than *your* circumstances would represent—represent—represent—"

On this innocent word he got muddled; but he bolted for the door without stopping to explain himself definitely.

As he passed through the gate, a few feet in front of the house, something happened him. The gate was a miraculously ingenious one, and it required careful study to be able to manipulate it successfully. The unfortunate who did not understand it could scarcely open it or shut it without jamming one of his fingers. It played no tricks upon the members of the household, but it would nip the sad-eyed Rhode Island tramp with remorseless and unfailing regularity.

Now, our hero, the peddler, had worked himself up into such a state of mental excitement an account of losing five minutes of his valuable time, and not making even a cent, that a scene of violence ensued on his essaying that gate. In fact, he jammed three of his fingers as they had never been jammed before since his eleventh year.

His thoughts drifted back to a black day in his childhood when his father caned those self-same fingers because he had tried hard to make a canal-boat out of a new forty-cent straw hat. His eyes filled with scalding tears, then shot fire; and he articulated, loud enough to be heard around the corner:

"Jam ad lunas!" he said. "Jam id ducibus damnetur!"

Or it sounded like that, anyway.

THE RAILWAYMAN'S TRIALS.

ABOUT the 20th of March there appeared before a railway ticket-agent at Green Bay, Wisconsin, a determined-looking woman from the wilds of upper Brown County. She was accompanied by a red-eyed boy, just recovering from chicken-pox, who evidently was her son and heir. He took after his mother, in that he was rustic, fidgety, warlike, and wholly uncultured in all his ways.

"Is this where they tell you about the railroads?" the woman asked.

"Yes, madam," said the ticket-agent promptly.

"Do the cars run from here to Milwaukee?"

"Yes, madam, direct."

"Do they run every day?"

"Certainly; two through trains each way every day."

"And do they stop long enough for a body to get on and off?"

"Certainly they do; and you will be assisted on and off."

"Well, where do I get on? I don't see no tracks anywhere; you don't keep them covered up, I suppose, do you?"

"You board the train at the station, madam."

"Well, we want to go to Milwaukee. This here's Johnnie, and his paw's coming in to talk with you bimeby; so it won't be no use to try to cheat *me*! His paw druv us into town, and he told me to go to the railroads first, and then he'd tackle 'em. He's travelled considerable, and he ain't easy took in."

"It isn't my place to take people in; it doesn't pay," said the ticket-agent sagely.

"His paw reckoned a ticket shouldn't cost more 'n three dollars, and that the boy ought to be took along free, seeing he's been 'most dead with chicken-pox, and is going away for his health."

"Oh! Well, we'll see. When do you think of going?"

"We calculate to go to-morrow, and stop over night here to his sister's. It's my cousin's we're going to stop at to Milwaukee. Am I likely to lose anything if I go and buy my railroad ticket to-day instead of to-morrow?"

"Certainly not; it will save you the trouble of attending to it to-morrow. The morning train will be the best one for you to take, and then you will get there in good time for your dinner."

"Well, that's lucky, ain't it! But s'pose I buy it now, and the railroad should bust up before I want to use it—who's going to be liable for that there ticket? That's what I want to know. I don't mean to go too fur trusting any railroad."

"I—I don't—exactly—understand," said the agent.

"Don't, eh? Well, I guess I'm a grain too cunning to go and buy my ticket to-day, and perhaps wake up to-morrow and find your railroad is dead broke, or sold out—'specially when you stammer so about it. We'll look around some, and maybe get a ticket here to-morrow."

The ticket-handler smiled sweetly, as was his wont.

"Am I sure to get into the right cars?" she asked presently. "I don't want to get took off to Chicago, or New York, or any of them awful places."

"I'll go down to the train myself, and see you off."

"Off where? You needn't hatch no plot to abduct me!

I'll have his paw there, and he'll see that you don't play no tricks on a woman traveling alone with her sick boy."

The ticket-agent explained, as well as she would let him, that he would see her safe on the right train.

"Does cars ever get struck with lightning?" she suddenly asked.

"No, not that I ever heard of, madam."

"Are they liable to run off the track this time of year?"

"Not at all."

"I don't know much about railroads and such; but my cousin told me to take your railroad. You don't own it, though, I s'pose?"

"No, I do not."

"Are the bridges pretty good? Is there any extry safe cars you can put us in? Is any English lord likely to be going our way this week, so'st I can travel in his car and be safe? I reckon you don't dare pitch them fellows into the ditch."

"The train that leaves to-morrow morning by our line will be extra safe, for a Jubilee company will be aboard, and they *never* get killed—or hurt."

"Is *that* so? Well, if they do smash up, anyhow, I want to know how I can work it to sue the railroad."

"Take out an accident ticket, if you are afraid."

"What's that?"

When this was explained to her, she said, feelingly: "I shan't take out no accident ticket, for if I was killed his paw 'd get the money, and the hired girl would get him. He told me I'd better get one if I was afraid, and I see now what he drove at."

Here the sick boy who was not sick nudged his mother, and whispered something to her. Turning to the ticket-agent she said, "I hain't no goods to speak of, but I calculate to have when we come back. This boy here's got a handsleigh that he's going to take down to his cousin to Milwaukee. You see, the handsleighing 'll soon be done, and he reckons if he makes a present of his old sleigh to his cousin that he'll get something handsome in return. Sal always *was* that way; she'd make her boy give away everything."

"All right," said the ticket-jobber wearily. "They'll fix that for him at the baggage office."

"Oh, *you* needn't worry about that; his paw says he'll work it through for him. What I wanted to say was," as the boy nudged her again, "that Johnnie here wants to know if he can't hitch it fast behind the cars. He reckons there'll be some snow yet, and he thinks it would be fun to set and watch that sleigh slidin' along behind."

Again the boy whispered some more, and his mother said further: "He wants to know if he mightn't climb out, occasional like, and ride a ways on that sleigh when there seems to be plenty of snow. He's used to hitching on behind. Besides, the railroad couldn't conscientiously charge the poor boy when he traveled that way."

Ticket-agents do not express astonishment. This one, however, said, "Unless the boy is as tough as a wrought iron door-knob, you would be sorry anybody ever built a railroad. And as for the sleigh—"

"Well, the doctor's always saying he's got an iron constitution, anyway; and we wouldn't look to you to find no cord to hitch his sleigh fast, for Johnnie's pockets is always stuffed with cord."

"Do you really want to make our train ridiculous by tying an old home-made handsleigh to the rear coach? The very suggestion of such a thing is preposterous. And besides, your sleigh would be wrecked or lost in a twinkling."

This outburst seemed to impress the woman from Brown County, and saying she would be likely to come in again, she went out, followed by the boy who was used to hitching on behind.

In about an hour's time they came back, surely enough, and accompanied by "his paw."

"Well," she panted, "I've found out something sence I was here before. But first I want to tell you what this boy wants to know. We seen the cars down to the station, and the enjine; and he wants to know how soon he could learn to run them. He wants to know if he couldn't ride with the enjine-driver, and find out how they do run them cars. Couldn't he work his way down to Milwaukee that way, like? Or could he learn how to do the hull business complete?"

"He could not be allowed to bother the engineer, madam."

"That's what his paw jus' now told him; but I said I reckoned I had a way I could work it so'st he could."

"You are mistaken; I have no authority over any engineer. When do you think of going down to Milwaukee?"

"Don't be so sure of that; nor don't be in such a hurry to sell me a ticket. I've found out that there's another railroad that 'll take us from Green Bay to Milwaukee, just as his paw always said; and I guess it's our place to be independent now, and yours to be pretty meek. I told you jus' now we had a way to work it so'st you'd have to favor us a little."

The ticket-agent at last showed faint traces of anger. It was not often that he was so badgered—even by the stupidest of stupid old women.

The old lady remorselessly continued, "The other fellow said this boy here is as smart 's a 'coon, and that he 'd make an enjineneer before the President gets his cabinet broke in; but *you* never even spoke to him!"

"I? By the Lord Harry, madam, you didn't give me a chance. How do you do, my little man? You certainly pulled through the small-pox better than the Gov—"

"Who said anything about small-pox?" snarled the old lady. "*My* boy had *chicken-pox*. We ain't easy flattered, neither."

"So you want to run an engine, do you, Johnnie? Well, when you get to Milwaukee I hope you may," sardonically. "Here's a map of our road. You can see how straight it runs to Milwaukee. Well, that 's the way—"

"The other fellow showed us his map, too," said the old lady, "and it appeared to run 'most as straight as yourn, and was a sight bigger. It was 'most nice enough for Jinny to hang up in her room. But they do both look powerful straight."

"That's the way with them durn maps," said "his paw," speaking for the first time. "They all run terrible straight; but when you get aboard the cars you go 'most as crooked as a boy with a game leg a-chasin' up a Thanksgivin' rooster."

"Well, I want to ask you something partic'ler," said the old lady. "S'pose this boy here gets to clamberin' around on the top of them cars, what am I to do about it?"

"Is he so fond of climbing as that?"

"Land, yes! He's an awful boy to climb. T'other day day he clumb up a ladder twenty-four foot high."

"And doesn't he ever fall?"

"He fell all the way down plumb that time, and tore his coat fearful. That's just what I want to find out. S'pose he climbs them cars, and falls off, and gets killed; ain't that there company liable? I warn you that *I* can't hold that boy."

"How much is the boy worth?"

"Well, his paw and me reckoned he ought to be worth about ten thousand dollars, considerin' how much it costs to raise him, and how terrible sorry we'd be to lose him."

"Well, then, madam, the company can claim twice that amount from you if the boy kills himself in that way; while *you* can't recover a ragged dollar from them. So I would advise you not to let him monkey about the train, unless you share my sentiments, and would like to see him martyred."

"Great Scott!" ejaculated the boy's "paw."

"You great wretch!" screamed the boy's "maw."

Burning with righteous indignation, the party hustled out into the street.

The next morning the ticket-vender had the satisfaction of seeing mother and son leave Green Bay for Milwaukee—but not by his line.

"So the other road gobbled them, after all;" he muttered. "But we are well rid of them; well rid of them."

THE OLD LADY POSING AS AN EXPERIENCED TRAVELER.

ALONG in April the old lady who had journeyed from Green Bay to Milwaukee on a visit to her cousin, went to a ticket agency to negotiate for a ticket for herself and her son Johnnie to Green Bay. She now considered herself an experienced traveler, who knew all the wiles of ticket-agents, and who was not going to take advice from any person. She and Johnnie had visited the St. Paul and the Northwestern depots frequently, and they now knew all about " the cars."

"Well, young man," she said patronizingly to a spectacled young ticket-clerk, who happened to be in charge, "I'm out prospecting for a ticket to the city of Green Bay. Let me know the best you can do for us, and if it doesn't chime in with my expectations, we'll just step around to some rival in your line."

The young man quoted the rates for first and second-class tickets.

"It kinder appears to me," said the old lady, "that considerin' it's spring now you might do better 'n that. Me and Johnnie here is always favored when we travel, and treated well."

"So you will be on our line," said the young man. "There are porters to assist you on and off all trains, and to take all charge of your baggage."

"Well, that's lucky. But be they honest men? Won't they run away with any of my goods? I've got considerable stuff with me."

"They wouldn't dare. This is a civilized community, anyway."

"Well, I've traveled before. I ain't no greenhorn; you can't play no humbugging tricks on me."

"What have you in the shape of baggage, madam?"

"Well, if it's your place to know, I *have* got considerable. There's a big umbrella for his paw; and there's a leather bag with some of mine and Johnnie's clothes in it; and there's a box Johnnie's got, with one of them things you call an organette packed into it; and there's a toy locomotive his cousin bought for him; and there's a greyhound pup I reckon we'll carry in his cousin's fish-basket; and there's my shawl, if it turns cold on the way; and there's a pair of long-legged boots I got for Johnnie here to Milwankee to a bankrupt sale, to slosh around in this spring, so'st he won't get the quinsy."

"I would like to suggest to you the propriety of packing your stuff in a trunk, and not attempting to handle it all yourself," ventured the ticket-clerk.

"Mercy on us! Do you take me for a lunatic? Young man, I ain't so simple. Pack them things in a trunk, and have it bumped around, and not know where it was, and mebby lose it; and have it dumped out to Green Bay, and busted open on the platform! His paw's often telling about the time him and his other wife moved on the railroad, and packed five hundred pounds of household goods in an old sideboard he bought at a sale,— 'most all the things they had in the world,—and the men shoved the old thing off onto the ground, to change it onto a steamboat, and it busted open, and the contents were landed around there like as if a freight car had exploded; and they hadn't no more place to stow them in than a kitchen table, and an eight-day clock, and a cook-stove, and a tool-chest, and a powder-keg;

and his paw says the way them men swore was worse than if a pirate had sprained his ankle. No, young man, I ain't green; and you can rely on it that I don't pack my goods in trunks for them railroads to bust."

"I was only thinking, madam, what a bother all your parcels would be to you," said the ticket-agent meekly.

"Well, young man, it ain't necessary for you to worry about other people. Be you a married man?"

"Eh! Well—yes—I am, madam."

"Well, sir, it ain't none of my business if you go home to-night and forgit to take your wife the starch she may have asked you to get. It ain't none of my business if she jaws you about it all night; and I ain't going to worry about it."

"It's our duty, madam, to look after the interests of travelers," ventured the ticket-agent.

"It might better be your duty not to interfere where you ain't wanted. I tell you I've traveled before, and I'm considerable sharp. You can't take me in no more 'n you could his paw. You ought to take us cheaper now, because it's spring; and you hain't got no snow to shovel off your railroad, nor no water to thaw out for your bilers; and the men that runs the railroad don't need to wear their winter clothes, nor keep the cars so hot."

"I should like to inquire in what country you have traveled, and what manner of railroads carried you."

"You needn't do it, then!" screamed the woman from Brown County. "I *have* traveled.—There's my cousin, now," she said suddenly; "she's traveled all over creation; and she wouldn't think much more of going from here to Ohio, where she come from, than she does of going around in them street cars."

"So your cousin has traveled a good deal, has she?" said the ticket-agent, wishing to conciliate the irate old woman. "Has she ever been to London? to Europe?"

"What! You don't mean the London where them British live, do you? I thought you meant the London near Madison, or that there place in Canada. I should think you'd be ashamed of yourself, a young man like you, to talk about a woman going skiting around in that way—and away over the ocean to Europe! And her my cousin, too! You needn't try to insult me about my relations, if you please!—I should think them railroad fellows would be afraid to trust you here alone with all these maps, and pictures, and picture-books."

"I meant no insult, madam," said the young man, looking scared and bewildered. "In what places has your cousin been, if I may ask?"

"Of course you may ask, as long as you ask civil questions. She's been to Chicago, and to my place, and to Madison, and to *Niagara Falls!* and to *St. Louis!* And I think she CHANGED CARS IN CHICAGO on her way there! Mebby you'd know; mebby not. We ain't going to Green Bay till Thursday, so 'st the hired girl and Jinny 'll have most of the week's work done; so you see I ain't in no hurry to get my ticket yit. Good day, young man; you can think it over about them fares."

And the old lady went out, leaving Johnnie to close the door behind them—which he failed to do.

She had had a little further experience with ticket-agents; and the persecuted clerk—who had a yearning to learn the railroad business—had had a little further experience with traveling humanity.

THE FOLDER FIEND.

"LET me have any folders of the railroads here to-day?" queried a lank youth with sore eyes, as he stepped into the ticket-office at Bureau, Illinois.

"Do you wish to distribute them?" asked the ticket-agent, handing over half a pack of folders of his own road.

"'Distribute them?'" echoed the youth. "Oh, no; I'm collecting for myself. I like railroads, and I'm crazy about folders."

"Then you won't want more than one, I suppose," said the ticket-agent, handing him a solitary folder and shoving the rest back into the stand.

"No, not more than one of each road," said the lank youth slowly, looking wistfully at the gaudy folders of all sizes and colors.

"Here, you talk to him, and tell him what he doesn't know already about folders," said the ticket-agent, with a sly wink, to a grinning office-boy.

"Got many of 'em?" asked the boy coming forward, all besmeared with red ink and stamped on the left hand, "Secure through tickets *via* the Great Line."

"Many?" cried the youth who was crazy about folders. "I've got more of 'em than you ever saw!"

"Glad to hear it," said the office-boy. "But if you never had one of ours before, I'm mighty sorry for you."

"I have. Besides, I live here, and that makes a difference."

"Shouldn't wonder. D' you ever hear of the Goose-bone road? or the Squint-eyed road? or the Sad Farewell road?"

"Do—— do—— You don't mean the 'Nickle Plate' or the 'Scenic Route?'" stammered the folder fiend.

"No, I don't. We always mean what we say here, for if we didn't we'd be fined eighty per cent. on pro rates."

The youth who wanted folders looked dazed. He began to comprehend that there might be some things about railroads that he didn't know; some things that the folders kept secret, as it were.

"I'm always on the look-out for new folders," he said, "and I wish you'd give me those you mention. I always try to keep a weather eye on the railroads and the folders, and I'll bet you there isn't one I don't know, if you call it by its proper name."

"Shouldn't wonder," replied the office-boy. "But if you wouldn't try to keep your eyes on the weather so much, perhaps they wouldn't look so red. And as for the railroads and the folders, I'll bet you don't know three out of thirty-seven by nickname; and if you don't know the nickname you oughtn't to go nosing around for folders."

"Name one properly that I don't know!" cried the youth who wanted more folders.

"Sho! what's the M. C.?"

"Michigan Central! You see, I've got you this time."

"No, you hain't!" roared the office-boy. "There are three M. C.'s."

"Three? You—you must mean the Dining Car Line, then, or the Scenic Route."

"No, I don't. But, see here—which is the Scenic

Route or the Dining Car Line, anyway? Which is it, or where does it run, when there are nineteen of one and eighty of the other?"

"Nineteen! Eighty! Why, isn't the Denver and Ree'-o Grand'-ay the scenic line of America?"

"Is it? I thought it was that, and the Erie, and the B. & O., and one of the P. roads, and the Hollow Bell, and the Needle's Eye, and the Mournful Note, and the Shock-haired Crank, and the Seventh Son, and the Lonely Run, and the Goblin Eye, and the C. P."

"Central Pacific!" caught up the lank youth hopefully.

"Who said anything about the Central Pacific?" sneered the office-boy. "Don't you know there are seven C. P.'s, and three more building?"

"You don't say so!" cried the folder fiend.

"I don't, eh? I thought I spoke it right out."

"Give me some folders of them, then," with an eager look in his watery eyes.

"You wouldn't know them if you got them. Why don't you learn railroading, as I have done, and then you wouldn't have to go about asking questions and making a fool of yourself."

"There must be an awful lot to learn," sighed the sore-eyed youth, looking dejected and humble.

"Creation, yes! But you appear to know something already."

"Well, I hope I do—and I really think I do. Try me, now; give me a hard question."

"I'll give you an easy one—a beginner's. What's the route from New Glasgow, Nova Scotia, to Chihuahua *via* Long Island Railway? Also distance, connections, and fare. Not in money, but in the way of grub."

"The — the— I— That's not an easy question! I know better!"

"So do I know better; it's the easiest one in the book. Come, now; you wouldn't give it up, would you?"

"The *book?* What book?"

"Worse and worse! 'What book!'—Why, I mean the Railroad Catechism for Freshmen, put out by the Hanging Beam Railway Co."

"Will you let me have a copy, please?"

"Let you have one? I'd be hot-pickled by the company if I gave one away! Why, they pay sixty cents apiece for them, and they're secretly distributed by incognito book-agents."

"I never knew you have so much fuss and nonsense about railroading," sighed the lank youth, looking wearily about him. "But say, tell me what you mean by 'hot-pickled.' Do you mean *bounced*"?

"Bounced? I guess not. I mean ear-whiffled, that's all. But that's bad enough, you know."

"No, I don't! You're a humbug, you are. There are no such cranky railroads as you talk about."

"There ain't, eh? I wish you'd prove that!"

"Well, tell me now, *do* tell me, the inside name for your own road."

"The Rock Island, or the Rock Island Route."

"Is that all?"

"That all! Ain't it enough?"

"Hasn't it any nickname, outside of your own selves?"

"Not worth a cent."

"Honest Injun?"

"Certain sure."

"Well, I'm glad to know that, anyhow. I suppose I've got that solid. Say, what's ear-whiffled?"

"Shut up in a box car with the rats, where they're bunting and banging into you all day long. 'Sh! don't tell!"

"I won't. But does it scare you any?"

"Awful. Give you nightmare and makes your nose bleed."

"I don't believe you!"

"Then I wish you'd go away and not bother me. I've got to mail some matter to Denver."

"Have they many folders in Denver?"

"I expect they have."

"Denver, Colo.?"

"That's the Denver I mean."

"Many railroads?"

"U. P.; Burlington; Denver and Rio Grande; Texas and Gulf; Santa Fé; and some local Colorado roads."

"If you had tried to fool me there you'd have been sold, for I know Denver by heart. Got an uncle there, and I'm going too, some day."

"Glad to hear it. I hope we ain't detaining you.—But say, who talks of fooling anybody? You're too fresh, or you'd know better."

"Tell me the nickname of the I. C. road," pleaded the folder fiend.

"Which I. C.? Don't you know there are three?"

"What three?" defiantly asked the folder fiend.

"The Illinois Central, the Intercolonial of Canada, and the old Isinglass Co.'s road in North Carolina."

"Is there such a road? Give me a folder of it then."

"We're out. Go so fast we can't keep them."

"Well, tell me what you call the Illinois Central."

"The Dixie Hammer, or the Laughing Stepchild."

"Boy," here interposed the ticket-agent, "if you string off any more heroic legends I shall not be able to believe you myself.—Here, young man," to the folder fiend, "take this packet of folders I've carefully made up for you. The instant a company shall build an all-rail line to the Sandwich Islands we will remember you and send you a folder. Meanwhile, perhaps you'd better not call around again till next leap-year, for you have picked up information enough to last you till then."

"If we find we can't get along without you, we will certainly send for you," cheerfully said the office-boy.

The folder fiend snatched up the packet of folders and walked away, happy, yet feeling grievously discouraged. When he opened the packet he felt still more discouraged; for it contained time-tables only, with never a map.

"This is mean!" he exclaimed. "This is a mean joke!—Upon my word, it's All-Fools'-day!"

But genius is not easily dismayed. That night he wrote a peculiarly affectionate letter to his uncle in Denver, asking (apparently incidentally) if his uncle, the next time he went down to the Union Pacfic, Burlington, or Rio Grande ticket-offices, would kindly procure for him the following-named folders: The Goose-bone, the Dixie Hammer, the Needle's Eye, the Mournful Note, two or three of the different C. P.'s, the several Scenic Routes, the Intercolonial of Canada, the Hanging Beam, and the Mexican Central. Any others that might chance in his (the uncle's) way would prove equally acceptable. "You see, uncle," he wrote, "I'm determined to learn railroading, for I want to become a practical railroader."

I have found out that the great roads have even a literature of their own. But I have no intention of losing heart, even though I should be ear-whiffled when I do get on a road."

In five days he heard from his uncle, to this effect:

"*My dear Henry:*—Somebody has evidently been making a fool of you. I do not accuse you, you will perceive, of wishing to play an April-fool joke on me. As for railway maps (and this seems to be the *raison d'être* of your letter), get the names of roads from the daily stock reports, or, better still, from the Official Guide. Go down to the office in your own town, where they are very courteous, and politely ask for what you want. They have an unlimited supply of folders; but you must be polite. Of course if you dropped in to buy a through ticket to Yokohama, you might be as boorish as a Boston tramp on his travels, and they would forgive you. Go ahead and learn railroading, by all means, but don't suffer yourself to be guyed by anybody; and some day I will strike you for a pass to South America.

"Your affectionate uncle,
"WILLIAM SHIPYARD."

The folder fiend now felt utterly discouraged. And there was one thing that bothered him sorely: what on earth was the Official Guide?

How could he again ask for folders at the ticket-office? "I guess," he muttered sadly, "I guess I'd better give up railroading and study law. It will be just a little easier, and it can't be such a humbugging thing."

A SEVERE TEST.

"WELL, old pard, how are you, and how are you getting along now-a-days?" demanded a rough old barbarian, returned to his native district after an absence of many years, of a good-natured granger, who was trying to lead a better life. "Manage to live any better'n you used to? Manage to live without pinching and starving yourself?"

"Eh? Well, I guess I hain't starved to death yet, nor sponged my board off'n the neighbors. But, I say, you're looking first-rate. How—"

"Just so. But I hear your family is very much reduced in size, compared with what it used to be fifteen years ago. How well I remember, now, that when my missus give one of your boys and any of the neighbors' boys a hunk of bread and molasses, your boy'd gobble his'n down so almighty suddent that it would fill a tramp 'most with pity for him; but t'other boy'd nibble a mouthful off and on, and tell us the news about the folks to home and his sisters' beaux, and feeze off and on, and bimeby, if you didn't watch him pretty sharp, he'd up and give more'n half his piece to our old dog."

"Oh, that's how you kep' your dog, I suppose? That's why he always had the mange, and poor health, and a sickly constitution, ain't it, 'cause he got too much of your own bread and molasses?"

"I dunno about that; your boys always seemed to bear up under the diet my missus doled out to 'em—and thrived on it, too. But, I say, what's the cause of your family's being weeded out so? Hain't starved any of 'em sence our folks left these diggings, I reckon?"

"*Great Cæsar's ghost!*—Well, my girls are mostly married off,—and you bet they're well married, too,—and my boys are mostly settled down in Colorado and Dakota."

"I'm mortal glad to hear you say so, Hiram. Yes, I don't doubt it; wouldn't doubt it for a minute. The boys stood it just as long as they could, and then they cleared out. But it's a mortal shame for them new countries to be settled by underfed men. Likely as not they didn't grow their growth out, now, eh? I shouldn't wonder."

"See here! Do you take me for a meek man? Do you take me for a Quaker, now? Do you take me for a weak, helpless, worn-out old pop-corn man? Do you calculate on my muscles' being paralyzed, or on your tender spots' being bomb proof? I see you ain't drunk, and you needn't expect I hain't no feelings to outrage. Do you expect I am going to let this sort of thing continue? See here! I hain't joined no peace-at-any-price society; I hain't leagued myself with no anti-Nihilist gang. See here! If you don't look out, I shall be sent to jail for six months, for assault and battery;—and *you* won't be a mighty sight better off!"

"Come, now; don't get riled, Hiram.—But, really, now, don't you sometimes think that prison fare would have been a good change for your boys when—"

"I warned you!"

"Golly, Hiram! 'Pon my word, you can light out as reckless a blow with that fist of your'n as an old Revolutionary musket! You can rely on it this bruise 'll smell of Thomas's oil to-night. A little more practice, Hiram, and you'd 'a' bunged my eye into my brain. I didn't mean to wound your family feelings right up to a pommelling point; but I heard you'd swore off on all cuss words, and I told the boys I wouldn't believe it till I tested you. So I struck out on this here starvation racket, because I knowed it was a good one. I didn't make you swear worth a cent, though you came powerful nigh it once or twice; but I'd be some better off if things had turned out as I expected. All the same, I beg your pardon, Hiram, for you *was* provoked. I'll forgive you, too, for this here bruise; for I deserved it, and you always tried to be a pretty good neighbor. Let's call it square."

"Durned if I don't!"

THE LONG-SUFFERING TRAMP.

"GOT any employment here for an able-bodied man that wants something to do?" inquired a janty-looking tramp as he stepped into the printing-office of a local weekly newspaper that terrorized over a quiet Hoosier town.

"Want to make your fortune, I suppose?" said a blonde young man, who had begun parting his luxuriant hair in the middle the next day after his mother left off combing it for him.

"Yes," put in another cream-colored youth, who sported a black cord watch-chain, sagged down in the middle by a shining brass watch-key. (This young man had found employment in the newspaper office temporarily, and now had "something to do" for the first time in his life.) "Yes, indeed; he looks as if he needed to make a fortune pretty badly."

"A fortune—or even a hunk of a one!" supplemented the office-boy, coming out of his corner. "Say, mister, what kind of employment have you mostly been used to lately?"

"Oh, any soft snap like you fellows have, that pays a man's board for setting around and keeping his hair combed, and throws odd jobs in his way," said the tramp cheerfully. Then fiendishly: "I guess I know better'n to think there's any *fortune* to be made here."

"I don't suppose the man ever had more than two bits in his life," said the blonde with the luxuriant crop of hair, ruminating on his own princely revenues, which could afford him a treat of cigarettes and peanuts every other day.

"Hadn't, eh?" snorted the tramp. "I once owned a hull town in Arizona."

"But now? To-day?" insisted the blonde with the watch-key.

"Well, stranger, I ain't busted plumb to h—l to-day."

"No," said the carefully combed blonde, "I suppose you've got a brass watch, and an old satchel hidden away behind the freight-shed, and some cold goose somewhere in your frouzy overcoat, and a horn of apple-jack in your pistol-pocket."

"And 'most a dozen cigar-stumps tucked away in yer greasy vest," chimed in the office-boy.

"You be hanged!" snarled the the tramp. "How many times a week does your parents have to clean the cigar-stumps out of *your* pockets? Or," sardonically, "do you manage to find time to smoke 'em all?"

"What's the matter?" roared the "editor and proprietor," opening the door leading into his "sanctum," and craning his bald head into view.

"Oh, I'm poking fun at these chicken-pocked noodles here," explained the tramp.

"What you want?" shouted the "editor and proprietor," jumping to his feet, while all the ink which, in the course of years, had been absorbed by his fingers, oozed out again into his face, making it black.

"Well, I *was* thinking I'd like a little employment; but I ain't very particular about it to-day, I guess, anyway."

"I'll give you a little employment, though, all the

same. You just step down and out into the street, and turn towards the setting sun, and keep straight on till you begin to perspire freely."

"Well, old chump, I guess I'll accept your kind offer," said the tramp. "Good day, gamins; I'm sure you'll give me a good 'send off' in your snide paper."

"Good day," sang out the office-boy. "I guess 'keeping straight on' is the kind of employment you've mostly been used to lately."

Then the "editor and proprietor" locked himself up in his sanctum and wrote a double-leaded editorial on Rampant Vagabondism, proving conclusively that the Administration will lose the next Election if it cannot protect honest, hard-working citizens from the insults of the unshorn, ravening, audacious tramp.

REJECTED.

This wretched day could not be brief,
    But it has run its course at last,
    The storm-clouds ghostly shadows cast,
And I am left alone with grief.

The cruel truth to-day I learn,
    That she cares nothing for my pain,
    A life's devotion was in vain,
The old, loved days may not return.

My bird sits drowsy on his stand;
    The fire upon the hearth burns low;
    The little clock ticks faint and slow;
My old dog, trembling, licks my hand.

I shiv'ring sit, with head bowed low;
    The night wind moans adown the lane;
    Sad 'gainst my casement beats the rain,
As if in def'rence to my woe.

Then restlessly I move about,
    Reflecting o'er and o'er again
    How I have loved so long in vain;
While still the dull rain falls without.

The still small voice reproves: "Weak man,
    Have faith in God; lose not your soul;
    What though you did not reach your goal,
Perhaps 'twas not in vain you ran."

But still the rain falls sad and drear,
    Still moans the wind as though in pain;
    Both bear to me the same refrain,
" She loves you not, and naught can cheer."

Oft times her voice I'll seem to hear,
    Sometimes in sleep her face I'll see,
    Her sweet, fair face, so dear to me—
But only in my sleep, I fear.

Although I ne'er can break the spell,
    I can forgive her cold disdain;—
    'Tis nothing that I loved in vain;—
But it is hard to say farewell.

Whate'er betide in this world's strife,
    Of this my heart doth full assure,
    The love I bear her will endure
As long as God shall give me life.

THE HARDSHIPS OF A BRAVE MAN'S LIFE.

AN OLD-FASHIONED BIT OF HISTORY.

ABOUT the year 1787 Joseph Trickey, a you g mechanic living in Cornwall, England, set sail for Canada, with the intention of taking up land along the St. Lawrence River. He left behind him kind parents, a devoted brother, Henry, and a happy home; but being naturally of a roving and adventurous disposition he prepared to embark with a light heart and with no fears for the future. Before leaving home his friends from far and near came to bid him a tearful farewell and wish him every success in his hazardous undertaking. Emigration in those early days was quite different from what it is to-day; it was then only daring and resolute spirits that had the hardihood to seek their fortune in the wilds of the New World.

Joseph was to write home immediately on his arrival in America. But no letter ever reached the old home; weeks lengthening into months brought no tidings whatever from Joseph. At that period, the close of the last century, strange ideas were entertained in England respecting the newly-established government of the United States. There was still, of course, no little hostility felt towards the enterprising Amercians, who had dared to dispute the supremacy of King George, assert their independence, and maintain it, too. Not a few of Joseph's prejudiced friends in Cornwall boldly declared that the young man had been enslaved, imprisoned, or even murdered by the triumphant Americans for presuming to settle in Canada. Joseph's mother mourned long and sorely for him, and after eighteen months of weary waiting, sickened and died; while Henry Trickey senior, the father of the family, made strenuous but unavailing efforts to trace him, or to find out what his fate had been.

After the lapse of two years the younger Henry determined to go in search of his lost brother. He embarked in a merchantman from Plymouth for Quebec direct, "working his passage," as his brother had done before him.

In those early days every well-equipped merchantman carried at least one heavy cannon, and the good ship *Transport* manned a couple of redoubtable forty-pounders. Henry was a resolute young fellow, of dauntless courage; but the grim-looking cannons made him feel the more at ease. It chanced that these guns were needed. One morning, in mid ocean, as the sun rose a strange ship was descried, bearing down upon them under full sail—a piratical-looking craft, beyond all question. She had stolen upon them during the night, and could probably easily overhaul the heavily-laden *Transport*. The captain, however, determined to crowd on all sail, and do his utmost to keep clear of the stranger till night, when, under cover of darkness, he might hope to escape by changing his course. Captain Lucas, like all British seamen, was brave, even to recklessness; but his policy, as commander of a merchantman, was always to avoid a conflict with sea-rovers.

On sweeping the horizon with his glass, the captain

made out a brig to the southward, far in advance of him. He fancied he was making better headway than this ship, and if he could press on and receive assistance from her, the pirate (if such his pursuer should prove to be) would perhaps give up the chase. The sailors promptly manned the yards, and soon every available sail was set to the breeze, which was fair and steady. Next the captain had all the ship's small arms carefully inspected and cleaned, special attention also being paid to the big guns. The port-holes of these guns were then covered with canvas; the object being to deceive the pirate, and lure him on, so that in case a juncture could be effected with the brig to the southward, he might find that he had caught a Tartar.

The *Transport*, of course, was conspicuous both to the ship in advance and in the rear, although these had manifestly been unable as yet to glimpse each other. The piratical-looking stranger was perceived to be steadily gaining on them, and towards noon Captain Lucas, seeing that escape was impossible, calmly made every preparation for a struggle. But he did not slacken sail, wishing to put off the rencounter as long as might be.

The ship to the southward was now made out to be an American merchantman. Captain Lucas apprised her by signals of his danger, and she at once hove to. A further interchange of signals showed him that he could not look for any but moral support from his new-found friend, as she carried no guns ; but she made preparations to intimidate the pursuer.

Meantime, the pirate, for such she undoubtedly was, gained rapidly on the *Transport*. At two o'clock any lingering doubt as to her real character was dispelled by the running up of a black flag. The pirate ship evidently perceived that there was no time to be lost in attacking and disabling her prey. By taking the ships singly, two prizes would probably be secured instead of one. No doubt the piratical commander thought himself in great luck.

The *Transport*, under full sail, bore down towards her new-found friend, whilst the pirate steadily pursued, gaining on her uninterruptedly. Shortly after four o'clock a puff of smoke was seen to curl from the deck of the pirate ship, and a shot came crashing through the rigging of the *Transport*, carrying away her top-gallant sail and colors.

This angered Captain Lucas beyond all endurance, and he resolved on a spirited resistance, although the American vessel was still too distant to support him in any way. The canvas was removed from the port-holes, and the first mate, who was an expert gunner, he having served in the navy, levelled one of the *Transport's* guns squarely against the enemy. The aim was well taken, for the ball cut down the pirate's mizzen-mast. This feat called forth the liveliest applause from all on deck, and the American brig saluted them in triumph. To Henry Trickey, coming from an inland Cornish town, such scenes were inspiriting, and he was almost beside himself with delight.

So unexpected and vigorous a reply from the *Transport* seemed to impress the pirates strongly, and before they could recover from their consternation the mate of the *Transport* followed up his advantage by firing a second shot. This was a masterly effort. The ball struck the pirate hull fairly on the water-line, directly under the foremast, and staved in her bow. No ordinary ship in those days could withstand such an accident; and it was apparent at once that the pirate must go to the bottom. There was evidently a panic on board, but no demonstration came from the piratical crew. The black flag still waved—and, yes! another puff of smoke! The grim old pirate chief, who had probably never given quarter, expected none, and would strike a last blow before his ship went down. But the aim was hurried and faulty, and the ball flew harmless over the bowsprit of the *Transport*.

Captain Lucas at once ordered two yawl-boats to be launched and put off to the rescue. This was an act of common humanity on his part; but the pirates, thinking he wished only to take them prisoners, chose rather to put to sea in open boats, and cried sullenly to the rescuing party to begone. Two persons only remained behind on the sinking ship, who cast themselves adrift in a frail craft just before she went down, and were taken up by the *Transport's* boats.

The *Transport* waited to take on board her own crew and boats, when she at once made sail in pursuit of the escaping pirates, joined in the chase by the American merchantman, which had hitherto been a passive spectator of affairs. The two pirate shallops spread each their sails, and pulled away in different, but converging, directions, thinking to escape capture. The pirates knew that capture now by either of the merchantmen meant trial and execution as soon as the nearest port was touched at.

The captain kindly inquired after the rescued men, and it transpired that they were not of the pirate crew, but were prisoners among them. While refusing to take part in any of the outrages perpetrated by the pirates or to submit to their domination, these two young men yet consented, on condition of their life being spared, to perform the ordinary duties of seamen, and both were frequently called upon to practise their trade, the one as a carpenter and the other as a worker in iron, for the benefit of the *Freebooter*—which, they said, was the name of the scuttled ship. They were always confined in the hold when the pirates were in active pursuit of prey, and their life was at best a wretched one, but they were sustained by the hope of eventually making their escape. When the *Freebooter* received that terrible shot from the *Transport* and the pirates saw that she was doomed, one of their number came to the hold and set the two captives free, with a caution to keep well out of the way till they could make sure of escape and rescue.

Of the two rescued men, one was from Cornwall, and his name was Trickey—Joseph Trickey. He had recognized Henry at once; but it was with the utmost difficulty that Henry could recognize in this careworn and prematurely aged man his lost brother, whom he was crossing the ocean expressly to find. The ship's entire company shared in the joy of the two brothers in their strange, romantic re-union. Joseph's story was a marvelous one, but it can be given only in this brief outline: The ship in which he sailed for Canada had been attacked and scuttled by these same pirates, and he had been virtually a prisoner in their hands ever since, except for two days, he having once escaped only to be re-captured. His fellow-sufferer, Frank Miller, was an American who had fought gallantly throughout the Revolutionary war, and had been captured by the pirates at a later period. Joseph and he naturally became firm friends, and formed many plans to escape from their slavery on board the pirate, but were always too prudent to jeopardize their lives till the opportune moment should come again.

Captain Lucas hotly kept up the pursuit of the pirate crew in their open boats, ably seconded by the American brig. But for the providential destruction of the *Freebooter*, it would have fared hardly with this American vessel, as she would surely not have escaped, even though the *Transport* should have.

The two pursuing ships came within easy hailing distance towards evening, when the American brig proved to be the *Commonwealth*, of Philadelphia, homeward bound, under command of Captain Henderson. Not long thereafter both the escaping shallops were overhauled —one by the *Transport*, the other by the *Commonwealth*. The former ship was especially fortunate in capturing the piratical chief himself. The pirates, to the very last, doggedly refused to surrender, but, overawed by the *Transport's* guns—for which they had the greatest respect—were constrained to do so. They had to be ironed at the point of the sword, and were then incarcerated, twenty-five in the hold of the *Transport*, and twenty in that of the *Commonwealth*. It has not often happened in marine chronicle that a merchantman has so easily been able to overpower a corsair, and take all her crew prisoners.

The two vessels now lay to alongside each other, and the two jubilant captains resolved to spend the night together on board the British merchantman. The ships' crews also mingled freely together, and the greatest goodfellowship prevailed. Their triumphant shouts and songs rose high above the execrations of the wretched pirates.

It has been said that Joseph Trickey's companion in serfdom was an American. Joseph and he had mutually agreed, if they should recover their freedom, to take up land on the Hudson River, and settle down as farmers. Joseph, on leaving home, could not have been persuaded to settle in United States territory; but his friend had convinced him that his prejudices against the Americans were not only wrong, but absurd. In fact, he had become a thorough American in sentiment, and he purposed taking out naturalization papers if Providence should permit him to set foot in that land of promise.

Henry Trickey's mission might now be said to be accomplished. But he was easily persuaded by his brother to go with him and establish himself on New York's famous river. The entire crew of the *Commonwealth* took a generous interest in the young man, on account of his brother's and their countryman's singular history, so that he could not but have the most kindly feelings towards Americans.

It was this spirit of good-will on the part of his new friends that induced Henry to cast in his lot with Joseph. Accordingly, when the two ships parted company in the morning, the *Transport* to continue her course to Quebec, and the *Commonwealth* to Philadelphia, Henry had his simple trunk transferred to the latter, and sailed away in her with his brother and Frank Miller.

Piracy being a capital crime, it need scarcely be said that the pirates, when delivered up to justice, met their deserts.

Joseph and Henry Trickey and Frank Miller took ship from Philadelphia to New York, and thence up the Hudson River. They did not halt till in the neighborhood of the old Dutch town of Schenectady, whither Miller's relatives had betaken themselves during his absence. Here in the course of time first Henry and then Joseph married each a sister of Frank Miller, and settled down tranquilly to farming in the beautiful Mohawk valley. Joseph built his own and his brother's house, with the barns, outbuildings, and fences. As the years passed, the brothers prospered in their vocations, and sent for their father to come over and live with them. Henry Trickey senior came at their urgent reguest, but did not live long thereafter, dying about the beginning of the present century.

Strangely enough, Henry Trickey the younger removed to Whitehall, near the foot of Lake Champlain, about this time, two of his sons afterwards passing over into Canada, where they established a home near Kingston. In this new country the young men suffered much hardship, and went through many strange and trying experiences; but with these removals Henry Trickey and his family pass out of our knowledge, since it is with Joseph's fortune that this history has now principally to deal.

The years came and went, till in the eventful one of 1812, war with Great Britain broke out. At that period Joseph Trickey was a middle aged man, owning and cultivating a magnificent property, well stocked and equipped, but having little or no capital besides. He was not naturally a money-making man, and the large family growing up under his roof was always provided for liberally. The war had scarcely been proclaimed when his eldest son, John, a young man of twenty, enlisted under General Van Rensselaer, and afterwards took part in several engagements. On the 22nd February, 1813, he was with that unfortunate company at Ogdensburg that were compelled to "retire" before a British force—among which he distinctly recognized his two cousins.

The spring of 1813 finds our old hero Joseph Trickey entering into a contract to supply the United States Government with fifty tons of hay, to be delivered at Plattsburg in July. This was a considerable quantity for him to undertake to supply, yet he felt no uneasiness about being able to fulfil his contract, though the Government had of necessity to be exact and even severe in having their contracts carried out to the letter.

Misfortune, however, seemed to follow poor Trickey all that spring. He lost two horses in the Mohawk; three or four men that he had employed forsook him to engage in General Dearborn's attack on Fort George, and it was difficult to fill their place; and, last of all, a June freshet spread over his meadows, soaking and spoiling a large quantity of his hay. With his limited means he made good this loss by buying of his neighbors; but hay was scarce and dear, and all his profits were swallowed up by this outlay.

At last he was prepared to deliver the stipulated quantity of hay to the commissariat at Plattsburg. As it was all but impossible to procure teams to haul the hay, he conceived the idea of floating it up on a raft. With the assistance only of his younger sons he constructed a large and buoyant raft, and transferred to it twelve tons of hay, which was as much as he thought advisable to carry on a trial trip. Taking with them a small supply of provisions and an old flint musket, he and one of his sons pushed off the same day. To the boy it promised to be a glorious pleasure-trip, and even the man experienced a keen sense of enjoyment as they floated slowly away from their moorings. But again disaster only awaited him. The raft proved unwieldy, and a severe thunder-storm coming up, he ran foul of a sand-bar, and his entire load of hay was washed off into the river; whilst the bulk of what had been left at home was seriously damaged.

Trickey felt this loss keenly. He would not only be unable to fulfill his contract, but was losing time that should be devoted to his farm. But he gave way to no vain repinings. Again his brave and patient spirit asserted itself; he resolved to return home at once and make one more stenuous effort to redeem his pledge.

On reaching home he scoured the country far and near to make up the fifty tons of hay. He wrote to the commissariat at Plattsburg that he could not deliver the hay on the appointed date, but that he would certainly do so by the middle of the month, making no mention whatever of his many losses. This was his old English pride, that caused him to look on misfortune as a disgrace.

Trickey had made a rash promise, and one which he was unable to fulfill. Undue exertion and excitement brought on a fit of sickness, and when he got about again, on the 20th of July, all the marketable hay he could muster was thirty tons.

Two days later he was placed under arrest, by order from Plattsburg, for breach of contract. The hay was seized and taken away, while he, after an informal trial, was lodged in the Schenectady County jail.

This was a severe measure; but as viewed by the

military authorities, who did not inquire into the circumstances, it was justifiable. It was known that Trickey was a native Englishman, and unkind doubts were entertained of his loyalty to the United States Government, now that they were at war with Great Britain. The irascible officials did not know that he had had to contend with grievous and unlooked-for difficulties, nor consider that his son was bravely fighting the country's battles.

The jail in which the unfortunate man was temporarily confined was a primitive structure, rudely built of unhewn logs, and dating back to the seventeenth century. Trickey saw at once that he could easily make his escape from it, and he resolved to do so, trusting to Executive clemency for a full and free pardon. He bore his persecutors no malice, knowing that his case was misunderstood; but he wished to get back to his farming interests, and not remain a prisoner till his incarcerators should see fit to liberate him. Perhaps this was not logical reasoning, nor yet good policy; Trickey was rather a man of action than of reflection. It is certain that he accounted it no crime to effect his escape, in this instance, from jail. Brought up a carpenter, he had practiced his trade in his own interests ever since settling down to farm life, and he was seldom without a few simple tools about his person. The tools required for his purpose were an auger and a strong knife, and these and some others he now happened to have in his pockets. He had not been subjected to the indignity of being searched.

There was a barred window, none too secure, but it was above his reach, and he contemplated no attack on it. The walls were but wooden walls,—of logs a foot thick, certainly,—and beyond them was liberty. His jailer visited him but three times a day, to bring a scanty meal, and the time of his rounds was carefully noted. On sounding the wall of bare logs, Trickey found a spot that would suit his purpose admirably. His first move was to wrench a spike out of the floor, and thrust it into the wall just *above* the spot thus chosen. On this spike he wished to hang his coat. When the jailer came in the next time, Trickey took his coat off this spike and sat down on it to partake of his frugal meal. At the time of the next visit the coat was hanging on the spike, and this time was not removed. At the third round Trickey had his coat on, the air being rather chilly. The spike and the coat looked innocent enough, and the jailer paid no attention to them. But every time thereafter that he made his rounds the coat hung on its spike, and was never again taken off.

The captive had a stout inch auger with him, as before mentioned, but no handle for it. But with his clasp-knife he ingeniously fashioned a handle from a splinter cut out of the wall in the spot indicated as covered by his coat. He then proceeded laboriously to bore holes in this spot, with the object of removing a square block of wood, large enough for him to crawl through. This was a very slow and wearisome piece of work, but Trickey persevered in it manfully. How to dispose of the borings was a difficult problem, and at first he stowed them away in his pockets. Careful search, however, disclosed a cavity in the floor, where not only the borings but other fragments from the hole being made in the wall could safely be secreted.

After three days' hard labor with auger and knife the task was completed. Trickey had carefully measured his size at the shoulders, and a square of wood could now be taken out of the wall, leaving an opening large enough to admit the passage of his body. Hanging his coat on its spike again, and carefully spreading it out as usual so as entirely to cover the auger holes, he waited, with the same calm patience that he had exercised all his life, for the night to come. Then he removed the block of wood, squeezed through the opening, and quietly made his way home. Once safe at home, he did not fear re-arrest, though apprehensive of harsh treatment if detected in jail-breaking.

He was right in his conviction that no further attempt would be made to molest him. Several influential men in his district took up his case at once, and sent a memorial of the affair to General Dearborn and to President Madison. The result was that Trickey was pardoned for his successful attempt at jail-breaking, and released from his contract. Further, he received a check paying him in full for the fifty tons of hay.

Joseph Trickey prospered greatly after the war, and when he died, in 1835, he was universally regarded as a hero and a patriot. The patience and fortitude he had shown under suffering, oppression, and disaster were virtues which he was often called upon to exercise, and which distinguished him all his life. His descendants to-day are respected and prosperous men, settled in almost every State in the Union. His son John proved himself a hero in the War of 1812-15, and served again in the Mexican War.

Such is the true history of a sturdy pioneer who quietly lived an eventful life of hardship in the long ago.

HOW THE HATCHET CAME TO BE BURIED.*

AN ALLEGORY.

TO THE MEMORY
OF THE LATE LAMENTED CAPTAIN KID,
WHO NEVER DID ME ANY HARM,
AND FOR WHOM I CHEERFULLY SPEAK A GOOD WORD.

"ALL things come to him who waits," including the opportunity for vindication.

Thus it fell out with a young man, who apparently was as powerless to avenge himself of cruel injustice done him as the mouse caught in a trap is powerless to retaliate on its human captors.

But what is impossible to that man who is resolved to accomplish his purpose? In fact, in this case the ways and means came about so easily and naturally that it seemed a manifest destiny he should make use of them. In a word, he would write up the history of his wrongs, and give it to the world in the form of an amusing novel. To the comparatively limited number of people who were indifferently well acquainted with the facts, it would be a revelation; to the great outside world it would simply be another of those readable books that are at once vaguely characterized as having been written "with a purpose." As for the interested persons themselves, it would probably always remain a sealed book to them

---

*Thrown together hastily, to take the place of a better story, which I have remorselessly ruled out.—B. W. M.

for they were to be so mercilessly exposed that no sane individual could expect them to get beyond the fifth or sixth chapter.

It was a pretty scheme, and everything seemed to favor it. In the first place, he had several damning letters, which had been written to him, to quote from, so that he could condemn the enemy "out of his own mouth," and in the next place, by revisiting his old home he got possession of a great mass of evidence that would materially strengthen his case.

It was a complicated history, and the young man, who may be called Despierto Aniquilando Nemesis, (which is a more poetical and sonorous name than his baptismal one) soon found that it would not be necessary to deviate a jot from the truth to make it interesting. Indeed, every trifling incident seemed to fit into the frame-work of his plot so naturally that he could not help felicitating himself on his unique scheme of retribution.

It was not long, however, before events happened to induce him to call a halt, and he found that it would be expedient to drop out one or two supernumerary characters and quite necessary to introduce some others. Some whom he had fondly thought guiltless he found to be as culpable as the principals; and, singularly enough, they possessed characteristics that would show admirably in his story, and relieve its occasional monotony—a monotony that could not be avoided, so long as the truth were rigidly adhered to. For what is more monotonous than a life of hardship? This being the case, he determined to introduce some new features, and blend the pathetic with the ridiculous.

Everything favored the growth of the story. Despierto

was not altogether a novice with the pen; otherwise he would not have undertaken a work of such magnitude. But he was staking his reputation on the book, and he worked with extreme care and deliberation. He considered his cause a just and holy one, and wished to prove equal to the task he had set himself, and to make his book a faithful exponent of his wrongs.

It was highly important to him to know how a petty case in law would be conducted—and strangely enough a case arose in which he was first plaintiff and afterwards defendant. He thought this a hardship at first, as it consumed a great deal of his time and was an insufferable annoyance; but what of this, when he had obtained, from personal experience, the very information he so much needed? This was not all: the one thing that troubled him was how to wind up, exactly how to color the catastrophe; and here was his opportunity. He saw in a flash that this last event could be skillfully worked in, so artlessly that it would seem to have been predetermined upon from the outset.

All incidents in the book were now harmoniously balanced, and in its completed state he found that it fully justified his anticipations. An impartial critic would not hesitate to pronounce it worthy of Despierto's vengeance, and an intelligent public would not fail cautiously to admit that the new author had GOT THERE WITH BOTH FEET. At least, so reasoned Despierto. He went further; he even fancied that if his enemies (as he persisted in regarding them, though he never spoke of them, either for good or for evil, outside the family circle) could be brought to read it dispassionately, they would be obliged to acknowledge its merits. He forgot;

foolish fellow, that however just criticism may be, it is never tolerated by the criticized. And what is the truth but a species of criticism?

Yes, the book was written; all that was now necessary was to find a publisher worthy of it. And here is wherein lies the *raison d'être* of our tale. Despierto received a conditional offer from a publishing house. It was not specially tempting, but the house was an honorable one, and had prestige enough to assure the success of any book of real merit that it might issue, however obscure the author. One would naturally think Despierto would consider himself a made man, and accept the offer by telegram, instead of waiting for a letter to reach the publishers.

Instead of doing this he at once began to show symptoms of that strange contrariety that we sometimes see in human nature, but never in the lower animals, which proves that Solomon was in the right when he advised the sluggard to go to the ANT, consider his ways, and be wise. Briefly, Despierto repented himself of his scheme of vindication. He put the case to himself in a blunt, repellent way that fairly staggered him. "Because an Indian does his best to scalp me," he said to himself, "is that any reason why I should turn to, and scalp him, when chance throws him upon my mercy? For instead of Providence delivering my enemies into my hand to destroy them, perhaps it was to spare them. So I will do as David did to old man Saul, I will content myself with chopping off their COAT-TAILS, figuratively speaking. Besides, it may not have been Providence, after all, but chance. They never had any notion of magnanimity, and till now I have had none. Perhaps they are too old in heart to learn; but *I* am not, and I will think twice before I fire my bomb-shell into their camp."

The next day Despierto thought better of his good resolutions, and was on the point of writing the publishers, when he again hesitated. At length he decided on taking three days to think the matter over. He began to wish that he had not put his case quite so strongly—or rather, that he had not told the bitter truth with so much engaging frankness.

But it was not without a terrible struggle that Despierto's better nature finally triumphed and he was master of himself. Virtue in this instance was not its own reward. The young man's resources ran low, as he had anticipated them while engaged in writing his book, in the certainty of being able to effect its immediate sale. He was forced to get into debt, in a small way—debts that would not have troubled a careless man, but which Despierto felt keenly, as he had no instant prospect of paying them off. The precious time he had devoted to his new book was irredeemable. Despierto neither asked for nor expected sympathy, and told no one his troubles; but sometimes in his desperation he felt like cursing all mankind, and almost wished he had introduced a great many others into his book in the garb of villains, and painted all his bad characters blacker than he had done.

This period in Despierto's life is so dark that it were best to pass it over. He had waited before and the opportunity to vindicate himself had come, and now another weary time of waiting brought its changes.

He showed his manuscript, after the darkness had in a measure passed away, to but one friend—a friend who could be implicitly trusted. This is the conversation that was held when his friend returned it:

"If you have told the whole truth, and nothing but the truth," said his friend, who, since he could not easily be called a worse name, may be called Orgulloso Apesadumbrado Desagrávio, "I don't see why you should hesitate one moment to give this to the world, which always sympathizes with the down-trodden."

"It is absolutely true," replied Despierto, "even to minutiæ. Of course there are anachronisms,—lots of them,—but they don't count. You will have noticed that I show myself as having been in the wrong on one occasion. But I wish to forget my enemies, and so forgive them. You know the Divine command is, 'Judge not, that ye be not judged.' The chances are that at the last day we shall all need all the mercy we can get. Mind you, I don't lay claim to any great virtue in taking this course; it is as much a question of indignation that has burnt itself out as of forbearance."

"Yes, but as I take it, it never was a question of vengeance with you, but simply of vindication. I will confess to you, Despierto, that at first I was a little bit jealous of your work, and I was prepared to agree with you that it should be withheld. But I overcame my unworthy feeling of jealousy, and now I strongly advise you to publish it, and let your enemies take the consequences. Send it to the same publishers, if they are still prepared to accept it, and let your thunderbolt fall. According to your showing they had no mercy on you when common humanity should have prompted them to mercy."

"No, perhaps not. But why should I adopt their

tactics? '*Nemo me impune lacessit*' may be a good enough watch-word, but there are better ones."

"Do they know about this scheme of yours? And are you sure it would have the effect you anticipated?"

"Yes, they knew all about it from the first, and were ashamed enough. Their shame ought to satisfy me."

"No, Despierto; it is one thing to be ashamed, and another to be repentant. They will laugh at you for being so QUIXOTIC."

"They don't know the meaning of your QUIXOTISM. As for their bad opinion, I have always had it, and always expect to have it. It has neither hurt me nor annoyed me. If I can enjoy a tranquillized conscience and a feeling of being more civilized than I was before, what is the odds what their opinion may be?"

"I will speak bluntly to you, Despierto, and tell you that *you* don t know the meaning of the term 'civilization.' If you were out on the plains, in danger of being eaten alive by wolves, would your superior civilization forbid your shooting these wolves?"

"What would be the use of shooting them if I could intimidate them in some other way? If all the world went about avenging private wrongs, this planet would soon be given over to the wolves. Come, I don't wish to pose as an Indian brave, who must have the scalp of everybody who insults him. Besides, in this instance, some innocent people would suffer with the guilty, and that would be outrageous."

"That is your one rational argument. Is there no way to get around it, though? How many of these innocents are there?"

"Enough to form a picnic party all by themselves."

"Well, how do you know your book would affect anybody, in any way whatsoever?"

"Because I tried the experiment, in a small way, some years ago, and twice since; but I never learned its effect but once."

"Well, did it have the effect you anticipated for it?"

"Even greater; I was utterly astonished at the result. But I afterwards fraternized with my antagonist, and we called it 'square.'"

"And do you expect to 'fraternize' again, in this case, Despierto?"

"Oh dear, no; as I told you, I wish to forget, and so forgive. I never could bear to punish anything—not even my dog."

"And I dare say your dog was the most notorious one in the neighborhood. Your enemies will misinterpret your motives, and persecute you as of old, if occasion should arise. 'Even the worm will turn,' but you won't, eh? Then you may expect to be insulted and ill-treated; though I dare say you could once have quoted Scripture to prove you were all right in your scheme of retaliation."

"Certainly I could have. But I am not doing anything out of the common way; don't you remember that in Shakspere's play of 'MEASURE FOR MEASURE,' even the scoundrel Angelo is pardoned?"

"Yes; but he doesn't deserve it, and is first exposed."

"Consider Lynch Law, Orgulloso. It is better than no justice at all; but the vigilantes are not the most civilized men in the world. And I have found that others might have treated me almost as cruelly, had they had the opportunity. I thought I had a wide experience of human nature, but this spring I learned something new. Did you ever find yourself hard up, Orgulloso?"

"Once; and man's inhumanity broke my heart."

"Well, that was my predicament. If I had let the book go—"

"Exactly; you spared your enemies at the expense of ruining your fortunes."

"Yes; but, Orgulloso, it gave me the opportunity of a life-time to prove my FRIENDS. At one time I told everybody that I was going away next week—always next week—and they fell away from me daily. If they chose to think I meant mischief, I let them think so; till at last—"

"Proving your friends, eh? And how did you come out? Not much better than 'Timon of Athens,' I warrant you."

"Not a great deal better, perhaps. There were some old friends that stuck to me like a bur; and one, whom our people had befriended, away back in the 'Fifties, took half an hour to explain why—"

"I understand it all. 'Away back in the 'Fifties' is the name of your initial chapter. Say, what are you going to do with your book? Going to lay it in the grate, and put a match to it, and so sacrifice it to your absurd whims?"

"No; for that would certainly fire the soot, and so the roof. No; I will keep it; and if I ever feel the old bitterness again in all its intensity, I will dust it off and read it over—bitterness, book, and all."

"So you are content to have a year cut out of your life, to all eternity!"

"Not altogether lost time, however. I am stronger than I was a year ago—I hope, more generous."

"Don't you recall what the old philospher used to say, Despierto, that it is better to be just than to be generous? Are you wiser than he?"

"You put a wrong construction on that, Orgulloso. Besides, I mean to 'remodel' the book, and bring it out yet."

"You can't do that. A man-of-war might as well be cut down into a merchantman. It wouldn't prove seaworthy."

"You don't understand me. I shall re-write the entire book, using such timbers, to follow your nautical phrase, as can be made to fit into the new craft."

"Well, Despierto, if you leave out the twenty-eighth chapter you will sink your ship. If the first one never leaves port, the second will never make it."

"I hope the contrary, and will risk it."

"Your new book will be like a man without any nerves in his organization, or like a ship without any crew to man and sail her."

"Perhaps so; perhaps you underrate my resources. In any case, it will be more like the captain of a peaceable and respectable ocean liner than like a swaggering old pirate chief, with a blood-stained cutlass in one hand and a horse-pistol in the other, minus both his thumbs and short an—"

"Just so, Despierto; you will be taken for a boasting, blustering fellow yourself, whose words are mere bluff. And, see here, is not your pirate chief a greater favorite with the general run of readers than your ocean captain, who couldn't properly load a horse-pistol, if his life depended on it? But, seriously, you do wrong to instance the pirate in your comparisons; to suggest the commander of a man-of-war, commissioned to make reprisals on the enemy, would be a neater way of putting it."

"Yes, but you see in my book they are pretty much all rascals, and *quasi* pirates, and *id genus omne.*"

"To be sure; I counted them, and you have managed to pick up SEVEN DEVILS. Any one would naturally infer that you had been down to Jericho, and had fallen among thieves, surely enough."

"Just so; my ink ran a little too black. To return to our tomahawking Indian again, I may say of them as Mark Twain once said, the fact that an Indian likes to scalp people is no evidence that he likes to *be* scalped."

"What is the application, Despierto?"

"Because they enjoyed fixing up a gallows-tree for me, as high as Haman's, you surely don't suppose they would see any fun in being dragged round the walls of their own Troy, do you?"

"But, suppose they should open fire on you again; wouldn't you slip the cable, and let the good ship stand out into the open, with 'NO SURRENDER' flying slily from the mast-head?"

"I don't know; I think I have washed the war-paint from my face for good."

"Well, will you let me read your book again?"

"Why so? It must be such an undertaking to read five hundred pages of manuscript that I thought you would consider it a doubtful compliment to be asked to read it at all."

"It takes practice, that's all. I want to find out the reason why you weakened at the last minute. Why,

Despierto, you are throwing away the opportunity of a life-time. Your enemies could never pay you back in your own coin—that is, *they* could never write either a readable or a marketable book; and if they should attempt it, no reputable publishing house would take it up, for either love or money. So you had them in a tight place."

"I know it; but you know 'it is excellent to have a giant's strength; but it is tyrannous to use it like a giant.'"

"True; but when the parties of the first part were the giants, it was LAWFUL. These would not have given you leisure to moon over Shakspere, or to inquire into the habits of the genus pirate. However, argument is wasted on you, Despierto.—Well, in any case, you must have had lots of fun while writing that book?"

"Lots of it!"

"Come, now, what is your motive in throwing up the sponge?"

"I have hinted at it several times; now I will tell you: *I don't want to go into the White Cap business!*"

VERSE FOR THE TWENTY-NINTH OF MAY.

As this bright, glad, and heav'nly day,
　So may your life be ever,
A glorious, endless dream of May,
　With not a cloud to sever
A moment's sunshine from your life,
Or cause the least domestic strife.

May 29th, 1887.—A cold day for verse-making.

WHAT AUGUSTUS WROTE IN LUCY'S ALBUM.

You ask me for a paltry rhyme
　In the same free and cheerful way
As asks a beggar for a dime—
　But surely I'll not say you nay.

I on my part will be more bold,
　Will ask for more transcendent bliss,
Will for my rhymes ask more than gold,
　For in return I ask a kiss !

Quick as a flash Lucy wrote beneath it :—

Not having asked you for a rhyme
　I hope you'll think it not amiss
If I give you a beggar's dime
　Instead of giving you a kiss !

But Augustus got his kiss, all the same ; and Lucy got more than ten cents' worth of caramels.

SING ME A SONG OF THE OLD DAYS.

In the old days, at my request,
　　You sang me fiery songs of love;
Sing now a song with sad refrain,
　　Despairing as a mourning dove.

In this last meeting of our life
　　I do not wish to cause you pain;
To-day you are another's bride,
　　And my old wounds must bleed again.

My love for you has not grown cold,
　　Though low the flame has sometimes burned;
My faithful heart has never changed,
　　But thoughts of other sweethearts spurned.

For ten long years I've cherished hope
　　That your regard I might redeem;
Man's faith sometimes burns on alway,
　　While woman's love is but a dream.

The spring-time love of steadfast hearts
　　Is love that cannot pass away;
Time will bring care, and pain, and death,
　　But the first love knows no decay.

When you and I were sweethearts still,
　　You promised to be mine for aye;
I ask not now for more than this,
　　An old-time song of yesterday.

Sing me a song of the old days
　　When you and I were sweethearts true;
Those happy days I would recall,
　　Ere for all time we say adieu.

GIVE BACK TO ME MY DIAMOND RINGS.

Parody on Preceding Poem.

In the old days, at your request,
    I gave you diamond rings galore ;
Give now those battered rings to me,
    And I will trouble you no more.

In this last meeting of our life
    I have no harsh wish to raise Cain ;
This ev'ning you'll be "charivaried,"
    And your poor ears will ache with pain.

My love for you has grown ice cold,
    My courting-days have taken wings ;
Full many sweethearts I have lost
    For want of my engagement rings.

For ten long years I've cherished hope
    Some of the gems you would give back ;
Man's faith sometimes lasts several days,
    But to keep rings is woman's knack.

The lavish gifts of sweethearts green
    May oft again come into play ;
Time brought my *letters* back to me,
    The useful *rings* you kept alway.

When you and I at last fell out,
    You peevish said my gifts you spurned ;
Some gloves and songs and gimcrack'ry
    You sent—the rings were not returned.

You surely have no further use
    For your old sweetheart's diamond rings ;
Your happy husband had no need
    To court you with such costly things.

HER MAJESTY'S CUSTOMS.

I HAD been notified of the arrival at the custom-house of a box of books for me from England. I was densely ignorant of the constitution and by-laws of that great autocracy of Canada, and imagined that all I had to do was to dress with care, betake myself to the custom-house, present my paper, and pay the duties. Then, of course, I should be able to collect my goods, and go on my way rejoicing. This shows how deplorably ignorant I was.

I was graciously received at the custom-house by a benignant elderly gentleman, and given some papers to fill out. This looked simple enough; and as I proceeded to fill them out (a not difficult task) I mentally laughed at the cock-and-bull stories that had been told me about the red-tapeism of custom-houses. The benignant elderly gentleman moved away from me in the discharge of his duties, and my work of filling out the papers was all but completed when a spruce, mustacheless young man sidled up to me, and politely but authoritatively asked to see my papers.

I weakly surrendered them. The young man smiled a smile of profound pity for my dense ignorance as his eagle eye glanced over those papers. He was evidently a youth who, in moments of confidence, told his friends and his inferiors that he could always tell by instinct when a greenhorn was at large in the custom-house.

"You are all wrong, my dear sir," he said cheerfully. "It would be impossible for you to manage this sort of thing, anyway. The ways of the custom-house are peculiar, you know, my dear sir."

I replied that I really knew no such thing.

"They *are*, sir," he said, deliberately tearing up the papers he had taken from me. "The proper way will be to go to Mr.———, a custom-house broker, who will assume all responsibility, and save you all trouble. If you will mention my name," tendering me his card, " he will push the matter through without delay. And it will cost you only fifty cents."

Then he figuratively, if not literally, put me out of doors, and very carefully pointed out the office of Mr. ————. Of course it would never do if I should stumble into the office of some rival custom-house broker! But, begrudging my enterprising young friend the small commission he thought he had made sure of in my case, I threw away his card, and did turn into the office of a rival broker. This goes to show how churlish I was.

I had considerable curiosity to find out what manner of man the custom-house broker might be. I was prepared to face a portly, severe individual, who would try to extort some very damaging confession from me, but who would generously spare my life. I was therefore somewhat surprised to find myself confronted by a dapper little fellow, ballasted by a huge and extravagant eye-glass, but whom, for all that, even the slim senator from Virginia could easily have pitched out of the window. He looked as if he had been tenderly brought up on fish balls and tapioca, and carefully protected from the sun and from draughty doors. I have since made an important discovery, to wit: that all custom-house brokers are not cast in the same mold.

This young man soon made me aware that however frail and spiritual he might look, he yet rejoiced in a monumental intellect, and had ways and means of scaring timid people almost to death.

The first thing he did was to prove to me that my books had been wrongly invoiced, and that in the name of his Queen and his country he was authorized to increase the invoice price by twelve dollars. As the duty on the books was fifteen cents on the dollar, this did not seem so very terrible, and I agreed to submit to the overcharge, after a mild protest. I thought I would give him a fair start, just to see how far he would presume to go before I should suddenly check him. That was where I made an egregious mistake, for he seemed content to have raised and put into the pocket of his Queen and his country the sum of one dollar and eighty cents.

He now proceeded to lay before me such a pile of papers that I marvelled where they all came from.

"You will sign your name and address, please; your name and address in full," he said, at last, taking up the undermost paper.

I did so, remarking that I had no objection to give him the length of my arm and the name of my dog, if he so desired.

He regarded me with withering scorn, and placed another paper before me to be signed. I perceived that these papers were precisely the same as those I had been given to fill out at the custom-house, only that here there were more of them. This was not calculated to soothe my ruffled spirits.

"Don't you wish me to fill out these papers in full?" I blandly inquired.

"No; it is my clerk's business to do that," he replied haughtily.

His clerk! I was astonished! But on looking about me I espied an office-boy of tender years and in all the glory of curly hair, pensively chewing gum in a corner. So he had a clerk, surely enough!

A third paper was spread before me, which I was requested to sign in two places. Things were beginning to get interesting. I had the curiosity to read a few lines, first humbly asking permission to do so. I had thought Blackstone dry and dreary reading—but this!

"Where do you get all your census papers, if I may ask?" I suddenly blurted out.

A contemptuous curl of the lip was an unsatisfactory reply, and I made bold to tell him so.

"I see," I pursued, "that you have not inquired into my politics, idiosyncrasies, or superstitions. You will doubtless earnestly wish to know whether my father's stepfather drank tea or coffee; whether my grandmother said either or either; and whether I myself smoke a twenty-five cent cigar, or chew plug tobacco. I haven't the sligtest doubt that it will be necessary for you to know whether I brush my teeth with 'Sozodont,' or with some obscure tooth-paste; whether I prefer as a beverage hard cider, sasafras tea, water-works water, or buttermilk; whether I use hair-oil, or trust to nature and the barbers to take care of my hair; whether I prefer the music of the hand-organ to that of the mouth-organ, or the music of the tom-cat organ to that of the organette; whether I carefully measure patent medicine out in a spoon, or swig it down by guess work; whether I wind my watch when I get up in the morning, or when I retire at night, or whether I wind it at fitful intervals; whether I write my letters with a cheap lead-pencil, or with a fountain pen, and whether I strike my relatives for postage-stamps, or buy them singly at drug-stores. As I am somewhat pressed for time to-day, I hope I shall not hurt your feelings if I urge that you should get through with your inquisition as soon as may be. In case, however, it is necessary for me to undergo a medical examination, or be placed before an insanity expert, I hope you will allow me first to telegraph my friends and prepare a brief obituary for my tombstone."

This prompt manner of forestalling his programme seemed to jar on the nerves of the dapper broker, while it completely demoralized his "clerk." I presume it was not every day that they encountered a man who could thus easily take Time by the forelock and get ahead of their knotty questions. The young man upset one of his three ink-bottles, and the "clerk" lost his grip on his gum.

"Where do you deposit all these valuable documents, anyway?" I jeeringly inquired.

The eye-glass deigned me no reply, but the "clerk," on whom I seemed to have made an impression, gasped out that the papers were sent to Ottawa. For this breach of discipline I am sorely afraid that the "clerk's" magnificent salary was afterwards docked five cents, or maybe ten.

"Are they scarce of waste paper down there?" I asked, trying to be sarcastic.

"I meet with a great many fools in my experience as a broker," the young man replied severely.

I did not retort by saying that I also met with a great

many fools; I kindly and respectfully told him that I was very sorry for him.

Then he brightened up and told me confidentially that the Government had of necessity to use some formality in collecting Her Majesty's customs. This proves that it is better to be kind than sarcastic in dealing with the custom-house broker. If I had retorted gruffly he would not have vouchsafed me that piece of invaluable information.

I thanked him gravely, and said that if I had known my handwriting was to be inspected by the Queen of Great Britain and Ireland I should have called for one of his very best pens.

However it was necessary for me to sign my name two or three times more, and I will venture to affirm that I never took so much pains to write it well. What did this avail me, when I could not prevail upon either the broker or his "clerk" to tell me which one of all the papers I had signed would be reserved for Her Majesty's perusal?

All formalities were at last concluded, and I asked, in an easy, off-hand way, if I could get my books that afternoon.

The ethereal young broker became indignant at once. That afternoon! I might consider myself lucky if I got them inside of five days.

I paid him, in lawful coin of the realm, $8.30 (which included his own fee and the over-charge), and walked out of his office with a heavy heart.

I am happy to say that he over-estimated the time, as I received my books in good condition three days later.

A DISILLUSIONED INNOCENT.

A RECHERCHÉ ALLEGORY.

AN observing young man from a tranquil and guileless country place once made his way into a great city, and there made certain discoveries that shocked him. His secluded country life had fostered romantic ideas that he had always entertained about the habits and modes of life of distinguished men and well-known people generally. His disillusionment was so complete and startling that he sought out a shrewd old uncle of his, who knew something of the ways of the world, and unbosomed himself to this effect :—

"Why, uncle," he said, "I had the curiosity to call on the greatest newspaper poet of the day; and instead of finding a patriarchal-looking man, with the beard of a Moses and the eyes of a pirate, I found a man who looked hardly better or worse than the average New Jersey tramp. He was sitting by a grate, groaning and whining over a vulgar, insignificant corn; and there was an unpoetical look about his finger nails, and a shipwrecked appearance about his socks."

"Exactly, my boy; and if you had asked him what he had been doing all winter, he would have told you (if he had been honest enough to tell the truth) that he had been trying to find out how many newspapers had copied his poems. But perhaps he tore himself away from the grate after you went out, and wrote a neat little ballad about yourself, called 'Our Susan's Latest Beau.' In that case the poet would forget all about his corns. It is dangerous to go about the world intruding upon the sacred leisure of those petulant individuals to whom the gods have given a pen."

"And I found, uncle, that a great railroad king, who has more chimneys on his house than our postmaster has dogs on his farm, has a pimple on his nose, a more heathenish head of hair than a side-show Indian, and an eye that squints so savagely that he wears glasses colored so deep that he can't see to read the weather bulletins. Besides this, he wears such shabby clothes that his own daughter hates to recognize him on the street."

"Again I say exactly, my boy; but instead of worrying about these things, he was probably figuring on how much longer the company could stave off the expense of putting up a new freight shed at some little station along the line."

"And I went to a spiritualist's seance, uncle," pursued the youth, becoming more subdued, "and found that the medium's breath savored of onions that must have sprouted under the bountiful rains of 1882, and that he had less sense and less education than a scamp evangelist, and that he couldn't materialize well enough to humbug even a crack-brained believer in spooks."

"Quite so, my dear boy; and if the hobgoblins evoked had been sober enough to perceive what a noodle was in the audience, they would assuredly have told you that the shade of Simple Simon wanted to consult with you at your lodgings on hydra-headed asininity."

"Then," continued the young man, "I had pointed out to me the son of a great philanthropist, now dead; and the youth had just mustache enough to make him feel uncomfortable and look ridiculous, and his only ambition is to criticize the mayor of the city and be invited to dinner by some old friend set up in business by his own deceased father; while a gaunt-looking man, with an old gold mustache big enough and heavy enough to make him look handsomer than a peacock under full sail, is a dog-catcher in the summer season, a snow-shoveller in the winter, and a quack doctor in the spring and fall, when hoarse colds and influenza get in their best work."

"My boy," said the uncle, "you are working your intellect too hard. Two years ago you were throwing stones at the birds, and now you are itching to give points to old Rhadamanthus himself. You must learn that while a man who is not blind can see through a pane of glass, it needs an observer of fifty years' experience to determine whether an unassuming and quietly dressed stranger, entirely off his guard, is a reformed freebooter or a heartless railroad section boss. Learn also that fresh young men who go away from home and think they can learn everything there is to be known about mankind in six years—not six days—are far from being wise. But, for your encouragement, I may say that you have made commendable progress."

But after the young man had gone the uncle sorrowfully shook his head, muttering: "That boy is a trifle too smart for this reasoning world; he will soon be wanted elsewhere.—Elsewhere, where the spirits and the mediums can call him up from the 'vasty deep' to tell flippant ghost stories about lunatics who never lived, and who consequently haven't had a good chance to die. I think I must encourage the boy to ease himself of his Cyclopean omniscience and interest himself in municipal politics."

THE LITTLE LONE HOUSE.

A TRUE STORY.

AWAY out in the country, far from any other habitation, a little brown house stood on a hill by the road-side. Its occupants were a widow and her two little children, a dog and a cat, also members of the family. A small garden surrounded the house, yielding a scanty supply of vegetables.

Mrs. Carlyle eked out a living by teaching a small school. It was hard work to teach this school and take care of her children, while the remuneration was pitiful; but Mrs. Carlyle had a brave heart, and bore her privations patiently, hoping for brighter days.

This little lone house seemed to be strangely attractive to beggars and vagrants, and they haunted it by night and day. It was annoying to Mrs. Carlyle, and sometimes terrifying to the children, especially when, as often happened, a drunken man would stagger up to the house, pound on the doors, and even try the windows.

They had a dog, to be sure; a big, loafing, yelping creature, which had been a plaything for the children so long that its usefulness as a dog was a thing of the past. When an objectionable caller came to the house this dog would make a tremendous uproar, and scare the intruder away, if he were a stranger and unacquainted with the dog's peculiar habits. But once let the doughty dog out of the door, instead of flying at the intruder neck and heels, it would either profess the greatest friendship for him, or else chase hurry-scurry after a stray cat or a bird. Carlo delighted exceedingly in running promiscuously after flying things.

Again and again poor Mrs. Carlyle resolved that she would never pass another twenty-four hours in the house; but the place was her own, and she could support herself there. Further, it was her children's birthplace.

So they lived on in the little brown house; often harassed by beggars, tramps, and drunken men; often having a hard struggle to keep the wolf from the door. It was a hard life, and a wearisome one.

One day in winter the daughter of a neighbor, having been at school all day, was going to stay overnight with Mrs. Carlyle and her two little girls. The children were amusing themselves greatly while Mrs. Carlyle busied herself preparing supper, when suddenly a tall and gaunt figure opened the door of the kitchen and deliberately walked in. This alone was sufficient to alarm Mrs. Carlyle and the three frolicking girls; but—the man was an Indian!

There was really no cause for alarm, as a peaceably-disposed Indian was less to be feared than a strolling white man. But Mrs. Carlyle did not consider this, and she was more frightened than she cared to admit. As for the two little girls and their visitor, they had read that very day in their Reader about the barbarities practiced by the Indians in the early days of the country, and they sickened with horror, feeling certain that they should all be massacred in cold blood.

First the dog was appealed to. The three little girls motioned silently but beseechingly for it to attack the Indian. Carlo, noble dog, understood; he obeyed their entreaties without hesitation ; and squatting before the Indian he stretched out his paws to shake hands, opened his mouth, and panted contentedly.

" Poor dog," said the Indian. " Good dog, missis, this un."

" The Indian has charmed him," whispered the little visitor shrilly. " Indians always do charm people's dogs."

" Oh, I hope he won't poison him!" gasped little Edith Carlyle.

The three posted thems lves in a position from which they could watch proceedings, but from which they could beat a retreat at a moment's warning.

" Boss in, Missis?" asked the Indian.

" No, he is not," said Mrs. Carlyle.

" I don't care," whispered Gertrude, the elder of the two sisters, " I don't care, I don't think it would have been wrong for mamma to say we are expecting our uncle from California."

" Can't you give me a bit of food?" asked the Indian. " I'm hungry. Victuals smell awful good."

Mrs. Carlyle, not so much frightened as confused, took up a generous slice of meat, and hurriedly gave it to the Indian. He did not ask for a plate, but said politely, " Needs knife to cut it with, Missis. My own all 'baccy."

Mrs. Carlyle was so confused that she gave him the first knife that caught her eye. To her own and the little girls' consternation, it proved to be what is familiarly known as a butcher's knife ! The poor Indian gave a grunt of disapproval, but did not ask for a better one.

It was high time for the little girls to retreat. There was a patter of little feet over the floor—they had fled.

The sanctuary they sought has probably been sought by every little girl (and boy, too) that the sun ever shone on. They hid in their bedroom! Here they felt quite safe for the time being; but Lizzie, their visitor, quavered, "I'll never come to visit you again, Gertie."

"Oh, don't be afraid, Lizzie;" said Gertrude, her voice trembling; "we'll get him to let you go, as you're a guest."

"Oh, he'll kill us all with that big knife! I know he will!" sobbed Eidth. "Listen!" hearing a rasping sound from the kitchen. "Oh, Gertie! He is sharpening the knife to kill us! Oh, dear!"

There was a scrambling noise—Edith had disappeared. A moment later and Gertrude and Lizzie had also disappeared. They had not fallen through a trap door, nor been spirited away; they had only gone where they believed they would be safest—they had crawled under the bed.

Finding herself deserted by the three frightened children, Mrs. Carlyle felt her native courage return, and although still so excited that she made little progress, she went on with her preparations for supper. She recollected that the knife she had given the hungry Indian was the dullest one in the house; and perhaps this comforted her not a little.

The door of the little girls' room opened quickly, and a figure appeared in the doorway. Three stifled screams and three gasps of terror came from the trio, betraying their hiding-place, and they huddled more closely together.

"Gertrude," said Mrs. Carlyle's voice calmly, "come out; I want to speak to you."

Three little golden heads peered warily and fearfully out

from under the bed. Seeing no one but Mrs. Carlyle, and that she did not appear so very much frightened, three little figures emerged from their ambush.

"Gertrude, dear," said Mrs. Carlyle in a hushed voice, "I want you to put on your thicker boots and your wraps, and run up to Mr. Colfax's for some of them to come and take the Indian away."

"Oh, it's so cold, and the snow is so deep," sighed Gertrude.

"Yes, dear; but there is no other way to get rid of him."

"All right, mamma; I'll start, anyway."

Mrs. Carlyle's presence began to inspire them with courage.

"What's he doing now?" Edith whispered.

"He is still eating his meat, Edith. You mustn't be frightened, girls."

"Can I go with Gertie, Mrs. Carlyle?" asked the little visitor.

"Oh, do come, Lizzie! You'll be such company."

But when they had put on their wraps and started out, they found the snow so deep and soft that Gertie's poor little boots sank through it, chilling and wetting her feet.

"Oh, dear!" she said. "My feet are going to get soaking wet; and then I'll catch cold; and then mamma will have to make me onion syrup."

"I wish you had nice long-legged boots like mine, Gertie; they are just like boys' boots. Pa got them for me on purpose to go to school when it's wet and the snow's deep."

"I wish I had, too," assented Gertie.

"I'll tell you what to do, Gertie! Let us turn back, and I'll take off these boots and let you wear them."

"Oh, *will* you, Lizzie? How good you are! I shouldn't be a bit afraid. But what will you do, Lizzie?"

"I'll stay and talk with Edith till you come back."

"And won't you be frightened?"

"No, I'll try not to be; and perhaps if the Indian should go to kill your ma and Edith, I could help. Only hurry, Gertie."

Lizzie meant, if the Indian should attempt to kill them, she might help to resist him. She was a bright little girl, but she could not always say exactly what she meant.

So they returned to the house. Gertie drew on Lizzie's top boots, and then bravely went out into the cold alone. The snow was just as deep, but with the magic boots on her feet she did not mind it, though she sank into it the same as before, and progress was slow. But these boots kept her feet dry and warm, and she trudged on bravely and hopefully.

At last she reached Mr. Colfax's house. Her story was a startling one—so startling that it frightened the little Colfax girls so much that they declared they would never go to school again. But Mr. Colfax did not look frightened, though he immediately put on his cap and overcoat.

"Won't you please take your gun, Mr. Colfax?" Gertrude ventured. "I'm sure the Indian is all ready to fight any person."

"No, Gertie; he wouldn't be afraid of a gun."

Gertrude stayed a few minutes to rest, and then set out for home, half expecting to see her mother's house burst out into flames before she reached it. But no; there stood the house all right.

Mr. Colfax easily prevailed on the Indian to go home with him, where he was given a good supper and a night's lodging, and sent on his way rejoicing.

Once rid of their unwelcome visitor, the three little girls became exceedingly brave, and gravely told what they would have done to circumvent him in case he had attempted to kill them. But Gertie had proved herself a little heroine, and she knew it.

Some weeks after this occurrence another schoolmate was spending the night with Gertrude and Edith. This time it was one of those same little Colfax girls that had declared she would never go to school again. Far from doing this, however, she had gone to school regularly, and never rested till she was invited to "stay all night" at the Carlyles'.

"How romantic it must have been for you," she said, speaking of the Indian's visit. "It was just like a story, wasn't it, Gertie? So romantic."

Little Phœbe Colfax was a most "romantic" young miss, who, instead of writing compositions about sugar, water, lead, sleigh-rides, strawberries, etc., wrote painfully moral fables about sportive little dogs, big watch dogs, blind Negroes, good little girls, and bad little boys.

"Yes, it did seem romantic after it was all over, and we'd had our supper," said practical Gertrude.

"Do you suppose anybody will come to-night?" Phœbe queried.

"Oh, I hope not!" devoutly said Gertie and Edith in chorus.

"So do I," assented Phœbe, "unless it should be something romantic—that is, that would not be too terrible, and would seem romantic afterwards."

Romantic Phœbe's wish was partially gratified. After supper, while the three girls were getting up their lessons for the next day, Mrs. Carlyle heard the sound of a drum in the distance.

"Girls," she said, "I hear a drum beating. I think it must be some one getting up his enthusiasm for St. Patrick's day; don't you want to go to the door and listen?"

"Oh, yes!" said the three, laying down their books and running eagerly to the door. Gertie turned the key very cautiously, and then, with her hand still on it, listened intently. Hearing no one outside, she carefully opened the door a little way, and then shut it with a bang.

"Oh, dear!" said Edith.

"What is it?" whispered Phœbe.

"Oh, it's nothing," answered Gertrude; "I was only careful."

Then she opened the door again. All was still, except for the sound of the far-away drum. Growing bolder she opened the door to the extent of about two inches, and with her hand firm on the knob, held it so.

"Isn't it nice?" said Edith.

"Yes; but then it's only some common drum, you know, Edith, so it can't be much;" said Miss Phœbe, who did not seem to have a very exalted opinion of the music. Of course if she could have imagined it was a gallant drummer-boy drumming to his regiment, she would have been enchanted.

"I don't care; I like it," declared Edith.

"Well, if Phœbe doesn't care for it, we'll come in," said Gertrude. "I don't like to have the door unlocked, anyway; and it's pretty cold."

As she finished speaking she perceived that something was pressing gently against the door, trying to shove it open. This was so terrifying that she screamed aloud, though she did not quit her hold on the door.

"What's the matter!" cried two voices.

"Some one is trying to get in!" Gertrude screamed.

"Oh, hang on! Shove it shut! Quick!" cried Phœbe. Then, at the top of her voice, "Mrs. Carlyle!"

"Oh, it won't shut!" panted Gertie. "Help me, Phœbe! My strength is all gone! I can't shut it!—Ma! Quick!"

Poor little Phœbe! Poor little girl! She did what she knew she would never do; what she despised. She followed the example of Lizzie; she ran and hid with Edith in Gertrude's bedroom!

Mrs. Carlyle came into the room in alarm. "What *is* the matter?" she demanded.

"Oh, mamma! Some one is trying to get in, and I can't shut the door any farther!"

"Stop, Gertrude! It's Stripy, our cat!"

Yes, it was Stripy. Finding a crack of the door open, he had pushed gently with his head to shove his way in. Having got his head inside, he could neither draw it out, nor force his body through, nor squall; for the door, with Gertrude pushing on it, held his neck as in a vice.

Poor Stripy! With horrified eyes protruding from his head, he turned tail when released, and sped away like a mad thing. It was a full week before he came back, and then he did not come to stay.

Miss Phœbe was very quiet for the rest of the evening. It is doubtful whether she could ever look on that incident in a romantic light. But Gertrude had again behaved like a heroine.

One night after Mrs. Carlyle's little girls had gone to bed, she was sitting up late, making a dress for one of them. She was sitting in the front room, which faced the road. The lighted windows of this room could be seen from afar.

Busily sewing the dress she heard a stealthy step outside, and knew in a moment it was somebody prowling about the house. What sort of person was it? a housebreaker? a vagrant? or a drunken man? Certainly it was not a neighbor, nor yet a friend.

The stealthy steps drew nearer, and Mrs. Carlyle perceived that they were shuffling and unsteady. Evidently it was a drunken man.

Instinctively Mrs. Carlyle laid aside her sewing and put out the light. Then she flew to the three outside doors to assure herself that they were locked. Yes, they were fast, but the windows were none too secure.

She had barely seated herself when the door-knob was turned. Trembling, she waited to see what the drunken man would do next. Soon the rear door was tried, then the third and last door. Presently a violent blow was struck on the front door. The man had made a circuit of the house and tried all the doors. What would he do now?

"Can't you let me in, boss?" asked a thick voice. "I'm lost, and I want a night's lodging."

So, it was a stranger to the neighborhood—probably a

tramp. Mrs. Carlyle found courage to say, "No, you cannot stay here; you will have to go farther on."

"I won't!" replied the man doggedly.

"Oh, what shall I do?" groaned Mrs. Carlyle. "God help me!"

Then, one by one, the drunken tramp tried the windows.

This at once roused Carlo, and he began to bark vigorously. The tramp, undaunted, continued to try the windows, pausing occasionally to mock poor Carlo.

The dog's barking awakened the children, and springing out of their warm bed they ran to their mother, crying piteously.

"Now, girls," said Mrs. Carlyle, "sit quietly here and be good, and I will save you. Don't cry, or make any noise."

"Yes, mamma," they whispered; "we'll keep still."

Going to the stairway, Mrs. Carlyle called out in a loud voice: "Anthony, Anthony! come down! There's a man here, trying to break in!"

Then, with a whispered "keep still," she slipped off her shoes and darted noiselessly up-stairs. Groping her way to an old closet, the receptacle of disused furniture, heirlooms, and rubbish generally, Mrs. Carlyle hunted out a pair of her husband's heavy old boots, drew them on, and came stamping down-stairs with a crashing noise.

"I'm coming, Mary!" she said, in a hoarse and very loud voice.

Poor little Edith, not knowing what it all meant, sobbed as if her heart would break.

"Hush, Edith!" whispered Gertrude, throwing her

arms around the frightened child. "It's all right; it's mother, Edith."

"Don't speak!" said Mrs. Carlyle, in s tremulous a tone that Edith only sobbed the harder.

Striding noisily to the rear of the house, where the tramp was about to try the last window,—one which would certainly yield to his efforts,—Mrs. Carlyle, assuming a mascul ne voice as well as she could, said sharply: "Get away from this, you scoundrel, or I'll blow your brains out!"

"A' right, boss; don't shoot, an' I'll go," came the reply.

There was a ring of alarm in the tramp's voice. Soon they heard him shuffling along, past the house, and out of the gate.

This was Mrs. Carlyle's most trying experience with vagrants. A few days afterwards Mr. Colfax presented Gertrude with a lively and effective little gun, and taught her how to shoot it. At the same time another kind-hearted neighbor gave them a powerful and intelligent mastiff—a really valuable dog.

This new dog, Nestor, did not seem to have much respect for Carlo, and they did not agree very well; but they ate every day enough to sustain them for three days. Although they persisted in this reckless indulgence of appetite, strange to say it did not hurt them. But two dogs were a nuisance; and if the new-comer had not been endowed with much dignity and self-esteem he might have picked up some of Carlo's foolish habits.

How was Mrs. Carlyle to get rid of poor Carlo? One day a deliverer appeared in the person of a lazy, good-natured boy (the hero of Phœbe Colfax's stories about bad boys), who inveigled Carlo off into the woods on a squirrel-hunting excursion. Carlo enjoyed himself hilariously that day; but, for all that, he made a "mysterious disappearance." His fate is still unknown to the little Carlyles. Miss Phœbe insists that he must have met his death while "defending himself" bravely against some ferocious outlaw; but the boys look wise, and say darkly that he didn't go farther south than Patagonia, the *Ultima Thule* of their geographies.

SUCH IS LIFE.

I loved a lass of sweet sixteen
    As mortal man ne'er loved before;
Of my fond heart she was the queen,
    And should be so for evermore.

Her eyes were of the softest blue,
    Her hair was of the richest brown;
Her heart to me I felt was true,
    And on my suit she did not frown.

From March till June I wooed my love,
    And gloried in her gentle rule;
"My love," I cried, "for this fair dove,
    Can nothing sap, can nothing cool."

I raved about her silken hair;
    I feasted on her eyes so blue;
I said, "No other is so fair,
    No other is so sweet and true."

I swore that she should be my own;
    I swore to take a rival's life;
I swore—but when twelve months had flown
    Another sweetheart was my wife.

HOW A COOLNESS AROSE BETWEEN BILL AND NERO.*

THE dog Nero was destined to figure somewhat conspicuously in the family history, and it may be well to turn aside from these monotonous scenes and narrate a refreshing incident of his career. Nero had now reached the indiscreet and aggressive age of fifteen months, and one bright June day he went down to the "Corners" to pay his respects to the old people and to bark, in his genial but authoritative manner, at such teams as did not habitually pass his own domains. In this way he soon established a reputation for himself at both corners.

Nero vaulted over the east gate in his usual breezy style, and stalked straight into the kitchen. It was getting well on to dinner-time, and he expected, no doubt, to find both his kind old friends in the house. But the old clock wanted three minutes of striking twelve, so it was a little too early for that, though most of the dinner was indeed smoking on the table.

Great Caesar's ghost! What was this? There, on the "settee," lay a hulking yellow dog, as big as himself, fast asleep, but with that air of easy content that a dog soon manifests where it is made one of the family. This was Bill, of course, whose tragic history was briefly outlined in a preceding chapter.

---

*Taken from the MS. of my book, "THE GREAT TEN-DOLLAR LAW SUIT."—B. W. M.

Neither human nature nor canine nature can tolerate an interloper, and Nero was always an outrageously jealous dog. This was the first he had seen of Bill, and he determined it should be the last. With a snort of rage he made a lunge at the sleeping hound and dragged him sprawling off the "settee."

Bill was now thoroughly awake, and looking on Nero as an intruder, a desperado, and a maniac, the struggle began in earnest. It was not simply a fight for supremacy; it was a fight to the death. The space between the "settee" and the stove was too cramped, so, backing out into the arena between table and stove, the battle was begun all over again. Oh, how stubbornly they fought!

The pantry door promptly slammed to, and terrified cries of "Joseph! Joseph!" smote upon the air. These cries could not penetrate to the shop, but both dogs recognized what they meant, and redoubled their exertions. Bill, of course, being an older dog, had the science of fighting perfectly mastered; but Nero had carried some hard-won fields, and always fought with the impetuosity of vigorous youth. It was hard to say which one would annihilate the other. Suddenly a leg of the table was snapped off, and the steaming dinner was scattered promiscuously over the floor. With frightful yells (for Bill was scalded and Nero was burnt) the combat slackened a moment, only to be renewed the more determinedly. There were many dainties under their feet that at another time would have been swallowed, scalding hot; but this was no time to think of dainties. Bill was after Nero's scalp, and Nero was after Bill's whole hide.

Not even the dinner-bell could be found in the pantry, so, making a detour through the cellar, a scared, trembling figure appeared in the shop, almost speechless.

"Why, Jane, what's the matter?"

"Oh, Joseph! Those dogs!" was the only answer.

Dropping his hammer and calling upon Jim Paget, who was balancing himself, as usual, on the rickety stool, a run was made to the house.

At this juncture Bill had his mouth full of Nero's neck, and Nero was growling hideously; while Bill's feet, cut by the broken glass, were streaming with his patrician blood. Bill seemed to be getting the best of it, and Nero was ready to welcome outside interference. Not naturally a fighter, Bill was easily persuaded by his kind protector to loose his hold.

"This here sport," drawled Paget, "would be perhibited in the city; but they hain't hurt each other any, an' it's the natur' of the animile fur to fight."

"But look at our dinner!"

Seeing his second opportunity, Nero made a sudden and vigorous assault upon Bill, took him again at a disadvantage, and seemed prepared to fight it out, if it took all the afternoon.

"Now, look at that!" said Paget. "The little black feller's got fight enough into him fur a hull ridgyment, as the sayin' is. Ef I was a-goin'——"

"Just like you men!" called out an exasperated female voice from the "west room." "Why couldn't you lock up the dogs when you got them separated!"

Nero had the advantage this time, and was not so easily induced to let it slip. Paget, thinking it was now his turn to interfere, undertook to separate them; but his visible nervousness only encouraged the combatants.

"Bill is afraid of cold water, and Nero of a gun!"

It was a woman's suggestion, but both men hastened to act on it. Paget dashed off to the shop for the firearm, while his host quietly took up a pail of water and deliberately poured it over the dogs, thoroughly drenching both. But neither the drenching nor the formidable-looking blunderbuss brought in by Jim Paget had any effect on the enraged creatures.

"Joseph, shall I shoot into them?" asked Paget excitedly.

"It isn't a shooting gun that you brought," was the calm answer. "No, it isn't necessary to hurt the poor dogs."

Then, with his deliberate, habitual coolness he stepped between the two brutes, grasped either firmly by the neck, and forcibly drew them apart.

"Now, then," he said to the astonished Jim, "take Bill, he is the quietest, and shut him up under the shop, and I'll put Nero in the shop. After dinner we'll turn Nero loose, and he'll go home."

So the two dogs, Bill snarling and Nero growling, and each one, no doubt, claiming the championship, were led away to their respective places of confinement.

"They hain't hurt each other, but you'll never make them friendly together as long as they live," said Paget, coming back into the house and crashing into a dish of currant jam, that had escaped unhurt, though it was, of course, no longer eatable. "Well, I never did see," he continued, half-apologetically, "sech a ruin of a dinner. Joseph, ef it hadn't been fur me, them dogs would 'a' upset the stove an' burnt your house up."

"If they had been of a heavier build they might have," without the suspicion of a smile. "But what a terrible shame to put Jane to so much trouble."

"Yes; an' what a terryble shame to spile sech a nappertizin' dinner, as the sayin' is," said Jim, in his practical way.

"Well, it will do to feed to the chickens. James, I was just going to ask you what ever became of the young fellow who, you were telling me, lived with your son. He seemed to have been a clever young chap, from your talk."

"'Clever'? Well, that ain't exac'ly the word fur to describe him. I ain't so hungry that I can't give you the pertic'lers while the dinner gits cooked over agin. We'll set right out door, by the shady old well, ef our conversation wun't intyrupt Mrs.———"

"No;" came a voice from the cellarway; "it won't interrupt me. But dinner will soon be ready."

"You are the curi'stist folks not to git excited that I ever did hear tell of," said Paget. "Well, this here young man took to intyferin' into everybody's business. There's my little gran'children: they're the cutest fellers fur to study you ever see. Well, Joseph, that young man told 'em they'd got their jography all mixed up, an' discouraged 'em so they quit a-learnin' it fur a spell; an' then he tells 'em their grammars is writ wrong; an' their Readers was shaky in their hist'ry; an' he found terryble fault with the portry into them; said the meetter was a-skippin' a cog—no, went a-skippin' afoot now an' agin; an' talked so high-falutin' that the school-master threatened fur to report to the Eddication Trustees.

"Our folks let all that pass; but when he come fur to talk about things we could all understand, an' said we orter have an even six hours atween every meal; an' not have no pies an' things fur supper; an' that it was a-gittin' fashionable now-a-days fur to have nap kins onto the table; an' that I was dead wrong to help myself to onct, when I was hungry, we begun to see he was a-goin' a leetle too fur.

"Bimeby he told the hired girl she was puttin' too much shortenin' into the pastry, an' that she needn't cook no more onions, 'cause they didn't agree with him, an' we see a storm was a-comin'. The nex' day he told her that his faverrite preserve was huckleberry jam an' quince marmerlade; an' that her milk-pails wan't properly washed; an' that she didn't change her aprons often enough, an' we knowed the air was jest chuck-full of steamboat explosions.

"The hired girl hadn't got more'n half cooled down afore my youngest daughter comes in, an' he serlutes her with the informatlon that it tain't nice fur real stylish schoolgirls to take an' plaster their chewin' gum onto the winder-sill an' under the table, an' we see it was time fur to take in sail, as the sayin' is.

"The same evenin', or the day before, I 'most forgit which, he ups an' tells my son's wife that it wan't considered genteel any more fur ladies to wear all their jool'ry at the breakfast table, an' I mistrusted there was a dog-fight on the ticket, so to speak.

"'Twan't long afore he insisted that the healthiest way fur to sleep was to have your winders open to both ends; an' that beds orter be aired 'most all day; an' that it was pisen to bake pies onto a dish we'd had in the family fur thirty year, 'cause he said the cracks into it was full of germs, an' I could 'a' swore a earthquake was all but upon us.

"The nex' day he quorrl'd with the butcher, 'cause he didn't make his sausages accordin' to his stric' notions of proprierty, as the sayin' is, an' we felt it into our bones that something was dead sure fur to happen.

"The nex' thing he done he told my son it wan't etiquette to set down to the table into his shirt sleeves, an' that dogs an' cats orter be shet out door at meal time an' not be fed permisc'us like by the hull family, an' that it wan't considered perlite in these here enlightened days to bring in tramps off'n the street to set down an' eat along with the household. I see my son didn't like fur to have a teetotal stranger do the thinkin' fur the hull family, so I wan't surprised when he reached———"

"Now, then, dinner is ready, and I'm sure we are all hungry enough."

"Well! Ef your wife don't beat all creation, Joseph, fur to hustle a meal of victuals onto the table!" said Paget, striding into the house and taking the guest's seat of honor, directly under the old clock.

No traces of the late disaster could be seen. The floor was perfectly clean,—dry, almost,—the broken table was removed and another was in its exact place, and a counterpart of the "ruined" dinner was served.

The host followed more leisurely, and still more leisurely began to wait on the table.

This was too much for the impatient Paget, who broke in: "You're so slow, Joseph, an' I'm so hungry, I'll jest help myself; an' when you all come to see us you can pitch in an' do the same. The all-fired smart young man is *non compus mentus,* as the sayin' is, as I was jest perceedin' fur to tell you. I hope you'll both excuse me; but I know the size of my appertite better'n other people."

And he did help himself—to all the viands on the table at once, his most dextrous feat being the apparently accidental tumbling on his plate of two large pieces of apple pie. But it was not accidental; it was the result of adroit manipulation of the knife, and the deprecatory glance cast at his hostess was one of the little arts that invariably accompanied it.

His plate was now heaped so full of food that it looked as if nothing but the most expert jugglery could keep it all from sliding off into his lap. No doubt the fault-finding young man he told about so often had been paving the way for much-needed reforms in a benighted household.

The host smiled good-humoredly; but, woman-like, the hostess seemed hurt.

"How far had we got with that there story, Joseph?" Paget suddenly demanded, with his mouth full of the various dishes heaped on his plate. "I think I must be goin' home now in a few days. You see, they'll be gittin' kinder lonesome about now, without the old man, though I hain't hardly got started to make you a visit yit, an' we want to examine into them there patents."

"Oh, don't be in a hurry yet, Mr. Paget," said his hostess kindly. "Still, if you must go———There comes the stage now, back from Newcastle. I'll just ask him to call to-morrow for your trunk."

And she suited the action to the word, somewhat to the consternation of Mr. Paget, who went the next day, surely enough, leaving his interesting little story unfinished for ten long years.

His kind host said to him at parting: "I have enjoyed your visit, James; but I didn't expect you would be going so soon."

"No more did I, Joseph," was the lugubrious answer.

A QUIET EVENING AT HOME.

THE scene lies in a Mormon household. The family comprises Elder Sampson, his five wives, and his children—forty-two souls in all, not counting those who have become immortal.

"Where's my pen-knife?" roars the elder. "Can't a man be allowed to have a pen-knife to trim his nails? Was it you, Nancy, that borrowed it this time? How many pen-knives of her own does each wife of mine think she is entitled to, without borrowing mine twice a week?"

"I never touched your pen-knife, you old heathen! So there!" screams Nancy, who prides herself on being his spunkiest wife.

"Then it must have been—No, it was Johnny; I remember now. But which Johnny? Whose Johnny?"

"Whose, surely!" pipes up his youngest and newest wife. "One Johnny is a thief, and another is an idiot, and another is sick in bed this week with gluttony. Thank Heaven, that's all the Johnnies big enough to wield a pen-knife."

"Hold your tongue!' bellows the elder.

"You old fool!" retorts Nancy. "Why don't you stop her before she's said her say, or else let it alone. You had better follow your own advice, and hold your tobaccoed old tongue yourself; for if you don't keep still you'll waken the 'seven sleepers.'"

"Hang the 'seven sleepers!'" cries out the elder. "Haven't I been tormented by the 'seven sleepers' these ten years! It's the 'seven sleepers' at morning at noon, and at night. The 'seven sleepers' want this, and that, and the other thing; and they've always got the mumps, and the measles, and the sore throat. I tell you, I want the subject dropped for a fortnight. If the hang-dog Gentiles only knew what we faithful are called on to suffer, they would admit that we are justified in claiming the Seventh Heaven in the hereafter."

Then turning to his fifth wife, he says harshly, "Madam, I want you to learn that you will lose your hold on my affections if you don't cease carping about my family. It is a large family; and a healthy family; and a well brought-up family; and—and—the most creditable one, on the whole, in this place. Now, three or four days ago, (I haven't had a chance to speak about it before) three or four——"

"She'd better learn better than to make any remarks about *my* Johnny!" Nancy here breaks in, her eyes flashing fire at the remembrance of the fifth wife's satirical comments on the Johnnies.

"Nancy," says the elder, rising from his chair with an air that means instant obedience, "Nancy, you have work to attend to in the kitchen. You may come in again when I call you."

Nancy throws down a patch-work quilt with sullen vindictiveness, and strides out of the room.

"Now, then," says the elder, turning to the fifth wife, " I want to know what you meant two or three days ago by flirting with my second wife's young cousin? What sort of wifely behavior is that in an elder's household ? What sort of opinion do you suppose I can have of you when I find you out in such actions ?"

"Well, *he* is a nice young man; and he doesn't look like an old cannibal idol, either, as *you* do! And he isn't loaded down with a houseful of quarrelling wives, and running over with snivelling brats. So there, now!"

"Shades of Smith!" gasps the astonished elder. "Woman, do you know the penalty of such an outburst as this? Do you know wherefore I keep an old slave-driver's whip in my cabinet, under lock and key?"

"Curse it all!" he mutters to himself. "It is Nancy that emboldens all my wives to try to shake my authority. It was Nancy's jabbering that gave this woman the nerve to retort." Then he resumes aloud: "This is your first noteworthy rebellion, and I might be lenient with you; but the offence is too aggravated a one. My wives all have to undergo the penalty of wilfully insulting me."

The fifth wife shudders. But just at this critical juncture the second wife—whose cousin it was that had fired the elder with jealousy—hurries into the room with the intelligence that the fifth wife's child is almost dying with croup. So the fifth wife escaped the punishment that threatened her.

"The fates are against me!" groans the elder. "Not oftener than once in six months can I score a moral victory over one of these women. Just as I get worked up to boiling heat, and begin to strike terror to a culprit's heart, somehow the rest of them manage to upset things and stave off punishment till it is too late. They don't connive together to do it, either; for they hate one another all around like cats and dogs.

"See here," he calls to Susan, his second wife, whom he has not seen for three days, "what sort of report is this I hear of you?"

The second wife holds out a new smoking cap, which she has brought him as a peace-offering, but he refuses to notice it, though his stock of smoking caps is always depleted, as the youngsters cannot be restrained from making away with them.

She looks at him pleadingly and says, " Heaven knows what report ; we are all spies on one another."

" Spies be hanged !" roars the elder. " You spend altogether too much time reading them heathenish Gentile story papers. You clutch onto a *New York Weekly* the moment it comes into the house, and read, and read, without any judgment or common-sense ; and you neglect the work appointed for you to do. Your work is at the sink, washing dishes, not reading cock-and-bull stories in the only decent rocking-chair left in the house, and you know it right well. When your work washing dishes is done, you have the family darning to attend to. Here I go about with raggeder stockings than the scum of San Francisco ; and I'll wager a house full of them darned papers that everybody else in this household is as bad off as I am."

" Well, it was my own copy of the paper that I was reading, so I don't see why Lizzie need complain," replies the second wife, who is the meekest of them all, and consequently the worst abused.

" Who said Lizzie complained about anything?" shouts the elder. " What are you grumbling about now ? Can't you let a man have any peace ? Do you want to see him wear the wrecks of stockings, and then come and abuse him about it, and come in and interrupt him when he is having a talk with his only good-looking wife ? Where is that last paper, now, anyhow? If you don't know, who's going to?"

"My copy was snatched away from me when I was trying to read it and work at the same time. But there are two others who have them."

"Don't tell me that! I know that I subscribe for three copies of those papers, and get a slight discount off. I take them for the sake of peace in the family; but what good do they ever do me? Three of them, and I can't have one!—Go and call them all in."

"What, the children, too?"

"No; the wives."

"Now, I want to know," cries the long-suffering elder, as soon as they are all assembled but the fifth one, "I want to know if there is one solitary individual in this household that can locate any one of the three copies of the *New York Weekly*, or any other heathenish paper that I subscribe for, as I would like to look them over myself. If your tempers weren't all so sour, I might have a little chat with some of you; but that is out of the question. Come, now; where is Susy's, or Peggy's, or Lizzie's copy of that story paper—or of any other paper."

The four wives all begin talking at once, and each one suggests a great many likely and unlikely places where the papers might be. But when search is made no one of the three copies turns up. At length Nancy declares that the third living James had been seen to gobble up some of them to build a kite.

"Very good," says the elder, in a tone that means very bad for James the third. "Very good; where is the boy? Bring him to me."

Diligent search for James is made by Nancy; but he cannot be found. He has, no doubt, strayed off and got lost. No one seems much alarmed at this, however, as it was a weekly occurrence for a James or a William to lose himself—and he was generally suffered to find himself, too. The household was too busy or too much perturbed to go in search of lost members, and none were angelic enough or valued enough to excite the cupidity of kidnappers. So it is concluded that James will turn up in the morning; but the *Weeklies* are considered lost for good and all.

The four wives betake themselves to their several employments, and the elder is constrained to content himself with the *Salt Lake Tribune*. The threatenings breathed against him and his religion in that resolute, indomitable exposer of Mormonism are scarcely calculated to soothe him.

Throwing down the paper with an oath, he says to himself, "I believe I promised Susy's boy a birthday present, and to bring peace to this disturbed house I must fulfill that promise. But how many other birthday presents shall I in consequence have to make within a week? Let me see—fortunately, not more than two or three on this occasion.

"Susan," he calls, "come here."

Susan comes, in fear and trembling. But the elder says pleasantly, with a smile suggestive of inexhaustible benevolence, "I must give that boy a present, Susan, for he has been a very good boy, indeed. His birthday will soon be here now; on—on—next week—on Friday, I believe."

"*My* son's birthday will come on Friday, you heartless old man!" flashes Nancy.

"Well, well," says the elder, "let that pass; he shall have a present, too. This boy, Susan; his birthday—"

"Is to-day," says Susan, sadly. "You have forgotten."

"How can you expect me to remember everything?" snarls the elder. "It is *your* place to remind me of such matters, not *mine* to bear them in mind."

"I suppose she was afraid to mention it," sneers Nancy. "I take precious good care to remind you of what *I* want!"

"Have a care, both of you, carping viragoes, or neither boy shall receive any present at my hands! Susan, I like your boy, and he deserves it, I hope; but beware how you bring him into my disfavor!"

"What have you to say against *my* son?" Nancy asks fiercely. "If he isn't the best child you have—"

In good truth, the two boys under discussion—whose birthdays, unfortunately, fell so near the same date—were as little alike in their appearance and disposition as an English yokel and a German bauer. The advantage, it need scarcely be said, was in favor of Susan's boy.

Nancy leaves the room abruptly to call in the two wretched boys, and another disturbance seems imminent. But scarcely has she stepped out of the door when angry blows and execrations are heard, followed by feline screams of pain and fury. A look of distress crosses Susan's face, and the elder scowls savagely.

The noise increases; evidently the whole household is alarmed. The door opens forcibly, and Nancy bounces into the room, chastising with a hatchet handle a large, domestic-looking cat, which, frightened almost to death, springs towards Susan and finds shelter under her protecting skirts.

In the doorway loom the three other wives, together with ten or fifteen shouting, quarrelling children.

"What does this mean?" cries the elder, in his most appalling voice, rising majestically to his feet.

"Why," says Nancy defiantly, "that's Susan's thief cat, and I caught her stealing Lizzie's chicken pie!"

"Let Lizzie look after her own affairs!" says the elder, for once disposed to shield his wife Susan.

But the hubbub cannot be put down at a word from the elder. Dust darkens the air; the dignified elder himis jostled; the five wives handle their tongues with tremendous effect; one child gets off with a burn, another with a bloody nose, another with an ugly cat scratch. The offending cat, of course, gets off scot free. (The writer who sympathizes with the mild-mannered feline can generally work it, in romancing, to let the gentle creature go scat free.)

What a scene to enlarge upon! But who would be so morbid as to wish to enlarge upon it? Let us withdraw from so much of human depravity and wretchedness, sufficing it to say that neither of those misguided boys received his promised present.

Yes, I have said enough—and more than enough to suit the fastidious reader. However, I trust the fastidious reader (for such I hope to have) will allow that the motive is good, and that but for a profound ignorance of the "Question" I might have said a good deal more—and in still more vigorous language.

DISCOURAGING A JOURNALIST:

I. AS A MUTE, INGLORIOUS MILTON.

"So you would like to become a journalist, eh?" surprisedly asked an editor of a youth who had come to the office as devil a few years previously, and had been steadily advancing himself ever since.

"That's my destiny, sir," replied the young man grimly.

"Indeed? I've seen people attempt to drive their destiny before, and fetch up in the asylum, or turn out a horse-jockey. DESTINY, my boy, is a cruel despot that cannot be driven, nor led, nor wheedled, nor intimidated, nor hoodwinked. Destiny leads a man on as the current carries one in a boat without oars down an unknown stream, where you do not know from one bend to another what is before you. You may glide into a peaceful lake, or ground on a sunken snag, or be dashed over a frightful cataract. Destiny toys with a man as a mousing cat naively toys with a captive mouse. There is this great difference, however, that I must point out, even at the risk of spoiling my metaphors: Gliding along in a boat, as suggested, would have a charm and an excitement about it, and it could not be indefinitely prolonged; while Destiny drags along from day to day like a contented, leisure-loving snail, sometimes for seventy, eighty, or, in extreme cases, one hundred years, with provoking monotony, so that the only pleasurable emotion there is is in retrospect. You wouldn't like to glide in a boat at the pace of one inch per day, would you? Then as to the cat and the mouse: I have sometimes seen the mouse escape, but I never saw a man escape from Destiny. Yet a man may as sensibly yield blindly to Destiny, and idly be its sport, as to think of compelling it. I am a Fatalist myself, but I should not advise any one else to worship so cruel a god. Depend upon it, my boy, the only inanimate gods to serve are Industry and Perseverance. They *have* been known to check-mate Destiny."

The young man did not know whether the editor was moralizing for his benefit or for his own amusement. "Sir," he said timidly, "may I show you some of my immature effusions?"

"Certainly. But never call them 'effusions'—though I dare say 'diffusions' would do—'premature diffusions.' Wind-falls would come nearer the mark, because I doubt whether they are either immature or over-ripe. Let me see now what you have hammered out.—So! I will read it aloud, as it may scare away stray intruders.

"'WHEN I WAS YOUNG.

"' When I was young, as I used to be,
   Full many a year ago,
I used to think it was howling fun
   To "holler," and sing, and swim.

"' I went to school when I was a boy,
   And learned how to skate and fish;
I taught the boys how to rig a ship,
   The girls how to throw a ball.

"' I sharpened pencils for all the school;
   I learned how to shipwreck books;
I studied fireworks and other things;
   I learned how to build a dam.

" 'I made bon-fires and I found birds' nests;
    I inked desks and books with glee;
I made scare-crows and I set them up,
    To peg at with stones and bones.

" 'I had a dog, and his name was Grim;—
    A dog very fond of war;—
He used to bark like a tongue-tied cub
    At teams, and at crows, and boys.

" 'I used to sing like a homesick jay,
    And whistle all out of tune;
I used to laugh like a milk-maid belle
    At ev'rything that I said.

" 'I used to sport, sprawling o'er my vest,
    A chain that I hoped was gold;
I used to wear a great humbug watch,
    That never was built to go.

" 'I used to ride on a grizzled nag,
    In those happy days of yore;
His mane pulled out and his ears shot off,
    His frame very gaunt and gone.

" 'I used to sail in a crazy skiff,
    A craft very crank it was;
Too warped to sell and too good to burn—
    The boat for a boy like me.

" 'I used to hunt with a rum old gun,
    A primitive weapon, sure;
Too game to burst and too worn to kill—
    At last it killed me—all but.'

"I don't see that Destiny had anything to do with this, my boy—it was indigestion, or a 'premature' attack of cerebral jim-jams. Now, I turned out surer-'footed' verse at your age,—verse that would rhyme at chance intervals, too,—and Destiny only allows me, on sufferance, to preside over a piratical Democratic newspaper, that is unknown in Europe, has no paying subscribers in Canada or Mexico, and that will be forgotten within a year after Destiny winds up my career and shoves another man into my editorial chair, who will certainly run foul of the sheriff within one hundred issues of the paper.—Come, now, is this your first effort at verse-making?"

"Yes, sir; it is. I wrote that two years and three months ago, when I should have been still a schoolboy."

"Quite true," said the editor. "'Two years and three months ago!' Well, well! When you were still in the dark ages of your intellect, as it were. I suppose you are firmly persuaded that your intellect is now a nineteenth century one—whereas the truth is, it hasn't yet advanced to the Reformation period. To return to your lines, which are not half bad, after all. I would advise you to send this away to almost any editor in the land, not keeping another copy, draught, or memo. yourself. Said editor will fire it into the waste-basket, with unparliamentary language, and that will be the last of it. You see, my boy, you cannot be a poet all at once, any more than you can be a doctor or a banjoist. I am going to criticise you freely; but if I put the screws on too tight, cry out, and I will let up. Now, if you were a Wordsworth, you know, you wouldn't be so secretive about the nationality and breed of your childhood pets. To be sure, you *do* give away the gender of both dog and horse; but you don't explain whether the dog was a pup or in his dotage. If you were a Byron, your dog would have more horse sense and better morals than a white man, and the 'noble animal' would be no slouch of a steed. A Mark Twain would take us into his confidence just far enough to tell us that the dog was lousy and mangy, and the horse originally the property of a Nebraska half-breed. Almost any one would up and tell which one of the school-girls he married, and what Destiny has done for him now that he is older and wiser.—What else have you?"

"Here is an unfinished poem, sir, that—"

"There you go again! You must say, 'an incomplete poem.' 'The Admiral's Last Cruise; or, How the Battle was Fought and Won,' eh? Your title's too long; some compositors wouldn't know how to work the second half all in on one line. Let's see how it reads, anyway:—

"'THE ADMIRAL'S LAST CRUISE;

OR,

HOW THE BATTLE WAS FOUGHT AND WON.

"'The battered old Lord Admiral,
    With fleet of fifty sail,
Had long time cruised o'er heaving seas,
    And made his foemen quail.

"'One day, as thus he ranged about,
    A man upon the mast—
Who chewed tobacco, and did spit
    The juice down thick and fast

"'Upon the heads of those on deck—
    Thus bellowed, "I do spy
A craft that is so far away
    She looks just like a fly."

"'With that, the old Lord Admiral
    Did catch up his spy-glass,
And ran and swarmed up the tall mast
    As nimbly as an ass

"' Which makes a sudden move to kick
 The boy who bothers him.
"A hard-fought battle there will be,
 With loss of life and limb ;

"'"And many ships will swift go down,
 And many men will die."
Thus spoke the Lord High Admiral,
 When he the speck did spy.'

"Is that as far as you could get? Why, you don't even tell us whether the enemy was really in sight, or not. 'Fifty sail,' eh? and all up-set about a fly-speck on the vast ocean! What you want to do, my boy, is to heave some of your top-heavy conceit and ignorance overboard, and strike Destiny for a cargo of plain common sense, with a glimmering of reason and a little dangerous knowledge of inductive logic thrown in by way of ballast. Here we are all at sea as to whether the Admiral's foe was a white man or a Chinaman; or as to whether the Admiral ever found his foe at all; or even as to whether the stupid old fellow would know his foe if he should meet him on the street. Why, anyone would naturally infer that the Admiral must have had to turn to and lick himself out of his boots, for want of a better foe to tackle, while the 'fifty sail' stood around in easy attitudes, and languidly bet on how long it would take the old fool to get through pommelling himself. While your strong holt seems to be a graceful facility in spreading your titles all over the page, there is a certain deceptiveness about those titles that would make a subscriber think he wasn't getting his money's worth of tangible facts. A little more regard for perspicuity and a little less straining after outside show would about even up your poetry, though it runs too much to bear-garden slang."

"Yes, sir; but the poem is incomplete."

"To be sure; I had forgotten that important fact. Why didn't you remind me of it when I was sailing into your cock-eyed old admiral? What's the reason, though, you didn't wind the thing up ship-shape, and wipe up the blood, and holystone the decks, and clean the big guns, and look after the wounded, and shut sable Night over the scene, and ring up the pale round moon, and l'Envoi the reader yawning to a nightmare sleep?"

"It is too vulgar to be spun out further, sir; and besides, I didn't want to make it as long as a nursery ballad."

"Certainly; you're level-headed there. Better to cut it short and chaotic and leave the reader in the doldrums than trail an index and a sequel astern and subjoin a preface. Now, you leave this with me, and I'll trim the sails a little differently, and we'll smuggle it into Saturday's issue and note how many subscribers give us the shake."

"I am very much obliged," said the young man feebly.

"Don't mention it. I've seen older people than you put up with more abuse for the sake of shoving themselves into print. But haven't you any love songs? You're no poet of Destiny if you can't write that sort of slush. Why, your true *poeta nascitur* would rather scribble lovelorn poems than go courting."

"Well, here's a four-liner, for an autograph album—though I haven't had a chance to put it there yet."

"That's a bad practice. Flee the insidious little dog's-eared album as you would the Latin humorists.—But still there's no occasion for you to be so distressingly frank about it. You were too reserved about your idiotic dogs and ponies, and now you fly to the opposite extreme. Why, if you hadn't told me, I shouldn't have known but you had written it in the album of your own sweetheart and also in the albums of every other fellow's sweetheart. Let's see it.—Hum; just 'Verse for an Album,' when you might have given it a heading longer than the 'pome' itself. Attention!—

> "'Why should you ask me for my name,
> When I would give you heart and hand,
> And all I have at my command,
> You so have set my soul aflame.'

"Now, as you haven't written it, you say, in any importunate—or rather unfortunate—person's album, here is your golden opportunity—DON'T! Next year about this time you might find out that by some terrible mistake you had *inadvertently* written it in the wrong young lady's album.—Is this the best you have? Have you no pastorals or madrigals?"

"I will show you one more poem, sir; but it is incomplete, too, and I don't know what classification it would come under."

"You seem to have a penchant for leaving your poems at sixes and sevens. Vulgarly speaking, you bite off more than you can chew. Well, let me 'review' it for you; and if we can't call it a sonnet we'll call it a lyric.—So; I will read it:—

> "'A SHOUT OF TRIUMPH.
>
> "'Sing, oh my heart, in joyous strain,
> Sing great—sing wild, delirious joy!
> Thou art released from all thy pain,
> Delight has come, with no alloy.

"'Brave heart! thou manfully didst hope,
Through five long, weary, bitter years;
With giant difficulties cope,
Though racked by ceaseless madd'ning fears.

"'Sad days did but succeed sad days,
But now, true heart, all such are past;
The glad sun darts resplendent rays,
Thy day of triumph dawns at last.

"'I'll spread thy fame from East to West,
This big round earth thereof shall sing;
Not through one century's brief quest,
But through all time thy name shall ring!'

"My boy, there *does* seem to be an hiatus somewhere in this. Is it unfinished in the middle, or at both ends? The last stanza might be made impressive; but you have made it simply amusing. I suppose it doesn't refer to your heart-disease, but to some candy-loving sweetheart, eh? But you must muzzle that heart of yours, or put it under lock and key, for it is dangerous to let it go wandering about at large. Like your admiral, it doesn't seem to have any clear idea where to go or what to do with itself. Seriously, you will have to shout yourself black in the face before 'this big, round earth' will pay any attention to you, or your heart, or your sweetheart; or care a snap whether her name is Harriet Jane or Alice Maude Ethel. You see, 'this big, round earth' is so occupied in her leisure moments with the fame of her Shakespeares, Scotts, and Longfellows, that she will only grudgingly countenance a new-comer. She is notoriously cold and unjust to green poets; but this either puts them on their mettle or kills them off. However, it isn't many men that can't and won't get even with their enemies when their 'day of triumph' does really come.

"Well, my boy, I have kept you long enough for one sitting; to-morrow we will examine into your merits as a writer of modern prose. I will wind up by hazarding the opinion that you and Destiny may get there as poets— if you live—along in the early childhood of the next century—perhaps while the century is still in his swaddling clothes. During the exciting Election of 1912 you may be in a position to realize a dollar apiece for Campaign songs, or to wholesale them at six for five dollars. On the other hand, you may die of chicken-pox, or croup, or some other infantile disease. These things often prove fatal to embryo poets.

"Come, don't look sad; you may develop into an eerie poet like Coleridge or Poe, or a sentimental one like Tennyson. Meanwhile, you will have to go through a love-affair that will shake you all up before you can turn out anything marketable. Sorrow is about the best poetry-tonic, and the years of early manhood are fuller of it than an out-house is of spiders.—So long."

DISCOURAGING A JOURNALIST:

II. AS AN UNFLEDGED HUMORIST.

"WELL," said the editor cheerfully next day to the youth who aspired to be a journalist, "I'm in the humor to give you another sitting-on. The old proverb says, 'Never put off till to-morrow what you can do to-day,' and I suppose it refers to the bitter as well as the sweet; to the boy with a bag of candy to eat and to the boy with a garden to hoe."

"I have nothing in the shape of prose, sir, but the draught of a letter I wrote the other night to an old chum."

"I am very glad of that. Besides, what you write for one individual reader is certain to be a pure specimen of your style. To be sure, letter-writing is an art, but it is as different from story or editorial-writing as playing marbles is different from snow-balling a school-teacher. You see, I adapt my illustrations to your years and understanding.—Now, then, hand me your rough draught, please, and I will read it and comment on it at the same time. Is this really the first writing of it, or did you go over it again, with your pencil in one hand and your eraser in the other?"

"I touched it up a little, sir."

"Good. You would be foolish not to do that. Here goes:—

"'MY DEAR TOM:—I have intended to write to you for ever so long, but every time I have fixed a day for the fatal deed some person has inopportunely dropped in and juggled the afternoon or evening away from me. These Philistines have been *bêtes noires* to *me*—but then, on the other hand, they have proved a mascot to *you*. Not that my long-delayed letter is charged, either literally or figuratively, with dynamite. Neither can it unpardonably afflict its reader with grief, nor yet inspirit him; but that it will *bore* you is a foregone conclusion, for I am going to write entirely about myself. To equalize things, if my letter is tiresome, it shall be short.'

"Short, eh?" sneered the editor. "I never saw a letter start out that way yet that wasn't as long as an alderman's address. Short? Why, it's one, three, five, seven—ten pages long! Short? It must have cost double postage to send it; and if the mucilage on your envelope wasn't good, it will go wandering about the country like a Campaign liar. To resume:—

"'I was fully persuaded to write you last Wednesday, because it was my birthday—but again one of your mascots interfered in the person of a neighbor's son. Guileless young man! If I should address the term *mascot* to him he would certainly think I was swearing at him. You kindly asked about my birthday, Tom. It comes this year on the 2nd September.'

"'Comes this year,' eh? That seems to work in very neatly.

"'I was delighted with your racy and gossipy letter. The bold unconventionality of your style is decidedly a charm rather than a drawback, and I quite agree with you that in writing a friendly letter to an old crony one should not guard so much against being off-hand as against being too precise and particular. At any rate, I enjoy your vivacious letter every time I read it over.'

"'Vivacious—gossipy—racy—bold unconventionality!' Really, now, when your friend comes to answer your letter, the only qualifying terms the poor fellow can hit on will be 'droll,' and 'breezy,' and 'quaint.' And I have yet to decide that your letter is any one of all these."

"'Truly, as you say, I spent a month this summer in a quiet spot, and events—or rather, the want of events—made a great impression on me. My uncle's farm-house is old, and my uncle's family have their peculiarities. The venerable chimney was full of swallows; the garden-walks were burrowed with mice; the cellar was running over with rats; the door-steps were crawling with ants; the fences were loaded with gorgeous slugs; the stable was full of unheard-of noises; the driving-shed was full of foreign and domestic tramps; the air was full of noise from my uncle's unoiled machinery, and foggy with dust; and their patrimony was alive by day with "swarming" bees and melodious by night with feline professors of music. The dogs slept all over the house, and scratched off their fleas all night long; and sometimes I myself slept next day till the sun was half seas over. If anybody had been annoyed by this state of affairs my uncle would have stirred up strife between the bees and the rats, and have starved the cats into an ancestral relish for a mouse-diet; he would occasionally have let a flea-tormented dog loose upon the feline choir; he would have given me fifty cents to chop down the giant willow that rasped against the stable shingles and to liberate the bumble-bees that flopped inside against its panes of glass; and he would have placarded the driving-shed to the effect that a beggar died there the previous forenoon of yellow fever.'

"Now you are humping yourself, my boy! The great mistake you make is to open fire in a slip-shod way. Start with a laugh and wind up with a joke; but work in your twaddle, if you must have it, when you are 'half seas over.'

"'A neighbor of my uncle's isn't feeling first-rate this summer. He fell out *with* a homemade ladder in his grandson's leaky barn, and had a rough-and-tumble set-to with an insulted rooster in mid-air and with half a pound of new shingle nails on the floor, and he swallowed four of his sharpest teeth, and ruptured his left thumb, and hamstrung the muscles hitching his left arm to his shoulder-socket, and scared four out of the five children looking on into St. Vitus' dances, and startled a seven-year-old mare into a circus performance that destroyed eighty cents' worth of harness; and finally the injured man hobbled himself home in a "dead dream," not knowing afterwards whether he came through the carriage gate or crawled through a gap in the fence.'

"My dear boy, you are like all the rest of us in one important respect: you can't do good execution till you get warmed up to your work. You must have sweated out a couple of neck-ties in evolving this.—Or did you catch onto it all without an effort?"

"Without an effort, sir."

"Good! I begin to feel encouraged. All the same, I'm glad there isn't much more.—'The newsmongers don't disgorge here oftener than once a fortnight, so I can't give you much news. Mrs. Hildreth and all the pretty little children came scattering around one day about three months ago. Master Jimmy went over to Holloways', to see what a spring fire of Hollowayian rubbish smelt like, and presently came blubbering back, with the downy hide all singed off his manly face. He looked like a spring chicken that had had all its pinfeathers scorched off with a vengeance. And we got off without hearing much of what "they say." Jimmy is of a most inquisitive turn of mind. Just the other day I happened to be at the depot when the family party were laying in ambush for a mixed. Jimmy was determined to find out whether the rails are fastened together with hair-pins or carpet tacks; so he smuggled himself up the platform to the freight-shed, and then jumped down to the track. Before he was found the mixed came grinding along, and rasped a whole pocketful of ornamental buttons off his richly embroidered little coat. I am sure everybody was anxious to find out what system of punishment the boy's father favors, but he was mean enough not to give it away. The poor child was hustled into the car with reckless haste and quite unnecessary assistance, and that is all I know about it.'

"I don't like the chipper way you talk about little children and big men having their necks all but broken. It makes a writer out a heathen, or exposes him as a greenhorn. Another thing you want to do is to weed out some of your adjectives. I don't suppose you have more than eight hundred in stock, and at this rate your supply would soon be exhausted. Now to conclude:—

"'I can now calmly proceed to fire my empty inkbottles out of the window, and distribute some toil-worn pens among my unobtrusive relations. I might have said *importunate*, but my relations are not importunate.

"'Yours sincerely, HEINRICH.'

"'Hen—Hannibal—Hannah!' What have you signed yourself, young man?"

"Heinrich, sir—German for Henry."

"I dare say it is, my boy. I am glad you are so completely master of the German language; but if your letter should hang fire and not reach its destination, you will some day get it back in an official envelope from the Dead-letter office, addressed to 'Mrs. or Miss Hannah!' Then perhaps you will be sorry that you hadn't signed your full name in English, like a white man."

"Well, may I ask what your verdict is, sir?"

"Can you shoot a gun?"

Visions of a turkey hunt with the astonished and delighted editor flashed through the young man's mind. His genius had been recognized at last! "You are too kind!" he cried, grasping the editor's hand. "I *can* shoot, and should be delighted to go."

"Well, then," calmly continued the editor, "I would advise you to tear off the first part of your draught and take it along for wadding next time you feel impelled to shoot. As for the rest of it, make a nice little sketch of it, and almost any editor will accept it; but he won't pay you for it, because Rhadamanthus isn't built that way.

"But what's the matter with your relations that you should insist on working off your damaged pens on them? Didn't they buy you jack-knives or take you to the circus when you were young—that is, younger than you are now? Or did they vaccinate you too often? You needn't let on but that your ancestors came over with Leif Erikson, and that your nearest relatives to-day are living a luxurious life in the most exclusive penitentiaries in the West."

"Then you really think my prose better than my verse?"

"Decidedly. Writing a letter, with your heart in it, is head-work; writing a pretty little story, loaded up to the muzzle with good precepts and pointing a solemn moral even if looked at upside down, is brain-work; writing a rattling good humorous item is mind-work; but writing clear-cut verse, that the matter-of-fact man and the cultured man alike will read with keen relish, and then file away in a disused cigar-box for future enjoyment—that is soul-work.

"Yes, my boy; you must quit flirting with the Muses, for every one of them, including Thalia, will give you the mitten. Strike up a friendship with the old man, Apollo; then, if you will curry-comb that spavined old nag of yours that we read about yesterday, and expose him where some journalistic cow-boy can stampede him away for good and all, Apollo may some day take you up behind him on Pegasus for a little turn when the atmosphere seems fairly clear. You mustn't expect the careful old fellow to trust you alone with his steed yet awhile. I shouldn't like to see *you* break your neck, you know. Meanwhile, there's lots of hard work before you.

"Now, if any unshaven poet comes around this afternoon, tell him it's a cold day for bards and a good one for barbers, and persuade him to bring his little manuscript around next week."

"And Destiny, sir?"

"Won't bother you, if you stick to prose."

"Heinrich" did not commit suicide in despair; he wrote more picturesque letters to his chums, telling them that he had "captured" the editor.

TO MIGNONNE.

A Boating Song.

On the bosom of the great sea,
Like a wild rose of the ocean,
Rests a lovely, perfumed island,
Coral-bastioned, ruby sky-spanned,
Tranquil 'mid the waves' commotion
As a flower on a lone prairie;
Peaceful as a child when sleeping
With his playthings round him scattered;
Where no harsh gales, ocean-sweeping,
Cast up brave ships, torn and shattered.

Here are men the slaves of science;
Slaves of reason; money-branded;
Slaves of pedants, idlers, dreamers;
Slaves of theorists with streamers;
Slaves of Anarchists red-handed,
Who to all laws breathe defiance.
No man's time is here his birth-right;
False-tongued guests breed life-long rancor;
There the great ships, in their earth-flight,
Distant pass, but ne'er cast anchor.

In that free yet sinless region
Wild, unfettered birds victorious
Pipe their rhapsodies sonorous
In a wayward, untaught chorus,
With exuberance uproarious,
Voicing Nature's pure religion.
More in sadness than in pleasure
Winds and waves chant solemn anthems;
But in soft, harmonious measure,
Soothing as majestic requiems.

Here the winds moan sullen dirges;
The poor captive song-bird, lonely,
Hymns his weary supplications,
Tinged with bitter lamentations;
From the cold, sad sea rise only
Threnodies of boist'rous surges.
Here the native songster's wary,
And his madrigals in full joy
Carols but from strongholds airy,
Where he flies the tricky schoolboy.

On this calm and glorious even,
With the stars our only pilot,
Let us sail away together,
With this fav'ring breeze and weather,
To this lone and lovely islet,
Which shall be our earth and heaven,
In the vast Pacific waters,
Where the warm waves bathe the shingle,
Where the moonlight longest loiters,
And where seasons soft commingle.

HIRAM'S OATH.

CHAPTER I.

THE Wolfe estate was a noble one, stretching along the Shenandoah River, in Virginia, near the old town of Winchester. The family traced their ancestry back to the Plantagenets, and boasted of having been cavaliers under Charles the First, in England, and patriots under Washington, in America.

But a curse rested on the family—the curse of hereditary insanity. Sooner or later almost every male member of the family became hopelessly demented. Those who escaped lived to a patriarchal old age, with intellect unimpaired; but they were exceptional cases. Still the family existed, for most of the young men, on attaining majority, believed they would be exempt from the general curse, and so married. But there had been some who had forsworn marriage rather than rear up children to inherit the fatal malady.

In ante-bellum days Reginald Wolfe was the representative of the family, and his heir and only son was Hiram—one of those noble ones who had vowed to live and die alone. He was a resolute young fellow, with a grim fixedness of purpose, and he seemed capable of keeping his vow, without unhappy repinings on the one hand, or considering himself a martyr worthy of canonization on the other hand. Yet he made the not unnatural mistake of keeping his resolution too prominently before him, so that it influenced him in every act of his life.

"I do not reproach you," he said to his father, "but no son shall ever turn to me and say, 'You have exposed me to the curse.' The race dies with me; but it shall die nobly."

"It is a resolution worthy of you, Hiram," said his father, "but remember that the physicians think your chances of escape are exceptionally good."

"True. But that would not prevent the curse from descending to my posterity. I have made a vow, and I will keep it; and my life shall be a cheerful one, too."

"God help him if he ever falls in love!" Mr. Wolfe said sorrowfully. "God help him, for his resolution will be sorely tried."

But Hiram, while assisting his father in the superintendence of the plantation, devoted all his leisure to books, going into society but little. He went about his daily duties with a brave heart, and never wavered in his resolution.

"I shall never be a madman," he said gaily, "nor shall I ever have cause to repent of my vow."

Mr. and Mrs. Wolfe insisted on the gratification of their son's every wish, but grieved about him almost as much as if he had shown symptoms of insanity. "Poor fellow!" the former often sighed. "His life will be the life of a hermit! But would that others could have done as he will do."

"If five generations could escape the curse, it would become extinct," said Mrs. Wolfe. "Could not this be, Reginald?"

"It has been the dream of our family, but I am afraid it is only a dream. Five generations! More than one hundred and sixty years! In five generations there has always been at least one in the direct line who has succumbed, and the probabilities are that there always will be. Hiram knows he could not live to see the curse removed, and he knows the cruel risk there is that a son or grandson might become insane. So perhaps it is best that Hiram should never marry, since he wills it so. But God help him, poor fellow!"

Hiram lived to see the twenty-fifth anniversary of his birthday without having cause to repent of his oath. On that eventful day he was to take a trip to New-York, on business for his father.

"I think I am invulnerable, mother," he said at the breakfast table, in answer to a solicitous inquiry from his mother. "I am twenty-five to-day, and as happy as any man can hope to be. So keep a good heart, mother, and don't look so sad. I shall come back all right, never fear."

"I think perhaps I had better go, after all, Hiram," Mr. Wolfe said slowly. "It—it—"

"No, father; it will do me good to see New-York; I have not been there since I was a boy. Don't be afraid for me. I am a monomaniac on the subject of our family affliction; but, for that very reason, I shall see the curse removed, because it shall die with me. So I have reason to be happy—and proud, too."

Mrs. Wolfe bade Hiram good-bye with tears in her eyes.

"Have you a presentiment of evil, mother?" he asked.

"Yes, Hiram; I have;" she answered sadly. "Couldn't you give it up, even now, and not go at all?"

Hiram hesitated. He loved his mother devotedly, and would gladly sacrifice his own pleasure to humor her; but this seemed only a whim of the moment, which they would laugh at together when he came back safe and well. Besides, he must occasionally go out into the great world; so why should he hesitate about going now?

"No, mother," he said at length, "I will go. But don't be alarmed about me. Depend upon it, no one shall capture me and spirit me away. I have made a vow; 1 am safe. Good-bye."

He was gone; and Mrs. Wolfe kept repeating to herself, "'I have made a vow; I am safe.'"

Hiram transacted his father's business in the great city, and said to himself as his train drew out of the Jersey City depot: "Just three days since I bade my mother good-bye, and now I am ready to go home and see her again. Poor mother! how fond she is! How we shall laugh at her presentiment! But I am glad that I have got along all right, and that I have made a beginning in seeing the world. The world! What do I care for it and its mockeries?"

The return journey was without incident till shortly after leaving Baltimore a pleasant voice nearly opposite asked, in a subdued undertone, "Who is that grave young gentleman, Herbert? Did you know him at Yale?"

"Don't know; don't want to know. Some lucky dog with lots of funds, from his appearance," said a gruff voice.

Hiram glanced amusedly towards the speakers, and saw a fair young girl, with an exquisite physiognomy, spiritualized by sad yet bewitching eyes. Beside her sat a spare and morose-looking young fellow, with a dare-devil air— evidently the person addressed as Herbert.

Their eyes met. The young lady blushed, for she knew her question had been overheard, and turned her eyes away quickly. Hiram felt a thrill of pain or pleasure, he knew not which, and as quickly turned away.

But that fair face haunted him, and soon he turned to steal another glance at it. Again their eyes met; again both looked away.

"This won't do!" Hiram said to himself. "I must remember my oath, and avoid temptation. A child must not play with fire; and in many things I am but a child."

He took a newspaper out of his pocket and was soon engrossed in reading it. He thought of the young couple opposite, and reflected that they would probably leave him at Harper's Ferry; but he did not again even glance in their direction.

The conductor came hurrying through the car, with a troubled look.

"Sir," piped up a venerable old woman, "is anything wrong? If something is going to happen I want to know it."

"There is danger," acknowledged the conductor, passing on and out of the coach.

Every one heard the dread words, "There is danger." Every face grew pale, and many a stout heart quailed. But what should they do? Was the danger imminent? What was it?

Hiram was not afraid, but he thought of the loved ones at home. "Poor, dear mother! Is this her presentiment?"

Then his thoughts reverted to the fair young girl, and he wondered whether she was still in the car. He stole a glance—yes, there she sat, looking pale, yet resolute.

"She is brave," commented Hiram; "braver than many a man in this carriage."

A loud and long whistle, or rather shriek, from the engine. Then the door opened and the conductor shouted, "Save yourselves! A train is coming! Jump to the right!"

There was a panic. The passengers rose to their feet and strove desperately to reach the door, but becoming pressed together, blocked the passage.

"Which is the right? Which is the right?" gasped terrified men and women helplessly.

Seeing the forward end of the coach free, Hiram forced his way through to it.

"This way," he said to a portly old lady, and she came forward and jumped courageously off the train.

By ones and twos, Hiram assisted nearly twenty persons to jump off—among them, the fair yonng lady. Then the rest, having more room to move about, scrambled out of the coach and reached the ground.

The train was now at a standstill, and there were but a few in this or any car, when there came a terrible shock, and Hiram and the other unfortunates with him were buried in the ruins of a wrecked railway train.

Those who had escaped did everything in their power to save the victims buried under the broken carriages. But they could not effect much till a wrecking party came to the relief, when, after a few hours' imprisonment, the poor sufferers were liberated and taken to Baltimore or elsewhere for treatment, some of them succumbing to their injuries.

CHAPTER II.

WHEN Hiram Wolfe recovered consciousness he found himself lying on a sofa in a darkened room. He wondered what it all meant, when a shooting pain in his knee brought back to his memory that awful scene on the train. He groaned, and moved restlessly.

A figure in white softly drew near him; a sweet young face bent pityingly but gladly over him. It was a face that he knew—the face of her whom he had seen and saved on the train.

"Are you feeling better?" she asked, in so musical a voice that Hiram started, and looked long and intently into her eyes.

"You are right, Alice," said a gruff voice; and the young man who answered to the name of Herbert strode into the room. "He is the same fellow, and his name is Wolfe, poor devil."

"Oh, hush, Herbert!" said the young lady reproachfully. Then she whispered, "He is conscious now."

"Is he?" and Herbert walked softly to the sofa, and looked compassionately at the poor sufferer. "Poor fellow!" he murmured. "He is indeed a hero, and," under his breath and glancing towards Alice, "he has met a hero's fate!"

But Herbert had a warm heart, and he said warmly, "Mr. Wolfe, we owe you a debt of gratitude that can never be cancelled. You nobly saved my sister's life, and the life of many on our car. You must be our guest till you are entirely restored to health; and everything that medical skill and good nursing can do, shall be done. I myself will be your nurse, and I will administer your medicines and see that you obey orders."

"Thank you," Hiram said faintly. "But am I so badly hurt that I cannot be taken home?"

"Doctors' orders are positive that you must not be moved; so make the best of it, my dear fellow, and be contented. You shall be well taken care of; and I will telegraph for any of your people that you wish to have come."

"My father would have detained you here, Mr. Wolfe, even though you had escaped unhurt, to express his gratitude to you," said Alice.

"Yes," said her brother ruefully, "you robbed me of the honor of saving my sister's life."

Not another word of explanation from the young man, but, as Alice afterwards explained, he had thought her safe and had gone into the next car, where they had noticed a helpless blind man, whom he found and assisted off the train.

"All this excitement and trouble has caused us to take an extraordinary interest in you, Mr. Wolfe," continued Herbert, with an arch look at his sister. "If you hesitate to remain as our guest, you must remember you are our prisoner. So say the physicians, my respected parents, and every one concerned."

"You are bent on acting the good Samaritan, in spite of me," Hiram said laughingly, "and I can only assure you of my deep obligation to you all. What is the name of my kind benefactors, and where am I?"

"Sinclair is our patronymic; and I am Herbert J. Sinclair, the most graceless good-for-naught of my day and generation. But this," with an involuntary softening of his voice, "is Miss Alice, my sister, who atones for all my short-comings. As for the scene of this interview, it is the home of our ancestors,—that is, of my deceased great-grandparents, who were emigrant vagabonds,—in Frederick, State of Maryland. Excuse me, Mr. Wolfe, while I call my mother in."

"Don't think my brother has lost his wits," smiled Alice. "He talks in that absurd way for his own amusement."

"Come, Alice; don't talk about my own 'amusement,'" said Herbert, in a hard and bitter tone, as he left the room. In a moment he returned with Mrs. Sinclair, whom he formally introduced to the sufferer.

Mrs. Sinclair was a refined, elderly lady, of a deeply sympathetic nature; and as the mother of this singular brother and sister, Hiram became interested in her at once.

"What is the extent of my injuries?" Hiram asked, after Mrs. Sinclair's kindly inquiries were satisfied.

"Broken bones; contusions; a shock to the nervous system; cerebral disturbance; divers wounds that will leave scars as mementoes of this event," Herbert made answer.

"No, Herbert; it's not so bad as that!" Alice said quickly.

"A business-like inventory of my hurts," laughed Hiram. "And now, how long before I shall be convalescent?"

"Depends on the doctors," Herbert said grimly. Then carelessly, "Oh, two months, or thereabouts, and you will have so completely recovered that you will be ready to pack up, and off, and forget us. Meanwhile, you will not suffer much pain, Mr. Wolfe, and I will give you a recipe for dulling pain—that is, mental pain."

Herbert Sinclair left the patient's couch and strode towards an outer door, softly whistling "*Die Wacht am Rhein.*"

But he had whistled only a few bars when he checked himself abruptly, flung open the door, and clapped it to behind him with a bang. In a moment he opened the door softly, thrust his head in at the opening, and said shortly, "Excuse me." Then the door closed softly, and they heard him craunching rapidly away in the graveled walk.

Hiram said nothing, but he noticed that tears stood in Alice's eyes and that Mrs. Sinclair looked sorely troubled. "A clear case of an undutiful son and brother," he reflected, in his naive inexperience.

Mrs. Wolfe came immediately on receipt of a telegram, and saw at once that it was out of the question for Hiram to be taken home till he should be convalescent. A warm friendship sprang up between her and Alice; and Hiram, cared for by these two and by Herbert, soon began to mend.

Hiram was thrown much upon Miss Sinclair's society. When he was able she read to him and sang for him, and seemed to take the greatest pleasure in ministering to his comfort. One day she revealed the story of her brother's unhappiness, which was becoming a sad puzzle to Hiram.

"Mr. Wolfe, to remove any harsh opinion you may have formed of my poor brother, I will explain to you the cause of his erratic conduct," she began. "It is not mere eccentricity, as he would have you think, but a settled grief, that I am afraid will be life-long. Four years ago, my brother was to be married to a beautiful young lady, an actress. No one can know how he loved her, and she seemed to love him. The day of their marriage was set, and everything seemed to be going on smoothly. My brother's happiness was so great that he was almost beside himself. On the day before the wedding he went to Washington, where they were to be married. He reached Washington late in the evening, but late as it was, he wrote us a long letter. Poor Herbert! We have that letter yet, and it almost makes me cry to think of it. He said he did not know what good he had ever done (and he was always doing good, in a quiet way, Mr. Wolfe) that God should permit him to enjoy such happiness, and he hoped he should prove worthy of his treasure. The next morning Herbert went to the church where they were to have been married; but oh, Mr. Wolfe! she had deserted him!"

"Deserted him?" queried Hiram, aghast. "How?"

"Yes! The evening before, she married an old Jew, a millionaire, and stole away, leaving only a cruel note for Herbert."

"Poor fellow!" sighed Hiram. "I had misjudged him."

"Herbert as a boy used to delight in the air you heard him start to whistle the other day,—'*Die Wacht am Rhein*,'—and the woman he loved used to play it for him. He forgets himself sometimes, poor fellow!"

"This is a sad story, Miss Sinclair, and I feel for your brother as if he were my own. He would have been a noble man; but now his life is blasted."

"Yes, his experience has been bitter enough. But pray don't let him suspect that you know this. I have told you it in confidence, so that you should not judge him hardly."

It was fated that these two should love each other, and under all the circumstances it was inevitable. Hiram struggled against it resolutely, knowing that it must end in a bitter parting. But his love grew stronger every day, and his resolution weaker. His health ceased to mend, and there was danger of a serious relapse. Still he fought against the inevitable, though his struggles became feebler from day to day.

"If I could only get away!" he murmured. "How can I help loving her, when I see her every day? And then she is so good to me. A man may think himself in love with a woman, not knowing her inner life, because he cannot see it. But here am I in Alice's house, with every opportunity to know every phase of her character. And what is she? All that is unselfish, and artless, and pure, and noble. God help me! it is hard! What makes it harder still, I feel that Alice loves me!"

In this way Hiram battled with his love. He wanted to subdue this passion; to prove himself a hero. But what should he gain by it, after all? he asked himself. Was it the part of a hero to conquer his love for so noble a woman, because of his oath? Why should two hearts be rent?—But then the curse!

"Is that my fault? Did I bring the curse upon myself? Why should I not do as my fathers did before me? Why did I bind myself by such an oath? But no; I was right. I have not broken my oath yet, and God helping me, I will keep it, and so do right."

Hiram was right; Alice loved him.

Mrs. Wolfe and Herbert Sinclair discovered that these two souls loved each other, and that one, Hiram, was fighting against it.

One day Herbert seated himself beside the sufferer, and said bluntly, "Mr Wolfe, did it ever occur to you that you have won my sister's love?"

Hiram quivered from head to foot, and said faintly, "Have I, Mr. Sinclair, I—I—can only say that it is a most unfortunate mistake. I—"

"'Mistake'? What sort of mistake do you call it, pray? I don't understand you at all. I am blunt myself; and I want you to be blunt—or, at least, frank."

"I can never marry," Hiram said sadly.

"Never marry, eh? Come, now; whose husband are you, or have you been?"

"There is a curse in our family—the curse of insanity. I have sworn never to transmit that curse; I never will."

"So, is that your reason? What sort of insanity? suicidal mania? hydrophobia? delirium tremens? consumption? fanaticism? or," scowling at Hiram, "family pride?"

Then followed a long talk, which resulted in a good understanding between the two young men.

"And you do love my sister?" Herbert queried.

"Love her? Oh, Herbert! if you could know what I have suffered!"

"'Suffered'? That is good! You have suffered!" with a hard smile. "Well, a lesson in suffering will do you good. But as for what suffering is—Pshaw! what cause have you to suffer? Hiram, do you remember Alice's question on the train?"

"Whether you had known me at Yale? I am not a Yale man, but I attended our own University of Virgina."

"Don't!" cried Herbert, with an impatient gesture. "You demonstrated the fact that you could read when you took up your newspaper. Hiram, it was a case of love at sight with my sister."

"How do you know this?" Hiram asked eagerly.

"Because my sister is so artless that I read her every thought."

Hiram groaned, and said desperately, "Don't you think I am strong enough to go home, Herbert?"

"Are you engaged to my sister yet?" was the surprising question.

"Engaged? Herbert! How can you ask that, after what I have told you?"

"Because after your engagement to my sister you will rally so fast that you will astonish yourself."

"But the family curse?"

"What do you know about the 'family curse?' It is all moonshine—in your case."

"What do you mean by that?" Hiram demanded peevishly.

"This: whatever fools or lunatics your ancestors may have been, your mind is sound. You will never be insane —unless you are now!" grimly.

"What does all this mean?"

"I once made demonology the study of my life."

"What?" asked Hiram, in sad perplexity.

"Dementia—psychology—anthropology—phrenitis—to use a generic and explicit term, insanity. You see, I once contemplated lunacy myself."

"You are an unconscionable joker," laughed Hiram.

"No; I am a pathologist. I have arrived at my own conclusions about your case, Hiram, and you will be exempt from the curse. Twenty years from to-day, unless you experience some maddening grief, or reverse, you will be safe, and the curse will be extinct; for, I venture to predict, the last of your race to suffer from it is in his grave."

"Are you sure of this?" Hiram asked doubtfully.

"I pledge you my word of honor for it," Herbert said solemnly. "Hiram, I had heard of the Wolfes of Virginia, and I made your case a study the moment you came to us."

Hiram looked up surprised. "I—I can hardly believe

that the curse is removed," he said, with tears glistening in his eyes. "But I did not know that you are a physician. Have you been treating me? or is your practice so exten—"

"Practice?" broke in Herbert, with a bitter laugh. "Oh, I don't 'practise' anything."

After a pause Hiram said hesitatingly: "This is so sudden, so unexpected, so incredible, that it seems altogether visionary. I—I must have time to consider this; I—"

"I expected you to doubt me," Herbert said dryly. "But do you really think I could trifle with you? Do you suppose I would see my sister married to a madman?"

"You honestly think, then, that I can shake off the curse?"

"'The curse!' Hiram, I have heard enough of this; it indeed a curse to you. Come, now; what about this horrible resolution, or oath, of yours? Have you it in writing?"

"I—I—. When I first formed the resolve, Herbert, I did not know what it is to love; so I relied on my own strength of will, and simply bound myself by swearing an oath."

"But since you came here?" Herbert questioned.

Hiram started, and moved uneasily on his couch.

"I see," Herbert pursued. "Since you came here you have drawn up a fresh resolution, and signed it with your blood, perhaps. Let me take a look at it, Hiram."

"Promise me not to destroy it, Herbert!" pleadingly.

"I promise nothing. Let me see it. Oh, Hiram! have you so little faith!"

Reluctantly Hiram drew a paper from his bosom and silently handed it to Herbert. The writing on it was almost illegible, as Hiram, to strengthen his resolution, had written it while suffering mental and physical pain. It was of the nature of an oath, calling down an imprecation upon himself if he ever deviated in the slightest degree from his vow.

As Herbert ran over this paper a suspicious moisture dimmed his eyes. He grasped the sick man's hand, and said brokenly: "Forgive me, Hiram; I have treated you inhumanly, when you were most in need of gentleness and sympathy. You mean well, Hiram, and you are fighting your battle stubbornly, but against dreadful and hopeless odds. I see that you have suffered,—are suffering,—and I ask your pardon. But will you let me keep this for you for just one week? You can trust me with it?"

"Yes."

"Hiram, did you ever hear of Dr.———, the great specialist?"

"Yes, I have," said Hiram eagerly.

"Well, I have sent for him to come down to Frederick to-morrow to see you. Can you rely on *his* opinion?" reproachfully.

"Oh, Herbert! what a strange man you are!"

"But if he confirms what I insist upon?"

"If he confirms it, I accept my freedom, thank God!"

"Hiram," gaily, "you look better already! You will be down street, buying your own cigars, in ten days." Then in his old, cynical way: "Don't take it too much to heart; but doesn't it seem to you that, sickly novels aside, a man is a downright noodle to try to play the hero in love-affairs? Why should a sensible man affect to be a great moral hero, when he might far better be the husband of the woman he loves? It's all bosh; the modern high-flown novel is stultifying us all; and I say we ought to legislate against them and against the sighing 'noble men' outside of them. Some men are born to suffer for a life-time, eh? Poor devils! let them suffer, then! That does not concern *you*—Pshaw! Hiram, I am worse than Job's comforters, eh? Or does the word 'noodle' grate painfully on your ear?"

With a hard smile on his lips Herbert tore out of the room. Hiram had come to know what that hard smile and rough language meant,—that Herbert's old wound was bleeding again,—and he was not angry with the restless, unhappy mortal, who could not apply his philosophy to his own case.

"In any other than he, I should suspect lunacy," Hiram mused.

CHAPTER III.

THE next day the venerable old doctor arrived from New-York, and carefully examined into Hiram's case. After hearing the family history from Hiram and Mrs. Wolfe he reported most favorably, advancing the same hope that Herbert had done, that the curse would be removed.

"By taking the greatest care of yourself, by having no anxiety to prey on your mind, and no business or family cares, in twenty years or so all traces of insanity will have disappeared," said the great doctor.

Herbert looked triumphant—pleased, no doubt, that the learned mind-doctor was merely echoing his own words. Mrs. Wolfe stood by with tears in her eyes. No others were present at the interview, or guessed its purport.

"What do you advise me to do meanwhile?" Hiram asked.

"During these twenty years? As your mind must be free from care, I should advise that you go and establish a home for yourself on the plains—a ranch in Texas, say. Avoid undue excitement, but keep yourself employed all the time, even though you have to do all the work yourself. Keep a spirited horse always in your stables, and whenever you feel low-spirited, mount it on the instant, and gallop away as if you were pursued by Comanches or hobomokkos. What you want is, to keep your spirits up,—not too high, not to excitement,—and always to be cheerful. Whenever you begin to feel depressed in spirits, have something to do that will engross your attention wholly. Secure Dickens' novels, Shakespeare's and Molière's comedies, anything diverting; and, above all, don't forget that wild horse. A horseback journey through the new State of Texas, or even through the Union, would be a good idea, if you didn't attempt it all at once. Don't permit any cares, great or small, to prey on your mind, and—that is all."

"And so in twenty years the curse is extinct! A long time!"

"Now, don't chafe about that, Mr. Wolfe. In twenty years you will have removed the ban of the house of Wolfe. Let that—"

"The wolf's-bane, so to speak!" Herbert broke in.

"Let that," continued the doctor, "be your watchword. It is a long time, it is true; I shall not live to see it; but twenty years hence you will look back upon to-day as not so *very* long ago."

"And if I pass through this period I am safe, unless—"

"Unless some great trouble should come upon you. But hope for the best, and trust in Heaven."

"One word more, doctor: Could you have removed the curse from our family earlier, by the same method of treatment?"

"That is a question that I cannot answer, Mr. Wolfe, without data respecting the temperament of the victims."

"Is he not a fine subject for the experiment?" Herbert inquired, with an admiring glance at Hiram.

"Yes, indeed; this is the hour and the man," laughed the doctor.

Mrs. Wolfe had a long talk that evening with Hiram. She earnestly advised him to tell Alice everything, and give no further thought to the family affliction. "Your oath is not binding now, Hiram," she said; "your vow is the same as accomplished."

"No, mother; not for twenty years;" Hiram said sadly.

"But you will speak with Alice?"

"Yes, mother; in the morning."

Then Mrs. Wolfe left him, and soon afterward Herbert strode into the room.

"Well, Hiram?" was his greeting.

"Well, Herbert," returned Hiram; "you may give me back the paper you are keeping for me, if you please."

"To be sacrificed?"

"Yes."

"That is good;" said Herbert, surrendering the paper. "You don't know why I wanted it, so I will tell you: A scrap of paper, anything in the shape of a document, will fortify a man's courage, either for good or for evil. Yours is a sort of mental thumb-screw, and I wished to deprive you of its moral support. See how cruel and crafty I am! But isn't it so? I don't know how it would apply to womankind," petulantly; "I don't know anything about them, nor do I wish to know."

"But your sister?" prompted Hiram reproachfully.

"My sister is any exception; she is an angel."

Hiram asked for a taper, and was about to destroy the paper when he checked himself, and said abruptly, "I can't do it, Herbert; keep it for me; keep it for my sake when I am gone."

"I will do so, my dear friend, for its work is done. So you are tired of playing the hero, eh? You will make a clean breast of it to my sister?"

"Yes; and here and now I ask you to our wedding, twenty years hence."

"That is right; I will come. Hum, yes; a wedding! And so, in twenty years, the days of your heroship will be fulfilled."

"Don't add to my burden, Herbert!"

"Forgive me, Hiram; I am wrong. Now for my idea. Will you tolerate my company on your ranch, for twenty years?"

"Herbert! Will you come with me?" cried Hiram, with feverish delight. "Do you mean it?"

"Unless you expressly forbid it, I am determined to share your adventures, your privations, your solitude, and—your warhorse!"

"Oh, Herbert! How good you are!"

"Fiddle! I'm a wretch! a stoney-hearted wretch!

Hiram, do you know, sometimes I envy the world its happiness; sometimes when I see misery I rejoice in it. I—I wish Uncle Sam would go to war; I should revel in the carnage and havoc. Pshaw! I'll take it out in spilling the life-blood of the buffalo.—And so your love-affair will turn out happily, after all; and you will marry the woman of your heart; and you and she will grow old, and bald, and wrinkled, and childish, together. Hiram, sometimes I like to see things go to pieces; I wish somebody would write a novel and murder every soul in it! Come, when you and I live together on the ranch, I'll write one myself! I swear I will; and I'll be my own hero-in-chief!"

"Don't talk that way, Herbert; it isn't Christian-like."

"God help me; I know it isn't," Herbert replied sadly.

"Herbert, can nothing console you? Wouldn't it do you good to follow the prescription the doctor made out for me for low spirits? We will, on the ran—"

"'Console?'" broke in Herbert, in the old, bitter tone. "Why do you say that to me? Has any one been babbling my affairs? 'Console!' If you should see a man being tortured to death by Indian braves, would you step up to him and say, 'Can nothing console you, sir? Wouldn't a prescription from Dr.——be a good thing for your low spirits?'"

Whistling a lively Negro melody, as if he were as light of heart as a schoolboy, Herbert sauntered out of the room.

The next morning Hiram gave Alice the history of the family curse, and then told her what the great physician had said.

"Alice," he said, "would it be asking too much if I
8

should ask you to wait for me? Could you wait twenty years? But do you love me, Alice? Will you be my wife?"

"Yes, Hiram; I love you;" Alice said falteringly, her face hidden.

"And will you be my wife? Will you wait for me twenty years?"

"Yes," faintly, but firmly.

"Oh, Alice! Alice! You will indeed be my guardian angel!"

"It is a long time, Hiram; but I would wait twice as long."

"Oh, Alice! my darling! Come to me, that I may give you a kiss—just one!" Then passionately: "Alice! would you marry me as soon as I get well? to-day? now?"

"Yes, Hiram," said Alice slowly.

"Heaven forgive me, Alice. If you can wait, I can. You will be here all alone; while I shall be hard at work, or scouring the plains on my charger. It will be harder, much harder, and longer, for you than for me."

"But you will be lonely, too, Hiram."

"No, Alice; Herbert is going with me. Isn't that good!"

"Oh, I'm so glad—for your sake and for his, too. But," sadly, "I shall miss him so much."

"I did not think of that, Alice; I will persuade him not to go."

"No, no! I did not mean that! Besides, we shall see one another occasionally; the doctor did not forbid that—did he, Hiram?"

"No, Alice; that pleasure is not denied us."

"Herbert will be good company, Hiram, when you get accustomed to his ways. You won't fret about me, Hiram; I shall be all right. And don't think the time long, either. We shall each of us have employment for our minds and hands, and we will correspond regularly. You will try to wait patiently, won't you, Hiram?"

"Yes, dear Alice; and to prove worthier of your love."

"A life on the plains may do you both a great deal of good. I will try not to be uneasy about you, but you must promise me not to run into danger, of any kind. Herbert is so adventurous that he would storm an Indian camp, alone."

"I promise you, Alice. Do you think Herbert will ever get over his disappointment?—his grief?"

"I am afraid not. But he is not so bitter as he was three years ago."

"How was he the first year?"

"We did not see him for a full year after that fatal day. Some of his friends persuaded him to go off to Russia with them, and from that country he roamed over half Europe. When he came back, Hiram, we did not know him."

"He was so altered?"

"Yes. 'Am I so woebegone a ghost,' he said, 'that no one knows me?'"

"But sometimes he seems quite cheerful. I heard him whistling a lively air yesterday, as jantily as a young sailor."

"Yes, Hiram; but I often think he does that to keep from breaking down entirely."

"He must have been a noble fellow once."

"He was, Hiram; he was the best of brothers; so clever, good-humored, witty, and good. Now he is cynical, and—and at times a little inclined to be ill-natured, I am afraid you must think."

"No, Alice; he is the only man I could ever think of as a brother. In truth, he seems as near to me as if he were already my brother."

Hiram improved rapidly from that day. He schooled himself to wait patiently—even to look forward composedly till the years of his probation should be fulfilled.

One day Herbert came to him, and said: "Old fellow, did it never occur to you that Alice ought to have an engagement ring? You used to bind yourself with grim resolutions, and oaths, and such things, and yet you expect Alice to keep on being engaged to you for twenty years or so, without even a betrothal ring! You don't know much about womankind, Hiram."

"You are right, Herbert; I'll try and get out to get one to-day."

"No, you won't! Do you see this?" displaying a ring-box. "Or are you so unsophisticated that you take it for a Roman relic?"

"Herbert! How good you are!" was all Hiram could say.

"Enough of that; it is growing monotonous. I tell you, I am a heathen!"

Hiram opened the box and found a beautiful ring, set with two brilliants that dazzled his eyes.

The time came when Hiram and Alice should part. It was a sad moment, but each looked forward hopefully to the day when they should meet to part no more till Death should part them for a season in old age.

"I shall be an old woman to be a bride, Hiram," said Alice, smiling through her tears. "An old woman—forty years old! Think of that! Wrinkled, perhaps, and gray!"

"But the noblest of all noble women, Alice, and the best."

"Good-bye, Alice," said Herbert. "Keep a brave heart, my sister, and we shall weather the storms of twenty years. I am interested in his case; he is a noble fellow; I—love him—as it were." (Herbert could not bear to be caught uttering pathos,—bosh, he called it,—and always contrived to give it a ridiculous turn.) "Now, I am going to oversee everything, and shall negotiate for all our supplies, and manage affairs generally, so that he shall have nothing to worry him. I mean to secure a medicine chest, and be medicine-man to the camp. So, don't borrow trouble, Alice, for I shall care for him as I would for a baby—I mean, for a puppy."

"Dear Herbert," said Alice, "it is so good of you! You are going on purpose to take care of him."

"I'm going for my health," said Herbert shortly.

"He is so good a man—"

"He is worthy of you, Alice; that is all. Yes, he is a noble fellow. Good-bye, dear sister; I will be my brother's keeper. Yes, poor soul, he needs some one to look after him, or he would be binding himself by some of his horrible 'resolutions' not to neglect his work, or not to read any books, or not to write—hum! Good-bye, for a time."

CHAPTER IV.

It was in ante-Pacific railway days, and the journey to far-off Texas was a great undertaking. Hiram suggested that they should travel the entire distance on horseback, but Herbert promptly vetoed that as too fatiguing. The better way would have been to take ship from Baltimore to New Orleans or Galveston; but finally it was decided to go by rail to the Ohio, thence down that river and the Mississippi to Memphis, and thence across the plains by caravan train, or on horseback by easy stages, to Austin. All necessary supplies, of course, would be procured at Memphis.

At that period the old B. and O. was completed beyond Cumberland almost to Wheeling. This route they took, staging it over the "gap" to the Ohio. Their journey was delightful, but uneventful, till Memphis was reached, whence, after a week's halt, they leisurely continued on their way on horseback, with a retinue of pack-horses and slaves—or rather, as Hiram afterwards discovered, manumitted blacks, liberally paid by Herbert. The long ride across the plains, though wearisome, was bracing and exciting, and they enjoyed it so much that Hiram began to feel very hopeful.

"The years will glide away peacefully and happily for us," he said; "but poor Alice!"

"He mustn't fret, poor fellow, even about Alice," thought Herbert. "Hiram," he said, "what do you suppose is in those packs in front of me?"

"Powder?"

"You guess as wildly as a parrot, Hiram, and that is the worst guesser I ever saw. The right one is full of comedies, for you; and the other is full of tragedies, for me."

"There you are again, Herbert!"

"Well, I am going to reform; I am going to take your medicine with you. When we feel low-spirited we'll both go coursing over the country full chase, eh, Hiram? Marry! as Shakespeare sometimes says, marry! we'll dose ourselves to death. Our mounts now are only gauls, as the Germans put it."

"Herbert, why should you not confide in me? You are helping me to bear my burdens; why should I not help you? Some cruel grief is preying on your mind, Herbert; why should we not sympathize together?"

"Enough of that!" said Herbert severely. "I always suspected somebody had meddled with my affairs. Say, Hiram, did you ever see me in a rage?"

"No, Herbert; you have too much self-command."

After a long interval Herbert said slowly: "Hiram, I will unbosom myself to you; I will unfold the story of my woes; I will lay bare the tragedy of my life."

Hiram listened intently while Herbert told the story of his love. He did not spare himself in the rehearsal, but seemed rather to take a savage delight in giving every torturing detail of the tragedy, as he aptly called it.

"Now," he said when he had finished, "now, do you wonder that I am a wreck? Do you wonder that I hate myself and everybody else? Do you wonder that I am an outcast, a Pariah, hating the very word 'happiness,' which to me is so bitter a mockery?"

"You have suffered, Herbert, as few men have suffered. I do not wonder that you laughed at my suffering, as after twenty years it would be over, while yours would never be over."

"Just so; you have something to live for, to look forward to; I haven't."

"But has nothing blunted the edge of your grief?"

"Don't be so metaphorical. No, nothing; the edge of my grief is still so keen that it cuts to my heart's core, as it did at first. Constancy, Hiram, is in our family. My parents were engaged for ten years before their marriage, and Alice's loyalty to you will never waver. Can you guarantee yourself to be as constant?"

"Herbert! How can you question it?" asked Hiram angrily.

"I don't. I have seen greater constancy in mankind than in womankind, and I know your heart, Hiram. But unfaithfulness on your part would kill my sister, and if I thought you capable of it I would shoot you as mercilessly as I would any other traitor. Aren't you afraid?" laughingly.

"You are a modern Horatius. No, I am not afraid that you will ever shoot me, Herbert. If it came to *that*, I would shoot myself. But wasn't your grief harder to bear at first?"

"I don't know; I was away, in Europe, somewhere, or everywhere, ranging about like a madman. I suffered least then, Hiram, for I was not conscious of my sufferings. Would you believe it? I know scarcely anything of what I did. But I was awakened one day in Paris. It was a rude awakening: I saw *her* and the Jew, looking as happy and innocent as twin statues of Charity."

"That must have been hard."

"Yes, rather; it made me what I am."

"Was she so beautiful?"

"Don't think me a fool, Hiram—at least, if you think so, don't say it. I trust to your honor. Here, see for yourself," handing Hiram a worn picture-case. "But, yes; I *am* a fool; an ass; a noodle."

Hiram opened the picture-case. "And this was the woman you loved?"

"Put your sentence into the present tense throughout," bitterly. "Well," roughly, taking the picture, "what do you think?"

"She is a master-piece of nature, Herbert."

"Her treachery so unmanned me that I have never been fit for anything since, and never expect to be. Now, according to romance, she and the Jew should have come to beggary in six months. Then she should have written an appeal to me, and I should have—hum! Marry, I abominate romance! Then there is another way for the romancers to figure it out, and happify me, in spite of myself. They should have a daughter, the image of her mother, and I should marry her, fortune and all! I'll organize a crusade against romancers, I swear I will, and poison them off with their own absurd theories."

"Have you ever heard from them? Have they a daughter?"

"Don't, Hiram! Don't! I've said too much; I must cool down, or I shall be beside myself." Then calmly, "What did you ask? No, I've never heard anything about them. But they are all right, never fear! Pshaw! Perhaps I wouldn't marry her, were she a widow and had I the chance!"

"Herbert, it is strange that it did not embitter you against all lovers. Yet you have worked hard for your sister and me, and you have removed the shadow of the curse."

"Those are the most sensible remarks you have made, Hiram. And you are right; it did embitter me; it incensed me almost beyond endurance to hear anything about love or lovers. But in my sister's case it was different. When I returned from Europe, the most wretched mortal on earth, my sister was everything to me. She was so kind, so compassionate, so unobtrusive. She put up with all my vagaries and perversities, and never vexed me. In short, if it had not been for my sister, I should now be a grinning lunatic in some private asylum. I did not notice for some time how good she was to me; but when I did notice it I swore that I would work for her happiness, if the occasion should ever come. I saw that a love-affair with her must be a life-affair, as with me. The occasion *did* come, Hiram, and you know the rest. I did my duty, and—I feel better for it."

"You have done enough to secure your happiness hereafter, my more than brother."

"And yet I am unkind to her, my sister."

"In what way?"

"I am so rough. God knows I regret my harshness towards her. My mother and sister find traces of my tears, poor souls, and they think I cry myself to sleep for the woman I love, when it is often because of my brutality at home. Never mind; now that I am away from home shall rival you in writing kind and encouraging letters to Alice. I *can* write a kind letter, Hiram, though perhaps you cannot believe it."

"I can believe you might be the kindest of men."

"Pshaw! I am used to my misery now. In fact, in a mild way, I enjoy my misery and my chronic peevishness."

Hiram and Herbert established themselves on a fine ranch on the Colorado River in Texas, north of the State Capital, at that time a town of less than 4,000 inhabitants.

Deer, buffaloes, and wild horses were all about them, and Indians were near enough to lend a spice of danger to their surroundings. They expected to occupy their new quarters for nearly the entire period of twenty years, and they made themselves as comfortable and their home as pleasant as if they would spend a life-time there. Austin was their post-office and base, and Herbert undertook the management of everything, so that Hiram had absolutely no cares whatever.

Each one procured a spirited horse, to which Herbert gave fantastic and sonorous names, and whenever Hiram seemed at all depressed the horses were promptly called up and saddled. Then together they galloped over the country, sometimes taking a run of fifty miles. The old doctor was right: a wild gallop on his mettlesome steed never failed to exhilarate Hiram's spirits.

They prospered as ranchers, but did not devote all their energies to money-making. They had come for no such purpose, and were not disposed to neglect health, exercise, or recreation for it. Herbert read his tragedies, and wrote long letters to Alice; Hiram read comedies, tragedies, magazines, anything readable, and also wrote long letters to Alice. Herbert was right; they vied with each other in writing loving and cheering letters. Besides this, Herbert frequently wrote to the old doctor and to Mrs. Wolfe about the "patient," as he styled Hiram. But they were almost 1,800 miles from home, and it took time for letters to reach their destination.

So they lived, a sort of Robinson Crusoe life, which was good for both. Each one enjoyed himself, and took kindly to his pursuits. Hiram did not complain, or get low-spirited; and even Herbert seemed to grow rational.

This life had continued about a year when one day Herbert said resolutely: "Hiram, the books I read when I was a boy harped incessantly about a man's having a purpose in life. That was good, though it never did *me* any good. But now I am going to have one; I am going to coin money; I am going to be a miser."

"What for?"

"Oh, you'll see. Perhaps I am going to pension the man who will be blood-thirsty enough to write a novel to my taste"

"But how are you going to make the money?"

"On this ranch. I am going to work in earnest, and not watch the overseer smoke, and look on, and talk in his ingenuous way, any longer. Or I can speculate in real estate in Austin; or dabble in medicine,—patent medicine, for instance,—or write poetry that would brand me as a madman. To-morrow I shall buy a slate and a slate pencil and figure out how long it will take to equip a new navy for our marines."

"Is *that* your game?"

"No; it isn't. Hiram, you have something to live for and work for, and I mean to have, too."

Long afterwards, when Hiram found that Alice, with a party of friends, was traveling in Europe, he learnt that Herbert had supplied her with the means to do so. "She needs change and amusement as much as we do, Hiram," he said deprecatingly. "You must hoard for an heir; I mustn't."

"Herbert, you are a noble fellow."

"Fiddle! I wanted to learn practical farming, and I was too lazy to learn it without an incentive to work Poor Alice! She would never have thought of going off to see the sights of Europe if some one hadn't proposed the idea to her."

Years rolled away, and still Hiram and Herbert lived their lonely life on the ranch, took their long rides, and wrote loving letters to Alice. Every Christmas they spent in Maryland, and twice Alice came to spend a few days with them on their plantation.

The air was filled with rumors of war; the nation was trembling on the verge of a rebellion.

"Hiram, I was born to be a soldier, even though I fall in the first battle. The spirit of fighting was strong in me when I was only a hobbledehoy. We will not part, Hiram, (and you shall not go to war, do you hear?) but I can aid the cause of right out of my private means, and now and then see and smell the smoke of War."

"As a Southerner—" began Hiram.

"As a Southerner, I have no sympathy with the North; but," resolutely, "as a man, *I will stand by the blacks through thick and thin!*"

"And yet your father is a slave-holder, and we have blacks on our estate!"

"You know my contempt for quack politics; you know my hatred of slavery; you know my dogged resolution when I set about doing a thing. We have blacks on our ranch, it is true; but they are not slaves, if laborers' wages make free men. Hiram, I have long groped as a blind man for a purpose in life, and I have found it now, thank God! Come, let us write to Alice about it."

"Yes, Herbert; for I am with you heart and soul. I have suspected this about our blacks; but," laughingly, "I don't know what other secrets you are keeping from me."

The years rolled on; the war was past. Hiram and Herbert were forced to give up their property in Texas, and even to flee for life—when their horsemanship stood them in good stead. But they were still alive and well, and Herbert took their misfortunes easily, though for a time he feared that if anything might unsettle Hiram's mind their reverses and troubles would. Groundless fear. So long as Hiram had Alice's love, he could smile at fickle fortune equally with Herbert.

The war effected a great change for the better in Herbert. Though still outwardly the same restless, cynical being, he had lost much of his heartache in the smoke of war. He had fought in many battles, with the indomitable courage of a hero. He had risen, too, to the rank of major—a distinction which he ignored.

"I advanced the cause; that is enough;" he said. "We have nothing more to fight about, and I never want to see the country plunged in another war."

The twenty years were all told but one. Hiram's eagerness to return to Maryland and claim his bride was intense; but in nineteen years he had schooled himself to wait.

One day Herbert said to him: "Hiram, old fellow, you have been everything to me; you and Alice; wife, children, everything. I can never leave you, for it would be like taking my life-blood. You will reserve a nook under your roof-tree for me—won't you, Hiram?" pleadingly.

"Herbert! you shall never leave us!"

It was the month of December, and the two men, no longer young, but middle-aged, were lounging about the streets of San Francisco. In just six months' time the engagement made nearly twenty years before was to be consummated by a marriage.

Herbert and Hiram were in good spirits, for everything was well with them. They were talking, as they had been talking for the last twenty years, about the reunion that was to take place in the June of 1872.

"Time goes fast, after all, Hiram; six months will whiz past before we know it. It has been about the best love-test I ever heard of. I have had no occasion to shoot you, eh? You and Alice can stand fire after this; there will be no danger that I shall ever pick up a paper and find your names figuring in a list of divorce cases."

As Herbert spoke he lazily turned into a newstand, and bought a newspaper for the day. His eyes caught a heading that almost paralyzed him.

"Awful loss of life at sea! Wreck of the steamer *Phœbus* and loss of half her passengers. Details of the catastrophe. Etc., etc."

Alice was again in Europe, and this was the steamer in which she was sailing on the Mediterranean, before she should come home for the last time.

A glimmer of hope that Alice might not have been on board, or that she might have escaped, penetrated to Herbert's brain. But, no! There was her name among the names of those who had perished.

All sense forsook him; he dropped down helpless. The paper slipped from his nerveless hand, and Hiram cried aloud for help. Then, with a quick prescience that it was something Herbert had seen in the paper, he picked it up.

"Poor fellow! Perhaps it was something about the woman who has made his life——"

Hiram said no more, for he had taken in at a glance all that Herbert had read.

CHAPTER V.

It was two days later. Hiram was delirious in the hospital off Montgomery-street; Herbert had so far recovered as to be able to watch by him, but his thoughts were too chaotic to be chronicled.

A messenger-boy brought in a telegram for one Herbert J. Sinclair. It was only because the newspapers had published among the city items that two robust men, Sinclair and Wolfe, had swooned away on reading an account of the disaster in the Mediterranean, and been taken to one of the hospitals, that the operator, from the purport of the telegram, had known where to find him.

"Read it, my boy," said Herbert wearily, when the telegram was tendered him. "Read it; *I* can't."

"'Herbert Sinclair:—Fearing you might have heard of the wreck of the *Phœbus* and think me lost, I telegraph to let you know I am safe in Genoa, having left the *Phœbus* two days before she went down.

"'Alice Sinclair.'"

Herbert broke down and wept as he had not for thirty years. For years no great joy had come to him, and this was almost too much. But he recovered himself and sent a cablegram to Alice, saying everything was all right, but begging her to sail for home immediately.

Then he went to Hiram's bedside, hoping to make the poor fellow conscious of the life-giving news. But that was out of the question; Hiram was raving piteously about the oath he had made when twenty-one.

"Poor Hiram! His reverse has come! Oh, that he may recover! Has this been my doing? Have I been wrong in having him live in Texas, and here, and there, and everywhere? Was the sacrifice made in vain? Has it *all* been in vain? Was I wrong in having Alice travel abroad, and so incur danger of being killed? Am I directly responsible for all that has happened? God help me! I am! I was a madman myself, crazed by my love troubles, when I brought the old doctor to see Hiram, and I must have distorted the facts to him. God help me! I was a madman!"

An hour later Herbert was in a coupé on his way to the telegraph-office. He feebly made his way into the building, and asked to see the messenger-boys.

When he returned to the hospital again he muttered: " A troop of poor little messenger-boys will think kindly of me to-night,—one of them, in particular, and he a little Jew,—but that will not make *me* any better."

The new year came, and with it came Alice and Mrs. Wolfe. Hiram was hovering between life and death, but the doctors held out hope that he would recover. Again Alice and Mrs. Wolfe were his nurses, while Herbert looked sadly on.

Slowly life and reason came back to Hiram. His ravings were less violent. Instead of fancying himself and Herbert on their ranch in Texas, his thoughts went back to the days when he had first known Alice. Then he would speak of the day when he had first seen her, on the train. From that his thoughts would drift to the terrible scene when the train went to pieces and he was buried under its ruins. This had made a lasting impression on his mind.

So passed January, February, and March; and spring had come again. Still Alice watched over Hiram, though he had long since been removed from the hospital to a private house, which Herbert had rented.

"Alice," said Herbert one day, "do take a little exercise. Why, you look like a vine that has grown in the cellar, and never seen the sun! You will be ill yourself, Alice; and then what should we do? See here! Be ready for a drive at six, p.m., for if you are not ready we shall have to take a close carriage, and I have ordered an open one. Poor girl! When you came back from Europe this time you didn't look more than thirty, but now you look fully forty."

Herbert was right; she was so wearied, and worn, and sad, that she seemed no longer the bright Alice of old.

As they turned into Golden Gate Park they almost collided with a gay equipage, in which sat a lovely woman, robed in sombre black, but looking supremely happy and good-humoured.

"At last!" sobbed Herbert. "Alice," brokenly, "that is the woman I loved; that is my *wife!* And we might have killed her!"

"Oh, Herbert! Drive after her! She is a widow now! Drive——"

"No," said Herbert sadly, "I must not. I am a child again, and I wish to have it so. My heart is ashes, but I have you and Hiram to love me; that is enough."

"But, Herbert, she is in black! She is a widow! And she looks as beautiful and as young as ever. You must see her!"

"Don't, Alice. The awful past is dead. We have the happy future before us, and that is enough. Let me be a child again."

Reason came back to Hiram Wolfe. The twenty years were all but told, and again he was himself. After a touching interview with Alice and his mother, he asked to see Herbert.

"Yes, dear Hiram," said Alice, "I will call him. It is hard to realize that all is well at last. The suffering is all passed now, but it has been bitter enough. You are weak yet, Hiram; but you have a month and a half to get well in."

"Till June," said Hiram, faintly and sadly.

"Yes, Hiram; till June. But don't look so sorrowful; the tide has turned; our days of happiness have come."

She kissed him tenderly, and he passionately returned the kiss.

Herbert came into the room, to find Hiram wasted to a shadow, but with the old resolute look in his eyes.

"Sane as a legislator, old fellow!" was Herbert's greeting. "Now, this is something to live for, isn't it? And you haven't lost a day, either; for the date we fixed on hasn't passed yet.. I believe I must sell out my woes, wholesale, and champion lovers every time."

"Herbert, listen!" said Hiram, in so strained a tone that Herbert started.

"You are weak, Hiram," he said; "too weak to talk."

"I must. Herbert, the curse is not dead! I know it is not. The siege I have gone through has only intensified the latent insanity in our family. I could not escape it, Herbert."

"No, Hiram! No; it is dead. All this suffering and waiting have not been in vain! Think of yourself! Think of Alice!"

"It is of Alice I think, Herbert. The oath made long years ago must be renewed. Answer me truly, Herbert; is there not danger? The curse of insanity would follow—"

"Oh, I don't know; I don't know; I had not thought of this. Oh, Alice! Hiram! Would to Heaven—"

"Be calm, Herbert. My strength is gone; my constitution is undermined; my mind is shattered; I shall die. The great doctor is no more, but I know what he would say. We did not tell him that I wished to marry at the fulfilment of the twenty years, but he knew it. It was tacitly understood, Herbert, that if the malady should return the curse would likewise return."

"He said nothing about that; he simply said in twenty years you would have left it behind you. So, it is bosh; I don't believe it."

"You *do*, Herbert; and *I* do. He did not say it, because—"

"Because he never dreamed of such a thing!" broke in Herbert.

—"because he did not wish to trouble us. But it was understood. Herbert, in a few days I shall die, because I, too, have nothing to live for. What I said years ago was sadly prophetic: 'I have made a vow; I will keep it.'—Herbert, my brother, don't grieve; devote your life to Alice, as you have devoted it to me."

But Herbert could no longer control his grief; he groaned in agony.

"Herbert, I did not destroy the foolish oath I drew up; you kept it for me. Give it to me, please, if you have it still; I wish to destroy it now, before I die."

Shaking from head to foot, Herbert slowly drew a heavy metal case from an inner pocket, and took therefrom a paper. Faithful Herbert! He had carried it about him all these years, the metallic case preserving it intact.

"It once saved my life from a Confederate bullet, Hiram."

"Thank God for that! But Alice must not see that wicked oath; burn it in the grate, before me.—That is good. I made my will long ago, and you will find it with our lawyer. It leaves everything without reserve to Alice. We shall all meet again, Herbert."

These were Hiram Wolfe's last conscious words. His sufferings were not prolonged; at midnight he called deliriously:

"Herbert! Herbert!"

"Yes, my brother; I am here."

"Herbert, it is pressing me hard. Call up the horses, and we will take a long run together. Then—we will write—to Alice."

A labored breath, and all was still.

"He is gone!" sobbed Herbert.

Hiram had kept his oath; he had removed the curse.

Alice, Herbert, and Mrs. Wolfe went back to Virginia, taking their dead with them, and thence to Maryland.

Spring had come, but it had no charms for them. The years rolled on, and they mechanically went through with their duties. But Hiram could never be forgotten.

VAIN TRIUMPH.

(A FRAGMENT.)

In the days of my young manhood,
At the golden age of twenty,
I looked out upon a bright world
Full of beauty and of gladness;
Saw in Nature only sunshine,
Saw in mankind only goodness,
For I lived at peace with all men,
Though by no man was befriended.

*   *   *   *   *   *

From that time came premonitions,
Dim forebodings, transcient glimpses,
Of a phantom, weird and sombre,
That in future days should haunt me.

*   *   *   *   *   *

For this was no boyish passion,
But a 'ove to last a life-time,
To survive all evil fortune,
E'en the grave, and live triumphant
In the glorious Hereafter.
Soon I won my darling's promise
To be mine, now, and forever.
And thenceforth how bright was Nature,
Filled again with joyous sunshine!
Strong and pure my faith in Heaven,
And in the Almighty's goodness.

*   *   *   *   *   *

Then began the phantom visits
That had long been full expected.
'Twas no monster that came to me,
No forbidding, cruel spectre,

But a slow, dim-outlined figure,
Partly spirit, partly vision,
With grave gestures and sad accents,
Oft alluring, oft consoling,
Vaguely whispering of Nelly,
Then again of disappointment ;
Friendly towards me, and yet mocking,
A pursuer, no inspirer.
Still I, awe-struck, clung unto it,
Nightly waited for its coming,
Though too oft it came to torture.

* * * * * *

"Never more," she said in anger,
"Can I speak to you or see you.
I am promised to another ;
My old love for you is conquered,
And the past is past forever."
 Thus she heartless broke her promise,
Heartless left me to my mis'ry,
Left me, with this grave suspicion,
And would hear no explication.
 How I longed for night to bring me
Counsel from my sage familiar ;
But, alas ! it came not nigh me.
Could it be it was connected,
As had oft been borne upon me,
With the sweetheart who had loved me ?

* * * * * *

 As one who has been a captive
Half a life-time in a dungeon
Sees a day fixed for his freedom,
Then is thrust into a dungeon
Deeper, blacker, and more awful,
With no hope of future egress —

* * * * * *

As in dreams the old delusions,
The old faces, the fond mem'ries,
Are revived, and the old heart-break,
That in sleep is oft rebellious,
With o'ermastering vehemence,
Bursts the mighty Past's locked portals,
Brings the dead again before us,
Shows dim glimpses of the Future,
Then soothes all our fierce repinings,
Till we wake to dull reaction
And the sharp regret of living—
So now gliding like a phantom
Nelly's spirit came beside me,
With a calm, bright smile of greeting.
"Though on earth we parted strangers,"
Came a voice, a breath, an echo,
"Though I seemed but brief to love you,
And once goaded you to madness,
Yet my heart was with you alway;
And now from the sleepless Death-land
I am come to prove repentance
And redeem my girlish promise
That our love should be immortal.
'Tis for me to ask forgiveness,
And for you again to pardon."
　　With a quick, wild cry of triumph
I reached forth with frenzied gladness
To seize fast my death-won Nelly,
That she ne'er again should leave me.
　　But once more I grasped at shadows;
'Twas the old hallucination,
The old sombre, mocking phantom,
With his protean disguises,
Armed with means of keener torture,
Since he wore my loved one's features,
Had her air, her grace, her accents—
For now joyous first, then sadd'ning,
With life's vigor and life's clearness,

VAIN TRIUMPH.

Nelly's footsteps, Nelly's laughter,
On my ears like music falling,
Roused me from my trance-like stupor.
She was jesting with another,
Not for me her mirth or converse.
    So the smile was as the phantom,
And the words were but a mock'ry.

*   *   *   *   *   *

    This strange thought stirred all my life-blood,
Fired again my drooping spirits,
Brought new soul into my being;
And once more I sought my Nelly,
Still unwedded, still my goddess.

*   *   *   *   *   *

THE YOUNG VIOLINIST.

CARL ADLER was a romantic, indolent young man, with no capital in life except a genius for music. He was an expert performer on the violin, his favorite instrument, and could sing divinely.

Poor Carl! He did not support himself by means of either his violin or his voice, but worked hard day after day in a tobacco-factory, of which he was superintendent. He had ambitious dreams of some day leaving his work in this factory, and appearing before the world as a great violinist; but for the present there was nothing for him to do but to plod on steadily and accept whatever fortune might give him.

After working all day he would go home to his lodging-house, take his violin case, and wander out of the city to a quiet spot beside the river, where he would play sometimes till well into the night. This he would do every pleasant evening, playing softly in his own room when the weather was not suitable for him to go out. He preferred to be alone when playing solely for his love of music; but his landlady, who could not appreciate music —who, in short, cared for nothing but a confab with a gossiping neighbor—did not encourage him to play in the house.

"There is no one for me to love; no one to care for me," Carl would often sigh. "I have no mother, no sister, no wife; I am but a stranger in a strange land. I seem to have no particular friends; there is no one that could ever become well enough acquainted with me even to take an interest in my welfare. I must never dream of a wife and home; I must live for myself and fame, the only thing to love, my violin."

Month after month Carl Adler lived his solitary life; but one day a change came. It was evening, and with his violin case under his arm he was slowly making his way to his retreat up the river. As usual he was thinking of his art and his beloved violin. Suddenly a young lady and gentleman turned the corner of a street, and met him face to face. He stepped aside and was moving on, when the gentleman exclaimed:

"Here's the very person you want, Miss Archer." Then *sotto voce*, "An adept at the art, I assure you."

Carl paused, and the stranger continued, "Permit me to introduce you, Miss Archer, to Mr. Adler. Mr. Adler, Miss Archer."

Carl bowed in acknowledgment of the introduction. Though "only a workman," as he habitually called himself, he was a gentleman, and could feel quite at ease in what Charleston called the "best society."

"I am pleased to make your acquaintance, Mr. Adler," said Miss Archer, in a slow, musical voice. "Would it be convenient for you to come and give us some music to-morrow evening? Of course, if it would be at all inconvenient—"

"Certainly I will come," Carl replied, so promptly that the young lady for a moment fancied he was overpowered by the honor of the invitation. But a second glance at his face convinced her that such was not the case.

"You play Strauss's compositions, I suppose?" she asked.

"Yes, I have most of his compositions," Carl said modestly.

"Sind Sie nicht einer seiner Landsleute, Herr Adler?"

"Ich bin es; ich kam aber vor fuenfzehn Jahren, wie ein Kind, nach Amerika, und ich spreche lieber englisch als deutsch. Ich habe Musik hier studirt."

"Very well; bring all the best of Strauss's music you have, please, Mr. Adler."

"I will; but, excuse me, Miss Archer, you have not given me the address," Carl said, with a smile.

Miss Archer, taken by surprise, looked at Carl blankly, for she supposed that everybody knew where Justice Archer lived. Immediately she recovered herself and gave the address, adding: "Have you your violin with you in the case?"

"Yes, madam."

"I suppose you value it very highly?"

"Yes, Miss Archer," Carl replied, with a fond glance at the case. "I—I worship it."

"It's a Stradivarius, is it not?" asked the gentleman.

"No," replied Carl, "it's an Amati."

"Ah, well; both were the great Cremonese makers."

Then Miss Archer and her escort pursued their way, and Carl went on to his retreat.

"Of course it is my violin, not me, they want," Carl mused. "But all the same, I will go, and do my best to amuse the company."

The next evening he dressed with care, and bent his way to Justice Archer's big marble house. He was at once shown into a handsomely furnished *salon*, where he found a knot of fashionable people already assembled.

Miss Archer advanced and received him cordially.

Then she introduced him to two or three of those present as "Mr. Adler, a young violinist of this city."

Carl saw in what light he was regarded, and was careful not to obtrude. However, he had not come as a paid musician, and this thought comforted him.

Presently he was called upon to play. Feeling that some of the fashionable people about him were covertly laughing at him, and wishing, perhaps, to exhibit his skill before Miss Archer, who had already made an impression on his susceptible heart, he exerted himself to the utmost, and played as if by inspiration.

In a few minutes he became aware that his audience were drawing nearer and nearer—even crowding about him. But he took no notice of this, playing on with his whole soul in the music.

When the last strains of "Wein, Weib, und Gesang" died away there was a loud burst of applause. Carl bowed in acknowledgment, and coolly keyed up his instrument.

"That is grand," said a portly old gentleman. "I have not heard such music since I came from the land of violins."

"The instrument is a master-piece, the handiwork of one of the old classic makers," said the young gentleman who had introduced Carl to Miss Archer the previous evening, "but as much is due to the performer's talent and skill as to that."

"Yes, Mr. Adler," said Justice Archer, stepping up to the now blushing violinist, "you are worthy of your Amati."

But Carl knew his own worth, and this praise did not turn his head. "They rate me too highly," he said to himself; "it is the instrument. But probably they took me for a common scraper on a nameless violin." Then he said aloud: "Don't give me praise that I do not deserve. I have not handled the bow long enough yet to be master of it."

"How long is it since you first took up the violin?" asked one of the guests.

"Barely six years," Carl replied—not deprecatingly, for it is the work almost of a life-time to perfect one's self in playing on the violin.

More music was called for, and Carl delighted the company throughout the entire evening, sometimes playing alone, sometimes accompanied on the piano by Miss Archer or other young ladies. The uninitiated joined in the cry, and every one declared the performance exquisite. Some of the gentlemen were envious of Carl's marvelous dexterity and sympathy in wielding the bow; and some of the fair sex were desperately in love with him, and manœuvred adroitly to obtain an introduction.

The evening passed pleasantly until some person demanded why Mr. Adler had never appeared in public before. Then some one unluckily asked what Mr. Adler's occupation might be.

This was put as a direct question, and Carl did not hesitate to answer it. Feeling a little bitter, perhaps, that it was his music, not himself, that excited admiration, and being somewhat of a Socialist at heart, he answered bluntly, almost defiantly, "I am a workman in a tobacco factory."

There was dead silence for a full minute. Carl stealthily glanced about him, and saw the look of horror that transfixed the faces of several of those present. But he only smiled grimly, and said to himself, "This will be a severe test for some of them, it seems. Now we shall see who are truly ladies and gentlemen."

But a shadow crossed his face when he saw that Miss Archer herself looked inexpressibly annoyed, and he wished he could recall his hasty words. "But no," he reflected; "let me see whether she is like the rest."

"Mr. Adler," said Justice Archer, "I am glad to see you are not above your calling. As an American citizen, you are on a level with us all; as a musician, you are infinitely superior to any of us. The young man with a genius like yours need not be ashamed to stand before a workman's bench, because he is conscious that some day he will immortalize himself."

It may be the justice said this as a well-merited rebuke to such as sneered at Carl. The latter himself took it as a mild rebuke, and felt equally abashed with those at whom it was more directly leveled.

Soon afterward the party broke up. Several of the more influential people gathered about Carl, among them the justice, Miss Archer, and Mr. Melbourne—the gentleman who had given Carl the introduction to Miss Archer, and who had, in a quiet way, proved himself Carl's champion.

"I hope we shall hear you again," said the justice kindly. "Cannot you come in some day next week? What day shall we appoint, Mollie?" to his daughter.

"Could you come next Wednesday?" Miss Archer said.

"Yes, Miss Archer."

"Very well, then; we shall expect you next Wednesday."

"I will come. Good evening."

Carl fell in love with Miss Archer? Passionately.

"She does not despise me, at all events," he reflected. "In fact, she seemed to regard me with something more tangible than mere courtesy. Was it admiration? Oh! that the day of my triumph would come! But it seems as far away as ever."

Carl kept his appointment on the following Wednesday, and played as exquisitely as he had done before. How it thrilled him with delight to stand beside Miss Archer! As they both read off the same sheet of music he was obliged to manœuvre dexterously to avoid hitting her with the bow. It was a novel experience for him to have a young lady accompanist.

On this occasion it was discovered that Carl could sing, and he fairly electrified Miss Archer with his fine voice. How it rejoiced him to call forth approbation from her!

Before the evening was over a maid brought in substantial refreshments of cake and coffee; and when Carl rose to take leave he was pressed to come again.

Poor Carl! As he walked to his lonely rooms he swore that, God helping him, Miss Archer should be his wife.

"They treat me as hospitably as if I were the most stylish gentleman in all Charleston. I will hope for the best, and do my utmost to prove worthy of her and to win her."

The next time Carl Adler went to Justice Archer's he found Mr. Melbourne there. "I want to enjoy the music, too, if you will permit me," this gentleman said, smiling good-humoredly.

Carl felt a pang of jealousy; but he and Miss Archer were soon so much engrossed in playing that he almost orgot another's presence.

"Sing me 'The Archer and the Eagle,'" suggested Mr. Melbourne, with a provoking laugh.

The joke elicited an appreciative smile from the justice, but Carl started as if he already felt the "bolt." This whimsical allusion had never occurred to him before.

Again refreshments were served; again he was pressed to come and play.

So the summer passed. Carl had played at the justice's six times since the night of the social gathering. He was now madly in love with Miss Archer. She filled the void in his heart; she was his all in all. He cared to live but to see her, and counted on the evenings he was to spend with her as a schoolboy counts on his holidays. Not satisfied with seeing her occasionally at her own home, he neglected his beloved violin, and haunted the park and other places where he thought there was any possibility of seeing her. Then he regularly attended the church which she attended. Still he never intruded, never spoke unless she recognized him, and never presumed while in her father's house.

"She must be my wife, or I shall go mad," he said.

At length he determined to propose marriage boldly, but before doing so he would make a supreme effort to have the world recognize his genius. To that end he made application to Justice Archer and some others for letters of recommendation, and armed with these he went to Boston. There his wonderful genius excited the liveliest admiration from musical critics. The New England Conservatory of Music received him most favorably, and prophesied a brilliant career for him.

At last it seemed as if fortune had smiled on him.

"The factory will have to look out for another superintendent," he said gleefully. "But I must go back to Charleston and see my darling. An hour will settle my affairs there, and then hurrah for Boston again!"

Carl found that he was expected to give still another recital in Boston in the course of a few days, and that probably he would not get away for a full week. Too impatient to wait so long, he determined to write to Miss Archer that very day, telling her of his good fortune and of his ambitious dreams, and asking her to be his wife.

Full of his great love for her, Carl wrote a pathetic, yet eloquent, letter. Then there was nothing for it but impatiently to await an answer.

"It seems almost madness for me to do such a thing," he said to himself. "What has she ever said that I should suppose she cares for me? She has treated me with the greatest kindness and respect, but that is all. What cause have I to be so infatuated? But she loves me! she loves me! she loves me! I know it! Didn't she lend me some of her best music to bring here, and didn't she give me a boquet when I bade her good-bye? Oh, my love! my love! God has been merciful; he has helped me; and you will yet be mine."

The last day of Carl's stay in Boston had come. He had given one more exhibition of his genius, and his success was now assured. There was nothing more for him to do but to become famous, he was told.

To-day he might confidently look for a letter. What would the answer be? His letter was to be sent to the "general delivery," and as he walked to the post-office his heart was light and heavy by turns.

His thoughts reverted to the evening he had sung "The Archer and the Eagle," and these lines rang in his memory:—

> "With fatal aim the bolt she lanched,
>   And with a scream the eagle rose.
> His gaping wound can not be stanched—
>   His plumes are hers, the proud Montrose!"

His voice trembled as he asked the clerk to look for his name. A letter was carelessly handed him, and at a glance he saw that the handwriting was feminine and the post-mark Charleston.

He almost staggered as he walked out of the post-office. "She is the only one," he thought, "who would write to me; so it is from her. Heaven help me! It *must* be hope, for the tide has turned."

Turning up a quieter street, he tore open the envelope and took out the letter, which ran:—

"MR. ADLER, *Dear Sir*.—Though pleased to hear of your merited good fortune, I was pained and surprised at your proposal of marriage. If I have ever unwittingly given you cause to think I might be your wife, I sincerely regret it. I am truly sorry if you feel as deeply in this matter as your letter represents; but can only say, in reply, that I am soon to marry Mr. Melbourne. Try not to think of me at all; devote yourself wholly to the glory of your art.

"With sincerest wishes for your prosperity and happiness, I am, as ever, your true friend,   M. ARCHER."

Carl read this letter to the end, and then mechanically put it in his pocket. Then he went on, hopelessly, aimlessly. "I—I ought to have waited," he said aloud.

Presently he fell.

Two or three kind-hearted people ran up to him, and a crowd soon collected.

"Sunstroke," cried one.

"Heart disease."

"Apoplexy."

"Take him to the hospital."

Three days later this brief paragraph appeared in the *Boston Globe*:

"Sept. 7th.—At the hospital died yesterday Mr. Carl Adler, a young violinist from the South. It is said that he had just received an appointment from our New England Conservatory of Music. Doctors differ as to the cause of his death, but it is generally attributed to the intense heat, which has caused sunstrokes all over the country. In the young man's pocket was a letter from a friend in his Southern home. Contents not divulged."

The Boston doctors didn't believe in sentiment, but they could respect a dead man's secret. Otherwise the reporters might have worked up a grim sensation.

MAMMON.

A STRONG man, true, with noble mien,
Defiant, in his oft proved might,
   His steadfast dog erect beside,
   Reflecting all his master's pride ;
With firmest trust in maiden's plight,
And little reck for Fortune's spleen.

A maiden fair, with love of pelf,
And scornful of a brave heart won ;
   Fierce, taunting words ere she forsook
   A last embrace, a last sad look.——
A lean dog, dozing in the sun,
A madman, mutt'ring to himself.

TIME, THE HEALER.

Stoney-eyed grief—Christmas, 1885.

As looms against the midnight skies
   A lonely, spectral, blasted tree,
So shapes the past before my eyes
   Whene'er my thoughts revert to thee.

Chastened grief—Christmas, 1888.

As some loved picture in a book
   Recalls a cherished by-gone thought,
So thou, when on the past I look,
   Recall'st the happiness once sought.

THINGS BEGIN TO GET INTERESTING.*

AFTER a weary march due east, they came to a small, cleared space, in which stood a miserable hut. A faint line of smoke was curling out of the roof, but no person was in sight.

"Now, this isn't another powder magazine," said Steve; "therefore it must be a 'wayside hut.' My wounds have made me thirsty, of course, and we can probably get a drink here, whether any one is in or not, so I am going in."

The others, also, felt thirsty; and Charles was advancing to knock at the door, when Steve softly called him back.

"Now, Charley," he said, "I haven't read romances for nothing, and if there's villainy any where in this forest, it's here. Of course you've all read that villains have what is called a 'peculiar knock?'"

"Yes," whispered four out of the seven.

"Well, I am going to give a 'peculiar knock' on that door, with my sound hand, and you must mark the effect it has. You needn't grasp your weapons; but just keep your eyes and ears open. Then will you do whatever I ask?"

"We will," they said, smiling at Steve's whim.

Then the man who had not read romances for nothing stole softly to the door, and knocked in a "peculiar manner."

---

* Extract from my book, "A BLUNDERING BOY." Inserted here without a word of permission from the author or any of the mythical characters portrayed.—B. W. M.

Without a moment's hesitation, a voice within said, "Well done!"

Steve faced the others and winked furiously, while he reasoned rapidly to this effect: "Evidently, here is a nest of knaves. The fellow on the inside thinks his mate is in danger, and knocks to know whether it is safe for him to come in."

Then the voice within asked uneasily, "Jim?"

"Will," said Marmaduke, leaning over the litter, "we are certainly on the track of the man who stole your deer!"

"Oh, I had forgotten all about the deer," Will groaned.

Steve started, but collected himself in a moment, and whispered to Jim, "Come along, Jim; this fellow wants to see you. Now, be as bold as a lion; blow your nose like a trumpet; and observe: 'By the great dog-star, it's Jim; lemme in.'"

Jim managed to do this; but he basely muttered that he wasn't brought up for a circus clown.

"Then come in; the door isn't locked;" the voice within said harshly, but unhesitatingly.

Stephen flung open the door and strode proudly into the hut, closely followed by the others. One scantily furnished room, in a corner of which a man lay on a bed, was disclosed. This man's look of alarm at this sudden entrance filled Steve with exultation.

"What does all this mean? What do you want?" the occupant of the bed demanded.

"A glass of water," said Steve.

"Well, you can get a dish here, and there is a spring outside," with an air of great relief.

"Is this the man?" Steve asked of Marmaduke.

Marmaduke sadly shook his head.

"I am very low with the small-pox," said the unknown, "and those of you who have not had it, nor have not been exposed to it, had better hurry out into the open air."

This was said quietly—apparently, sincerely.

The hunters were struck with horror. It seemed as though a chain of misfortunes, that would eventually drag them to destruction, was slowly closing around them. Small-pox! Exposed to that loathsome disease! They grew sick with fear!

"Was it for this we went hunting?" Charles groaned.

For a few moments the hunters lost all presence of mind; they neglected to rush out of doors; they forgot that the sick man seemed wrapped in suspicion; they forgot that they had gained admittance by stratagem; Steve forgot that he was playing the hero.

A cry of horror from Jim roused them from their torpor.

"What a fool I am!" cried Henry. "I had the small-pox when I was a little boy; and now, to prove or disprove this fellow's statement, I will run the risk of taking it again. The rest of you may leave the room or not; just as fear, or curiosity, or thirst, or anything else, moves you. I believe, however, that there is not the least danger of contagion."

"No, no; come out!" Mr. Lawrence entreated, not wishing to be responsible for any more calamities. "Come out, Henry, and leave the man alone."

"Believe me, Mr. Lawrence, I run no risk," Henry declared. "I shall—"

"Ha!" shrieked the sick man. "Lawrence? Did you say Law—"

He stopped abruptly. But it was too late; he had betrayed himself.

"Yes, my man; I said Lawrence!" Henry said excitedly. "Come, now; explain yourself. Say no more about *small-pox*—we are not to be deceived by any such pretence."

The sick man looked Uncle Dick full in the face; groaned; shuddered; covered his face with the bed-clothes; and then, villain-like, fell to muttering.

After these actions, Jim himself was not afraid.

"Mr. Lawrence, Will, all of you," Henry said hoarsely, "I think your mystery is about to be unriddled at last. This man can evidently furnish the missing link in your history. He is either the secret enemy, or an accomplice of his." Uncle Dick trembled. After all these years was the mystery to be solved at last?

Stephen's hurt and Will's knee were forgotten in the eagerness to hear what this man had to say. All were familiar with Uncle Dick's story, as far as he knew it himself, and consequently all were eager to have the mysterious part explained. The entire eight assembled round the bed-side.

After much inane muttering the sick man uncovered his head, and asked faintly, "Are you Richard Lawrence?"

"I am."

"Were you insane at one time, and do you remember Patriarch Monk?"

"Yes, I was insane; but I know nothing of what happened then."

"Well, I will confess all to you. Mr. Lawrence, I have suffered in all these weary years—suffered from the agony of remorse."

"Yes?" said Uncle Dick, with a rising inflection.

"I will keep my secret no longer. But who are all these young men?" glancing at the hunters.

"They are friends, who may hear your story," Uncle Dick said.

"To begin with, I am indeed sick, but I have not the small-pox. That was a mere ruse to get rid of disagreeable callers."

At this Steve looked complacent, and Henry looked triumphant; the one pleased with his strategy, the other pleased with his sagacity.

At that very instant quick steps were heard outside, and then a "peculiar knock" was given on the door, which, prudently or imprudently, Steve had shut.

"It is a man who lives with me," Patriarch Monk said to the hunters. "We shall be interrupted for a few minutes, but then I will go on." Then aloud: "You may as well come in, Jim."

If this was intended as a warning to flee, it was not heeded, for the door opened, and a man whom Will and Marmaduke recognized as the rogue who on the previous day had feigned a mortal wound in order to steal their deer, strode into the hut.

On seeing the hut full of armed men, he sank down hopelessly, delivered a few choice ecphoneses, and then exclaimed: "Caught at last! Well, I might 'a' known it would come sooner or later. They have set the law on my track, and all these fellows will help 'em. Law behind, and what on earth in front!—I say, fellows, who are you?"

"Hunters," Henry said laconically.

Then the new-comer recognized Will and Marmaduke, and ejaculated, "Oh, I see; yesterday my ring was ruined, and now I'm ruined!"

The officer of the law, whose nonchalance had provoked the hunters in the forenoon, was indeed behind, and soon he, also, entered the hut, which was now filled.

"Just like a romance," Steve muttered. "All the characters, good and bad, most unaccountably meet, and then a general smash-up takes place, after which the good march off in one direction, to felicity, and the bad in another, to infelicity—unless they shoot themselves. Now, I hope Patriarch and Jim won't shoot themselves!"

"Jim Horniss," said the officer, "I am empowered to arrest you."

"I surrender," the captured one said sullenly. "You ought to have arrested me before. I'd give back the deer, if I could; but I sold it last night, and that's the last of it."

"That will do," the officer said severely.

* * * * * * *

The hunters now held a short conversation, and it was decided that Mr. Lawrence and Henry should stay to hear what Patriarch Monk had to say for himself, but that the others should go on with Will and Steve to the surgeon's.

The officer of the law thought it might be necessary for him to stay in his official capacity, and so he took a seat and listened, while he fixed his eyes on Jim Horniss.

And the confession he heard was worth listening to.

The hut was soon cleared of all save the five; and the six first introduced to the reader were again together, and on their way to the surgeon's.

"Well," said Will, "it seems I have lost my deer; but I have the comforting thought of knowing that the rascal will receive the punishment he deserves."

"How strange it all is," said Marmaduke, "that your uncle should stumble on the solution of his mystery when he least expected it; and that you could not find the thief when you looked for him, but as soon as you quit, we made straight for his house."

"No," Steve corrected good-humouredly, "that isn't it; but as soon as I took to playing the part of a hero of romance, 'events came on us with the rush of a whirlwind.'"

Leaving the wounded and the unwounded hunters to pursue their way through the forest, we shall return to the hut and overhear Patriarch Monk's long-delayed confession.

As soon as the door was shut on the six hunters he began. His face was turned towards Mr. Lawrence, but his eyes were fixed on his pillow, which was hidden by the coverlet; and his punctuation was so precise, his style so eloquent and sublime, and his story so methodical, complicated, and tragical, that once or twice a horrible suspicion that he was reading the entire confession out of a novel concealed in the bed, flashed across Mr. Lawrence's mind.

If this dreadful thought should occur to the reader, he can mentally insert the confession in double quotation marks.

* * * * * *

"I now surrender myself to outraged justice,—voluntarily, even gladly,—for I can endure this way of life no longer. Forgive me, if you can, Mr. Lawrence, for I have been tortured with remorse in all these years."

The villain's story was ended; and Uncle Dick, Henry, the officer of the law, and Jim Horniss, fetched a sigh of relief.

They felt extremely sorry for the sick man who had confessed so eloquently and prolixly; but Mr. Lawrence was not so "tortured" with pity as to plead for his release from punishment. In fact, he had nothing to say against the law's taking its course with him. However, he spoke kindly.

"Mr. Monk," he said, "I forgive you freely, for it was my own foolishness that led me into your power. As for the money, it seemed fated that it should melt away, and to-day not one cent of it remains. I am glad to see you in a better frame of mind, sir; but I must leave you now, to see how it fares with my nephew. Come, Henry."

"And *your* story?" asked the confessor, with a curious and eager air.

"Excuse me, Mr. Monk," said Uncle Dick; "but *my* story would seem prosaic, exceedingly prosaic, after *yours*. Good day."

And he and Henry brutally strode out of the hut, leaving the ex-villain "tortured" with curiosity.

SIGNS OF SPRING.

Signs of spring come thick and fast;
　　The toboggan is neglected,
Snowshoes, too, aside are cast,
　　And lawn-tennis resurrected.
　　　　The snow-shoveller's work is o'er—
　　　　Let us thirst not for his gore,
　　　　He will trouble us no more,
Careless lives he on his fortune.

Soon we'll read of baseball nine;
　　Jokes on blanket-suits will languish;
Steamboat jokes fall into line;
　　Ice-cream horrors swell the anguish.
　　　　Soon will gas-bills take a drop (?)
　　　　Roaring furnace fires will stop,
　　　　And the smart house-cleaner's mop
Will despotic make its circuit.

Small boys hie them to the brook,
　　With intent to get a wetting;
Scaly fish they joyous hook;
　　Hard at rafts they labor, sweating.
　　　　Soon the frog will serenade
　　　　From the friendly barricade
　　　　Of the dank pond's gruesome shade
Those who do not wish to hear him.

Loud, in tranquil safety placed,
　　Fiends will practice on the cornet;
Brisk the small boy will be chased
　　By the wild, bellig'rent hornet.
　　　　Soon the bumble-bee will come,
　　　　With the wasp, his huffish chum;
　　　　Soon will blithe mosquitoes hum,
Ere our blood they cheerful sample.

SIGNS OF SPRING.

The dog-catchers with their lures,
   Scooping dogs with gay abandon,
Will try hard—the blackamoors—
   Our pet dog to lay their hand on.
      Ere the sad-eyed Vermont tramp,
      With his lies of field and camp,
      Can his chestnuts quite revamp,
Watch-dogs fierce renew acquaintance.

Love-sick leap-year-privileged girls
   Now will have a little leisure
To trick out in monstrous curls—
   Trick'ry in which they take pleasure.
      Then, enchanting as a rose,
      As their woman mind well knows,
      They will bring to time the beaux
Who have courted them all winter.

Some spring poet soon will die,
   Martyr to his rhymes atrocious,
Slain, ere he can raise a cry,
   By some editor ferocious.
      Soon the peddler on his round
      At the door will gaily pound,
      And the old, familiar sound
Will remind us spring is coming.

OUR NEW GIRL.

SHE looked as if she would be equal to any emergency, in so far as mere physical strength was concerned; so we decided to give her a trial. We were a quiet family of four, and not very exacting.

Our expectations were grandly realized. The most determined tramp would meekly apologize for ringing the bell when her Amazonian figure appeared at the door in answer to the summons. Even a bailiff, who came around with fire in his cock eye to collect an account of seventy-five cents, only stayed to parley with her for the brief space of two minutes, when he, also, beat an inglorious retreat. For once he had met his match.

Going to the door was her supreme accomplishment. She took a ring as a personal insult; but would drop whatever she might be at, and striding to the door, would throw it wide open, stand squarely blocking the way, and glare at the unfortunate person outside with a gorgon look of haughty defiance. If running water from the hot water tap in the kitchen, she would march to the door if a ring came, leaving the tap wide open. But we knew she would never be detained long at the door.

It was not a week, however, before she began to receive calls herself from her numerous friends; and in these cases the interview never lasted less than fifteen minutes. A period in our history hinges upon such a call, one day when I had gone upstairs to take a hot bath. Just as I stepped into the bath, our new girl opened the hot water tap in the sink below. "Cæsar!" I groaned, "if that bell should ring!" Ring! ting! ting! went the bell, surely enough; and our new girl hurried to the door, leaving the tap below wide open. The ringer was a bosom friend of hers, and as no one came to my rescue, by the time they had exchanged their mutual confidences about their mistresses' affairs, my hot bath was gone up. This brought on such a cold that I was constrained to remain in my room for nearly a week.

The first morning I felt well enough to get about the house, the new girl, in opening the shutters, clumsily knocked one of them down into the street. It so happened that an old African rag-and-bottle fiend was trundling his push-cart along the sidewalk at this inopportune moment. The shutter rattled down so close behind him that he ran headlong into a hydrant—his cargo littered the walk and the boulevard—and he keeled over his cart all in a heap.

I saw this from a window, and hastened to the door—which was very rash and unfortunate on my part. The old fellow picked himself up slowly, and looked behind him in a very scared and deprecating way. On seeing me at the door and the grinning girl at the upper window, he heaved a sigh of relief, and exclaimed: "By gosh, boss! I thought it was a p'liceman a-goin' ter pull me fer runnin' this heah outfit er mine on the sidewalk."

"Are you hurt?" I asked.

"Well, between you and me, I was pretty badly scart. I *do* feel shook up, now I comes to raise myself, worse 'n if a gris'-mill had kersploded; and jes' look at them goods!"

"Too bad," I said soothingly, and turned to step back into the house.

"Hol' on, boss!" the old fellow cried out. "Let us estermate the damidge on the spot, so'st there wun't be no hard feelin's arisin' about this misfortune, and no unfair advantage took by either one er us; and so'st you, bein' a hones' man, can recoup me ter once."

"Will forty cents 'recoup' you, old man, if I throw in five more for your loss of time?" I asked haughtily.

"No, boss, it wun't; but seein' you're consposed to ack like a gennerman about it, and bein' as I'm handy with tools, and not above doin' a little repairin' myself in a case like this heah, we will estermate that my outfit is damidged to the tune of two dollahs. That's the way I figger it out, boss; but I'm willing ter make a perduction of twenty-five per cent. in your case, as it's sorter agin the grain fer me ter be downright hard on a gennerman, anyhow, bein' as I was brung up a gennerman, *myself.*"

I told him that he had found his vocation at last, and that I had no doubt he could outjew the ablest German Israelite in his trade. Then I weakly compromised on a dollar and ten cents, and hurriedly retreated into the house, as a crowd of gamins was beginning to collect, eager at the prospect of a free circus.

I found that the shutter was "damaged to the tune" of fifteen cents, and I felt all broken up. But what was my consternation next day to find that a mischievous reporter, who lived across the way, put a startling paragraph in his paper, to the effect that an inoffensive and much-esteemed old colored citizen, trundling a homely but respectable cart peacefully along the public highway, had been assaulted by an arrogant householder, and most shamefully handled. "But," pleasantly concluded the paragraph, "this man of violence was mulcted to the tune of $200, which will probably cause him in future to keep at a respectful distance from guileless old men of the push-cart fraternity."

Of course this mean joke was understood and appreciated, not alone by my intimate friends, but by those who had witnessed the mishaps of the old tramp and my parley with him. And by all these it *was* appreciated—for many long and weary days. The great army of friends—of all ages, and sexes, and colors, and creeds, and conditions—that our new girl would seem to have accumulated in the course of her life, likewise appeared to understand and appreciate the affair. But their covert ridicule did not affect me.

The day after this unfriendly encounter of mine with the swindling son of Africa, my mother directed the new girl to drive a strong nail in the wall in the dining-room, for the purpose of securing a bracket. In half an hour's time we heard a noise in that dining-room that shook the foundations of the house, and reminded us of Noah building his ark. We dashed into the room, and lo! there stood the new girl on the sewing-machine, wielding a neighbor's ten-pound hammer, and trying hard to pound into the wall a Northern Pacific railroad spike, which she had fished up in the wood-shed. Truly, she was energetic, but too impetuous.

Two days after this incident I was called to the door at the hour of noon by the new girl, who said, with a look of genuine alarm and horror, that "some man was asking for me, all tied up together and crunched-up-looking, like as if he had fell offen a house afire."

Full of curiosity to see what manner of man it could be that had daunted even our new girl, I inconsiderately went to the door without stopping to make any inquiries, and had hard work to recognize my friend of the damaged push-cart.

His right hand was painted livid with iodine. His left arm hung in a sling, and was bound with cloth—mostly venerable pantaloons, with an outside veneer of dismal, greasy cotton—till it was decidedly larger than a stove-pipe. His stomach (which he evidently considered the seat of life) stood out into empty space like the smock of an emigrant boy loaded with stolen apples; and was braced, guyed, stayed, and kept from falling off him by the voluminous folds of four different mufflers, or "comforters," in various stages of unwholesomeness. Besides these mufflers, his stomach was belayed by two encircling pairs of suspenders and a piece of comparatively new skate-strap. Verily, he must have harnessed on the entire stock of a rag warehouse. He would have afforded no inconsiderable load for an easy-going horse to pull. He took up as much room as a drunken man with a wheel-barrow, and would have crowded an alderman completely off the sidewalk.

"Well, boss," he began, in a voice that sounded as if he must have swallowed a piece of ragged ore, "that night after I seen you I was took *aw*-ful sick. The doctah says I'm terrible bad, and that I mus' go ter the infermery as soon's I seen you agin. The doctahs ecks-zamined me, and foun' that I'm damidged *in-ter-nal-ly* ter the tune er eight hundred dollahs. Now, that's pretty tough, ain't it, boss?" and he hitched his supports and looked very sad.

"Bein' ez me and you air both jus' men," he continued, "I'm willing ter settle this heah affair without any legul perceedings, 'coz I doan' want ter put you ter any trouble; (here he affected to be caught by a terrible spasm) and so I come erround heah, all weak and a-totterin' ez I am, ter say that I'll compermise with you in er quiet way fer five hundred dollahs, spot cash. And that's erbout the liberalist offah I ever heerd tell of, boss."

I listened calmly, with an inscrutable look that beguiled the old hypocrite to continue his argument. He went on to say, further, that if I would heed a friendly warning I would gladly compromise; as if he didn't collect that money to buy patent medicine and doctors' medicine, he would surely die. But the money would be collected, all the same; for he had seventeen able-bodied heirs, who would never give me a moment's peace till they had collected the full amount of eight hundred dollars, *with interest!*

No doubt the old fellow thought all this would stagger me. But a man who knows anything of the reprobate Negro is not easily staggered.

He next proceeded to say that if I could stand the expense of a great public trial, he would willingly unbosom all his frightful wounds and "damages" to a sympathetic court. But he believed I would spare myself this frightful loss of time and money.

It so happened that the Water-works Department had that very forenoon set about replacing the hydrant against which he had collided with a new one entire. Old age and last year's frosts had rendered this hydrant cranky and unreliable. The rigors of another winter might destroy it.

Perceiving my opportunity, I slowly and with much dignity pointed with three fingers to the dismantled hydrant, and said harshly: "Rash criminal! the relentless arm of outraged city by-law is waiting to snatch you up, and make a fearful example of you! If you had but dimly comprehended the *awful* pains and penalties inflicted upon those who demolish, impinge on, or tamper with the city hydrants,—thus endangering property and hampering the work of the city watering-carts,—you would at once have set out by rail for Canada. I, old man, am one vested with authority in this department of the city's welfare, and I cannot but do my duty. As soon therefore, as you recover sufficiently to be able to work hard for a living, the city will provide you with no light employment in the city *jail*; and the prosperous business which you are building up will go to the dogs. I am confident that a repudiator of your ubiquitary oneiromancy will at once solecize the invulnerability of the platitude. I wish further to impress upon you the vitiosity of the rhinoplastic turgidity and incompatibility which has predeterminedly crystallized the unctuousness of your ambiguous odontology."

This bloodthirsty and pompous bluster was not without its effect. The old African quailed under it, and I continued: "Think not to work upon my sympathies; for since this periodicity to a city hydrant has occurred, before my very door, I am steeled to pity and sworn to vengeance!" Again the old man quailed, and I wound up by saying that as a former Indian hunter and fighter under Wild Bill, I could perceive that his "damages" would not realize three cents on the dollar.

The old ruin, now thoroughly alarmed, gladly compromised by accepting an order on our druggist for a bottle of stomach bitters and a bottle of hair-oil.

The wicked old heathen looked so woebegone as he shuffled off that I relented so far as to hold out a promise that he and his family should have all our soap-grease, rags, bones, and bottles, *free* to the fifth generation. But I stipulated that he should never levy on my pocket-book again, and that, so long as he remained out of jail, he should give our new girl as wide a berth as a Gattling gun.

He tried to look grateful, but said I wasn't acting right through like a " gennerman," though he guessed he would have to give in this time. I warned him not to bother me about it if a street car should run over him on his way home; and so we parted. The two workmen now came back to the hydrant, and he slouched away with amazing agility.

The very next day our new girl set the kitchen on fire, so carelessly as to have invalidated my insurance policy. I saw clearly that she was likely to run some one into an untimely grave, and myself into the State's prison or the poor-house. So we made her up a purse of ten dollars, bought her a scalper's ticket over the St. Paul, and persuaded her to go and take up land in Dakota. We have since heard that she is doing well, but that no one has had the rashness to marry her.

I thought I had shaken off the enterprising accumulator of rags and bottles. But about two weeks after his last appeal to me, we were suddenly besieged one day by no fewer than seven tramps for free soap-grease, etc., etc.— evidently some of the old fellow's able-bodied heirs. That idle promise to him was a fatal mistake on my part, for he took it seriously. It wasn't so much a question of loss of revenue, but now that our new girl's sphere of action had been enlarged, who would scare away these fiends from the door? I plotted to secure the services of a couple of bowelless bull-dogs—but if the old man himself should come around again!

One-happy day we decided that the climate of Chicago wasn't cold enough to suit us, and removed to Minneapolis.

A MISSING TESTIMONIAL.

A MATRONLY cat that has successfully reared seventeen families that have all turned out well, sends in the following grateful recommend of Dr. Humbugger's unequalled "Proprietary Medicines." As the learned doctor cannot consistently publish it in almanac form at this inopportune time of year (the only mistake Mrs. Pussy Cat makes is in forwarding her testimonials in February instead of September), no time is lost in placing her letter herewith before "suffering humanity." It is manifest that these high encomiums are genuine and unsolicited.

"DEAR SIRS :—I beg to inclose you a photograph of my seventeenth family of triplets. From too much fondling by my genial host's impulsive son, they became reduced to a mere skeleton at the early age of seven weeks, and I despaired of saving their precious lives. But fortunately I got hold of a phial of your marvelous Lung-Waster Cordial, which I began using according to your printed directions. The first dose brought them relief, and three dozen bottles effected a permanent cure.

"This amazing result induced me to try your celebrated Angel-Maker Bitters for Tommy, an elder son of mine. Tommy was gifted by nature with a magnificent solo voice, and for months past has been the leader of our Harmony Club, and has organized many brilliant serenading tours. His midnight glees are everywhere greeted with tumultuous applause and peremptory encores of 'Scat! Scat!' from impulsive human-tribe beings, who cannot restrain their enthusiasm. In fact, their rapturous emotions often become so uncontrollable that they prodigally heave valuable kitchen and toilet articles out of the windows, and address congratulatory speeches to him, largely composed of those complimentary phrases beginning with 'By ——.' On more than one occasion Tommy has narrowly escaped being hit by elegant boquets of boot-jacks, thrown by some ardent admirer belonging to the impetuous human tribe. But one bitterly cold night Tommy came home at 3 a.m., complaining of a hoarseness in his throat. I naturally became alarmed, fearing it might result in pneumonia. The next day Tommy was worse, and imagine my anguish on realizing that his glorious voice was likely to be impaired! There were plenty of rivals who would have rejoiced to see my noble boy's star wane, and peter out. From this you will understand my intense satisfaction and overflowing gratitude to you; for twenty-two bottles of Angel-Maker Bitters and one two-pound tin of Don't-keep-it-in-the-house Salve restored his voice to its pristine vigor. He has since taken twice his weight of your Rough-on-Health Pills, with the very best results.

"But I must proceed to inform you of other incredible cures. Miss Minnie, a petted daughter of mine, was once out charivariing a white race tyrant who had annoyed several callers by turning an infernal-machine called a hose upon them, when she contracted a severe cold and was badly frost-bitten about the ears. I liberally applied your Out-of-the-frying-pan-into-the-fire Liniment to my darling's ears, and dosed her with your Stomach-Paralyzer Tonic. This is the triumphant result: She lost the tips of her ears, but her intellect thawed out, and her brain and stomach were saved! Far from suffering any ill effects from the loss of her ear-tips, Minnie thinks it gives her rather a *distingué* appearance, and I predict she has set a fashion that other feline belles and beaux will hasten to copy.

"Now we come to the most wonderful cures of all, the crowning work of your invaluable specifics. One awful day a playmate of my kind host's son committed the diabolical crime of assassination on a most dutiful and amiable son of mine, a little younger than my beloved Tommy, by drowning him in a bucket of abominable drinking water! I shudder to this hour when I think of it. Oh, he was such a promising youth! He is yet; for your Heart-Stiller Compound brought him back to life and health! In retaliation for this dastardly outrage on an innocent life, my heroic son Tom last week waylaid the canary-bird of the man-tribe assassin and made a bird's-nest pudding of it, and the next day captured his tame white mouse and brought it home, when we prepared a rich ragout and invited in two or three family connections. My restored darling, Pete, was able to digest a little fricasseed mouse, and is now able to go out into society again.

"We all thought this would crush the murderous white-tribe child, and bring his short black hair to a premature maturity. Alas, no! It is wonderful how quickly that race can throw off their griefs. Yesterday his papa brought him a monkey, and to-day the foul creature, as I was going upstairs for a nap in the work-basket, caught me by my terminal facilities (as my host, a railway man, enviously calls my graceful tail), and actually dropped me into a tub of filthy 'bathing-water,' which the deluded man-tribe animals prepare for a 'bath' every Saturday—or oftener! Of course *they* considered it clean, because it hadn't been used yet. I was never subjected to so shameful an indignity in my life. It makes my blood boil! You naturally ask in alarm, did I really get wet! Sirs, I sank beneath that hideous water, and with difficulty rescued myself. What to do I did not know till I remembered your Out-of-the-frying-pan-into-the-fire Liniment. Without doubt, this has saved my life. I have since started on a bottle of your Silencer Elixir, and after dinner shall try some of your Slow-Decay Preparation, and next week hope to feel myself again. To-night we purpose to charivari the monkey-monster, and may feel ourselves called upon to compass his ignominious execution. In case of any set-to with him, or in the event of any intestine strife, we must again resort to your remedies, when I will promptly write you full particulars.

"N. B. If you can make any use of this testimonial you are perfectly at liberty to use my name. May it do for other suffering mortals what it has done for me and mine.

"Sincerely yours,

"Mrs. Pussy Cat."

If a tramp evangelist from Kentucky, with a push-cartful of circus-poster letters of recommend, can wheedle a rising barrister of tender years out of his own good opinion of himself, what else need we expect from the discovery of these unforged testimonials but a renaissance of Scottish chivalry and a decadence of legal previousness?

ANOTHER VALUED TESTIMONIAL.

SURELY enough, within two weeks Mrs. Pussy Cat sent in another testimonial, which is herewith given to the reader in its entirety :—

"DEAR SIRS :—I again feel it my duty to inform you of the astonishing cures your remedies are performing. But for them, several old families would have been completely wiped out.

"We had a terrible time on the occasion of our last charivari. At my urgent request, Tommy did not start out with his famous crescendo, but contented himself with trilling a sonorous bass, which at intervals became an ecstatic tremulo. Tommy's versatility is past all belief.

"It was soon evident that our recital was awakening unusual interest in the man-tribe households, and that an unexpected demonstration from them would soon come. It did come; and it was both unexpected and undesired. Suddenly the monkey-monster himself shot sailing through the air, as though discharged from a giddy schoolboy's catapult. Did it mean that the motive of our clamorous protest was understood, and that the hideous creature was to be sacrificed to our outraged sensibilities? That is a disputed question to this day, since we cannot determine that any of the conflicting rumors are correct.

"The concert broke up in confusion, and many of our bravest veterans fled the field. In fact, the grandest hero of our community, who has carried off more scars, and bears more medals than any warrior of our contemporary annals—even he, our haughty generalissimo, precipitately attempted to scale an utterly unscaleable chimney. He fell, with his habitual gracefulness, fairly upon the monkey-monster, afterwards claiming his intention was to gain vantage ground for a reconnaissance. But Tom insists it was cowardice, unworthy of even the human tribe. My Tom is a musician, not a combatant, while Pete is a society pet; yet these gallant boys, seeing that the old general was on his mettle again and engaged in a victorious hand-to-hand conflict with the enemy, sounded a reveille, and bore down on the scene with intrepid valor. Tom encouraged the cowardly old veteran to fight it out to the bitter end; while Pete, with foolhardy but unheard-of daring, attacked the monster's unsightly tail. He said afterwards that he was never calmer in his life, knowing that even though he should be grazed by a parried blow, we had access to your System-Shatterer Specific.

"Tom and Pete had thus all but conquered the monster when a human-tribe woman appeared, armed with a broom, and prepared to do battle on our side. The monkey, in despair, at once gave up the struggle and surrendered to this person, who carried the crushed and abject creature away to some frightful punishment, we doubt not. Our humiliated veteran slank painfully away (he has since died of grief and shame for his cowardice), and several of the musicians, supes, and prompters returning, heartily congratulated my brave boys on their splendid victory. They have even gone so far as since to confer a new Order of Merit upon them—that of the Unterrified Bystanders. That very evening Tom and Pete began to take your Muscle-Attacker Compound, your Insomnia-Inducer Mixture, and your Mortal-Coil-Shuffler Prescription, and are now fast getting over the effects of the terrible scene with the monkey. I think if the cowardly old veteran had tried a little of your General-Debility-Bringer Ointment, or your Brain-Softner-Resolvent, or even your Sight-Dimmer Wash, he might be spinning his yarns among us yet.

"I must now acquaint you with the details of Tom's wonderful recovery from hereditary insanity—or incipient mumps, I don't clearly make out which from your diagnoses. The other day Tom scented a savory smell of fish, and found a rich treat of pure California salmon in a fish-can, which had been considerately opened and carefully carried out into the garden by one of our host's attentive children. Tom inserted his noble Egyptian head into the opening, and was enjoying a delicious repast, when suddenly a ferocious Dog bounded upon him! To his horror, Tom found he could not withdraw his head from the fish-can, nor shake it off! But with his characteristic courage he ran as only a feline hero can run. A terrific shock apprised him that he had brought up against the garden-wall (poor Tom could not see, you will understand, but he looked majestically picturesque as he dashed gallantly hither and thither), and he abruptly changed his course and eventually found himself in his luxurious nook in the woodshed; while the stupid Dog kept right on, and burnt his tail on the kitchen range. I promptly got out a bottle of your Apoplexy-Producer Preparation and placed it in plain sight, which enabled our host's daughter to remove the fish-can easily. We have been doctoring Tom ever since with your Cancer-Fetcher Gargle, your Nerve-Shaker Draft, and your various other specifics, to such good effect that Tom was able yesterday to attend a rehearsal.

"I had thought to write you of further unparalleled cures, but think I have done my share. It is sufficient to add that no feline nursery should be without your remedies.

"Respectfully yours, .

"Mrs. Pussy Cat."

If an unworthy disciple of Esculapius can successfully juggle two large-limbed executors, untrammelled by anything but their own Unpurified Conscience, out of twenty-two dollars in excess of his lawful hire, what else need the blindfold Goddess of Justice expect from all this but a frenzied entreaty to take her "darned old gun" and go in peace?

AN INTERVIEW WITH THE PROPHETS.

THE probabilities are that nobody will get left in predicting the kind of weather we may expect this month of March, as witness these conflicting forecasts : The settler from Manitoba, who pre-empted his claim away back in the 'Sixties, and who knows more about the idiosyncrasies of this particular month than the office-boy of the Meteorological Department, announces, with all the vagueness of an oracle, that there will be " some right smart flurries of snow, with considerable call for cough-syrup, and no end of bluster about March winds and dust "—and in this non-committal dictum he will come nearer the truth than any other of the prophets. Then the oldest inhabitant of Wentworth County will proclaim, in the emphatic manner of his tribe, that "there ain't goin' to be no sech airly spring sence 1871, when Benjamin Grigg sowed peas on the eighth of March ; " while his old maid sister, who has resolved on matrimony this spring, although it is not leap-year, and who knows that proposals in the rural districts need the bracing stimulant of a drive on runners under the keen and frosty moon, declares that the sleighing will last till the middle of April.

About the fourth of the month an editor out at Shanty Bay, who encourages Canadian literature in the same masterly way that General Middleton and the " boys " encouraged Louis Riel's little rebellion,—namely, by determinedly sitting on it,—will officially make this announcement, in his classical and vigorous style, unto all peoples conversant with the English language: "We speak in this morning's issue with no uncertain sound respecting the sort of weather that our prosperous and intellectual subscribers may expect during the current month. We are always logical. We are ever observant. We are at all times brief. The spring poetry sent us up to date is wanting both in respect to *quantity* and *quality*. It falls far behind that inflicted upon us during any previous year of our editorial experience. It is poor stuff. It is mawkish. It is peevishly puerile and uninterestingly unintelligible. *Ergo*, we argue a prolonged winter—a backward spring—an inclement season—an ice-bound March! Reader, it is not always May. NOW IS THE TIME TO SUBSCRIBE!"

The recluse professor of Toronto and millions of other awe-struck people will read and ponder the wise words of the Shanty Bay editor. But the learned professor alone will reply to him. He will come out with a carefully-written article on Commercial Union, in which he will satisfactorily prove that if complete Reciprocity were at once established between the United States and Canada, our "rough, raw, and democratic" March might be interchanged for a soft, southern, attempered month, of almost Florida-like geniality.

While the Indian agriculturists of Muskoka say they will continue to farm for muskrats for two full moons yet, a Grand Trunk freight conductor is morally certain that we needn't look for any more March weather at all this year, except in the almanacs and time-tables, because April is within twenty-four hours' run of Montreal.

In spite of these varying speculations, the sagacious small boy, with the instinct of his species, will see to it that his skates are kept fearfully and wonderfully ground, and that his broken hand-sleigh is promptly repaired.

From all this, what can we expect but an average March?

TO THE FIRST

Organ-Grinder of the Season.

I pray you, grind no more to-day,
    Or your small eyes may cease to gleam;
I'd rather hear a jackass bray,
    Or even a mad poet scream.
Oh, let me hear a raven sing!
It surely would less torture bring.

Your very monkey seems half crazed,
    And jabbers in a troubled way;
The gamins stare at you amazed,
    And hearken not to what you play.
When friendly critics of this stamp
Find fault, I think you should decamp.

Can you not grind some other airs
    Than " Put Me in My Little Bed "
And " Climbing Up the Golden Stairs ? "
    Play any other strains instead;
Grind chestnuts old from " Pinafore,"
Or newer ones from " Ruddigore."

Perhaps your intellect has fled,
    Perhaps, swan-like, you hymn your dirge:
To put you in a *narrow* bed
    My aggravated passions urge;
And though I fain would do no crime,
With you, I fear, 'tis scoot or climb.

TO THE FIRST ORGAN-GRINDER OF THE SEASON.

Our dimes for cough-drops yet we save,
    And boys their marbles still entrance ;
The spring-time bards now long to rave,
    E'en Jack Frost gives them now a chance.
Come, get thee to a peanut stand,
And cater to the rhymster band.

Forbear, rash man, to longer play,
    Prepare your spirit for its flight ;
I can my wrath no longer stay,
    Your death you premature invite.—
Cease, or you'll hear a maniac shout,
And you will think the sun's put out.

JUDITH'S DILEMMA.

JUDITH MARCHEMONT had a score of lovers. She was a beautiful girl, the pride of her parents, the admiration of her friends, and the envy of her less fortunate confidantes.

Two suitors were resolved to win her: one, a medical student, a romantic, handsome young fellow, with a pitiful income; the other, a practical youth, the heir and only son of a burly old Illinois farmer, whom ambition fired to become a civil engineer. Judith fancied herself most in love with the romantic young man, who could quote poetry, describe the pyramids of Egypt, go into raptures over Shakespeare, and explain why the U. S. must control the Panama Canal; but she would also smile sweetly on the young civil engineer, with his plain manners and hard common sense, who was so madly in love with her. Charles Montgomery, the first mentioned, prided himself on being the great-grandson of a Revolutionary hero, and was disposed to look down on Robert Richter, the son of a German emigrant.

At length matters came to such a crisis that both young men felt the time for a direct proposal had come.

Robert Richter bought a box of delicious bon-bons, and laboriously penned a little note on pink-tinted paper, offering his hand, his heart, and his fortune. At least, he thought he did. His proposal ran in this wise:—

"MISS MARCHEMONT: Dear girl, you know how madly I love you. I think I have sufficiently proved my devotion for you. I cannot offer you my heart in person, but to-day I have plucked up courage to do so by letter. Sometimes I have a moment of exquisite happiness, thinking that you must love me; then again I am goaded to frenzy, fancying that you are only trifling with me. You have so many lovers who are worthier, in every respect, than I, that my heart misgives me, even now. But if you can love me, ever so little, make me supremely happy by giving me just one word of hope, and I will strive to prove worthy of your entire love. I do not ask you to write to me; I will not intrude upon your time. All I ask is, if you could ever think of me as a husband, let a little ribbon band (blue, lovers' own color) stream from your window, or any place you think most suitable, to-morrow morning, and I will post myself where I can catch an immediate glimpse of it.

"Your own ROBERT RITCHTER."

Judith received this note and the box of bon-bons early in the evening. A boy delivered them, but amorous Robert was outside in the darkness, in the hope of catching even a glimpse of the girl he loved—which he did not.

Judith tore open the box and hungrily pounced upon the bon-bons. Then she leisurely opened the dainty note, and perused it. Her eyes sparkled as she read, and a smile parted her rosy lips. But this was not her first offer of marriage; if she accepted it, it would not be her first engagement. Naturally she was flattered and pleased; but she did not manifest much emotion.

"Dear Robert," she murmured softly, "how good he is! How modest and unassuming in offering his love! Who would have thought so grave a gentleman would indulge in such romance about a ribbon—a blue ribbon! Why, I should sooner expect Charley to be guilty of such an act! Poor Robert! I wonder what I had better do! Well, I won't decide till I consult mamma. How foolish of Robert to say he would not intrude on my time by asking me to write an answer, when he comes here and takes up my time evening after evening! But what good taste he has in selecting caramels. I wonder what Charley would have sent me?"

Mamma, on being consulted, congratulated her daughter on her good fortune. By all means Judith must accept this offer; Robert would be so good to her. The mistress of a happy home, with every luxury at her command, and with opportunities for foreign travel, would she not be happy?

So Judith Marchemont decided to accept the old farmer's son. She had plenty of time to make up her mind, if it was a question of doing so, but having once come to a decision she troubled herself no more about the matter, but spent the evening munching her bon-bons and reading a fashionable novel, wondering once or twice where Charley could be that he did not come in.

The night was a wretched one for Robert, whose sleep came in fitful catches. How he longed for the light of day, that was to make or mar his happiness.

Morning dawned, serene and balmy. Judith ate the last of her bon-bons, then opened a drawer full of delicate ribbons of various colors, and composedly selected one of blue.

"What a strange whim for Robert," she mused. "Let me see, what did he say? The window, I believe. Now, I've just thought of a lovely idea! I'll tie it to the bird-cage, the very cage he gave me, and hang that out of the window! That will please Robert; for he is always referring to the bird and its cage."

No sooner said than done. Judith thought the ribbon had a remarkably pretty effect, as it fluttered in the morning breeze, and as she was admiring it she caught sight of Robert standing on a corner of the street. He bowed profoundly, and then pretended to go away. But she noticed that he did not go out of sight of the ribbon.

She now discovered that Charles Montgomery was loitering on the corner, a block up the street, steadfastly regarding the fluttering blue ribbon.

"How provoking that he should see me!" she murmured; and instantly she took in the cage and detached the ribbon.

"How is it Charley never proposed?" she asked herself. "Such a scheme as this, now, would take his fancy. I wonder if he suspected anything? Does he lack the courage, or what is it? Well, I must think no more about him."

Judith tripped lightly down stairs, and told her maternal counselor what she had seen.

"Miss Judith," said the housemaid, coming into the room, "a boy brought a parcel to the back door last night, and asked me to give it to you. I'm sorry, Miss Judith, but," here she blushed, "Harry was in, and—"

Here the speaker stopped, and did not seem disposed to go on.

"Give me the parcel!" Judith said eagerly.

And Judith ran away from the breakfast table to her own room, with a rectangular parcel, securely tied with a long and strong cord. When opened, Judith found Dante's immortal poem, illustrated by Gustave Doré, in three richly-bound volumes. Her own name was emblazoned on a fly-leaf in each volume, in bold characters that she knew at once as Charles Montgomery's.

Beside her name in the "Paradisio" lay a note addressed to herself. It would have been a sardonic lover indeed that would have ventured to place a note in any other volume than this.

Judith literally tore the envelope to pieces, and her face blanched as her eyes ran over the note.

Almost in tears, she murmured angrily: "Oh, dear! That stupid girl! She is always making some blunder. Oh, Charley! Charley! I'll have mamma send her off this very day!"

Charley's note ran thus:—

"DEAR JUDITH:—I can endure suspense no longer. I love you, Judith, with my whole heart, passionately, eternally. Will you be my wife? You know my dreams of ambition; you sympathize with me in them; with you to inspire me I should become illustrious. I cannot pour out my heart as I could were I with you, but I will call on you to-morrow evening, to plead my cause and receive my fate at your hands.

"My dearest, I cannot wait so long. If you would be my guiding star, let a blue ribbon (your favorite color, dear girl,) appear a moment from your boudoir when you see me at the intersection of the Avenue to-morrow morning.

"Your devoted slave,

"CHARLES L. MONTGOMERY."

"Am I engaged to both?" Judith asked herself. "I certainly am engaged to Robert, and Charles as certainly believes me engaged to him! Each one thinks himself my future husband! Oh, dear! How unfortunate I am! My head is going to ache; I know it is! And Charles is coming in this evening! What was he thinking of just now? I half fancied he was laughing at me, when perhaps he was composing a sonnet! I wonder if they saw each other!"

Then she picked up one of the volumes, and reverently turned the leaves.

"What exquisite taste Charles has," she soliloquized. "He knows exactly what will please me. Who but Charles would have sent me these? It is only a short time that I have known him, and yet how quickly he anticipates all my wishes, and how thoroughly he knows my tastes. What is a box of confectionery, even of the choicest kind, compared with books worthy of Doré's art? And Charley knows I like sugar-plums, too; he buys only the best, if they are not so expensive as Robert's. Pshaw! What do I care for money!"

And Judith ran down stairs, with a good appetite for breakfast. After the meal was over she held another consultation with her mother.

Mrs. Marchemont was troubled. Clearly, Robert was the better match; clearly, Judith favored Charles. What should she advise?

"I don't see what I'm going to do," Judith said fretfully. "Charles is so handsome and gifted, and Robert appears so common-place beside him."

"Yes, Judith," said her mother gently, "but Robert

has a strong mind, rooted good principles, great resolution, and—and a fine property to recommend him."

"A minor consideration," said Judith. Then, with a smile: "Here I am, accidentally engaged to two gentlemen, at liberty to choose between them, and more undecided than ever! What a ridiculous situation! I do wish young men wouldn't try to be so romantic! It is all very well in romance, but in real life it is a bore. What could I have done if I had received both proposals last night? I couldn't have accepted either —at least, not by hanging out a ribbon."

"Well, you can decide better, perhaps, after you see both. I think it is all for the best," said Mrs. Marchemont decisively.

At eight o'clock that evening the door-bell rang gently. Judith, her face flushed, and her manner excited, herself answered the summons.

Robert Richter, his face radiant, stepped into the hall. He pressed Judith's hand and ceremoniously bowed.

"Step into this room," Judith said tremulously, opening the door of the parlor.

"Are you alone?" Robert whispered.

"Oh, yes," said Judith.

"Is your father in? I—I want to speak to him."

"No, he is out this evening, on business."

Then the two went into the parlor, glittering with its showy furniture and gimcrackery.

"My own dear little girl," said Robert, "how good you are!"

Then his eyes rested on the Doré volumes, which Judith had been examining while waiting for Charles.

Robert did not remember having seen these beautiful books before, and he took up a volume eagerly. As he caught the inscription and date on the fly-leaf he flashed Judith a look of ineffable delight and exultation, for he reasoned: "Some one—a lover, of course, Charles Montgomery, probably—gave her these yesterday, and she accepted me this morning! What further proof of her love can I ask?"

Laying down the book, Robert fumbled nervously in his pocket for a little box that enshrined a dazzling engagement ring.

Judith instinctively guessed what was coming, and, amazed at Robert's evident delight on examining the book, she looked at him vaguely, wondering whether he smiled because he had a more beautiful gift.

In the midst of her speculations she was startled by a peremptory ring of the door-bell. Charley's ring! She knew it was!

A look of vexation passed over Robert's face. He meekly dropped the ring-box, with the ring still in it, back into his pocket, and sank into a chair.

The housemaid answered the door, and Charles Montgomery was triumphantly ushered into the parlor.

On seeing Mr. Richter so comfortably seated *tete-a-tete* with Judith, Charles was visibly annoyed. His dark eyes flashed and his brow darkened. He shook hands with Judith as warmly and inquired after her welfare as solicitously as if he had just returned from Arabia, and then greeted Robert with ceremonious civility.

Judith now began to realize keenly the embarrassment of the situation. Each of these young men believed himself engaged to her; each one had come to ratify the engagement; each one probably had an engagement ring in his pocket.

Feeling that she must make an effort to talk, but not knowing how to begin or what she was saying, she queried, turning to Charles, "Is the skating good to-day, Robert?"

"I believe we have had no skating for the past two weeks," Charles answered drily.

"Oh, yes! how stupid of me!" said Judith, with a forced laugh.

"Have you seen these new books of Miss Marchemont's?" asked Robert, handing Charles one of the volumes in question.

"What do you think of them, Miss Marchemont?" asked Charles, without deigning Robert a look.

"I've been in raptures over them," said Judith, beginning to recover her equanimity. "I have studied the illustrations so carefully that I have not yet got out of the 'Inferno.'"

The young men did not perceive anything ridiculous in this, but Judith immediately did, and was amused, in spite of herself.

"Yes?" said Charles, looking pleased, but thinking that Judith spoke with too much constraint. "She is usually so unreserved and natural," he murmured.

"It was so good——" said Judith, and then stopped.

But Charles knew what she would have said. So did Robert; he drew himself up straight in his chair, and looked as grim as the Sphinx.

"Is your father in, Miss Marchemont?" Charles asked, in a low tone.

"No; he is out;" Judith returned, in a tone equally low.

If they fancied Robert had not overheard, they were mistaken. He glared at Charles, and then darted Judith a reproachful look.

"This soft weather will be bad for consumptives and such people, but good for you and your brother professionals, Mr. Montgomery," said Robert, with a palpable sneer that surprised Judith. In all her wide experience she did not yet know what discreditable things jealousy can prompt a lover to say.

Charles started as if he had been struck. Why should this humdrum fellow be suffered to come and pay his addresses to Judith? Why did Judith tolerate him at all? Should he not muster all his forces, and annihilate the clod? Should he not crush him so utterly that Judith would never look at him again? Should such a varlet browbeat Charles Montgomery? Never! In five minutes Charles Montgomery would so demoralize him that he would slink crest-fallen out of the house, never to re-enter it.

But it would be best to begin with musketry fire, and reserve his bomb-shells for a final effort. So he said, very calmly, as he supposed: "To be sure it will. But are you not afraid, Mr. Richter, that you will have to give up your intention of surveying railroads, and take to laying out grave-yards?"

Robert started in his turn, but replied sharply: "Oh, I didn't wish to insinuate that *all* doctors will kill their patients. It is the new men, you know, that always do the greatest 'execution.'"

Charles Montgomery winced, and a dazed look appeared

on Judith's face. How should she get rid of these two? If they were bent on quarrelling, as it seemed probable, it would be better to get rid of both. Did Charles and Robert differ in politics? She knew they differed in religion, and if they should get into a dispute about politics or religion, what would be the upshot? She shuddered to think of it.

"I—I wish Robert would go," she said to herself. Then aloud: "Oh, never mind such things," she said lightly. "Are you going to the next inauguration?'

This was a random inquiry, and Judith quaked as soon as she had made it, realizing that it would be almost certain to bring up the question of politics.

"Yes, I should like to go," said Charles. "What an attraction Washington proves to the rustics; they come even from the copper regions. It is as good as a fair for them."

"But then we thrust ourselves on our country friends, and make ourselves a nuisance," interpolated Judith, by way of saying something.

"Are your people fond of 'patronizing' such things, Mr. Richter?" Charles asked carelessly.

"My father sometimes had to do such things in his official capacity as Senator," Robert said quietly and with secret satisfaction at Charles's discomfiture. "But that isn't the place I should care to take a wife to, unless I lived in the vicinity, and could avoid the jam. I wouldn't see my wife fagged out for all the fairs, and so forth, in the universe."

"I was not aware that you have a wife," Charles said, tauntingly. "I thought you still enamored of schoolgirls."

Judith trembled. The two had seemed peaceably disposed a moment ago, and now another clash was imminent. And what if Robert or Charles, in the heat of the moment, should declare his engagement to her? She waited, breathless, to hear what Robert would say.

That young gentleman retorted boldly, and with ill-concealed exultation: " I shall be happy to introduce you to my wife at no distant day."

Charles thought that matters began to look serious. What was this fellow doing there, and why was he, usually so humble, putting on so insolent and triumphant airs? Pshaw! perhaps the fellow was intoxicated. In any case, he, Charles Montgomery, had nothing to fear, for was not Judith his promised wife? Yet, in spite of this comforting reflection, Charles Montgomery was uneasy.

"Unless a rival should step in your way!" he suggested.

Robert's eyes flashed fire. " Let a rival," he said, " beware!"

" Let a rival cross my path," said Charles impetuously, "and I would shoot him like a dog!"

Judith shuddered. She began to fear that the two young men might snatch each an umbrella or walking-stick from the hall, and fight a duel over her very head.

Robert looked up sharply. " Yes?" he said. " But unless you are as good a marksman with the shot-gun as you are with, say, the lancet, you would probably miss him, and so cause yourself much annoyance, and the other party much amusement. Of course, if the shooting were purely accidental, why, then, according to the newspaper tragedies, your victim would be pretty effectually put out of the way."

"Spoken like a Solon, my honest German," observed Charles, with a look that showed Robert's "shot" effective.

"Does not your professional experience bear out my remarks?" Robert asked.

"My professional experience has not yet begun," Charles said loftily.

"I beg your pardon, with all my heart!" Robert said drily.

"I have often been amused," observed Charles, "at the way sturdy old farmers send their sons away to study a profession, or seek some employment not quite so homely as farming. A farmer's son should, in general, be a farmer, except where he discovers special aptitude for some other calling. The higher walks require a finer organism and subtler intellect."

Charles thought this eloquent, and unanswerable.

"Yes," said Robert, "it would be better for a good many of us to till the soil than starve to death or go to the dogs by sticking to some beggarly profession."

This was intended as a home thrust, and Charles took it as such. "To come down to hard facts, what does pay, for young men?" he demanded.

"Well," said Robert slowly, "I don't know that anything does—except taking the census at four dollars a day, or starting out in the dime museum way."

Charles laughed, in spite of himself,—more at the accidental rhyme than at anything else,—while Judith began to hope that the two would now be civil to each other while they stayed.

But Charles again returned to the attack, feeling, however, that it was not so easy to disconcert the intruder. "You are almost as witty as my old Revolutionary great-grandfather," he said, with a lofty air.

"Oh?" said Robert. "Was your great-grandfather any connection of General Montgomery's, of Revolutionary fame?"

"No," replied Charles shortly, "he was my mother's grandfather." Then, brightening up, "Pray, Mr. Richter, what were your antecedents in the 'Vaterlander'?"

"We call it 'Vaterland,'" corrected Robert. "An ancestor is mentioned, barely mentioned, in connection with Charles the Fifth's Abdication, and another was one of Frederick the Great's favorite generals. My father has a medal, presented by the emperor himself, for some signal service that he rendered the Government. But all this reflects no credit on me. I believe that every man's reputation should depend on his own merit, and not descend to him from his forefathers."

A long and painful silence ensued. Judith warmed towards Robert on account of his ancestors, but still she wished he would go. However, it was a great relief that the young men were disposed to monopolize the conversation.

Then Charles took up a new subject. "What did you think of the play the other evening?" he asked Robert. "Was not that tragedy sublime? Or do you prefer comedy?"

"Well, I believe I was he—was—was engaged—otherwise," Robert stammered, appearing very much confused.

Charles looked angry, and Judith, uneasy.

Then Robert added, recklessly, defiantly: "I don't like such a comedy as this!"

Judith was angry enough now. Robert's cause was hopeless, if he could have known it—and perhaps he did know it.

Another painful silence. Judith felt that she could not endure this kind of torture much longer.

Nor did she. A side door opened, and Mrs. Marchemont glided in, bearing a tea-tray with cake and coffee. She courteously accosted the rivals, and deposited the tea-tray on a table.

Charles and Robert drank their coffee so incautiously and feverishly that they scalded their throats; but Judith knew that a little moderation was always advisable in sipping the family beverage.

"Can't you play something, Judith?" Mrs. Marchemont asked.

Charles and Robert greeted this proposal cheerfully, the latter observing that it would be better than so much monotonous talk.

Judith played one of her most soothing sonatas; then, thinking her mother would remain in the room till one or both of the rival suitors had taken leave, she returned to the table.

But such was not Mrs. Marchemont's purpose. She had determined that, as Judith could not decide on any course of action, she would bring matters to a crisis herself.

"Mr. Montgomery," she said, "Harold would like to see you a few minutes in the library."

It certainly cost Mrs. Marchemont an effort to say this, as her manner and voice betrayed; but she knew her duty, and could do it bravely.

Charles looked stupefied, then indignant, but grandly rose to his feet, bowed mockingly to Robert and profoundly to Judith, and marched out in the wake of Mrs. Marchemont.

Judith looked indignant, too, but said nothing; while Robert made no attempt to conceal his intense delight and relief.

Charles was ushered into a bright and cheerful room, and Harold, Judith's brother, a thirteen-year-old schoolboy, rose from his seat at a table and grinningly stretched out his paw to shake hands. Charles frigidly extended his hand, saying nothing.

"It's too bad the sleighing's all gone," Harold sighed.

"I think so," Charles replied absently.

As Harold ventured on no further regrets, Mrs. Marchemont explained that he wished to ask Charles a few questions on some mooted points in history, in which the dear boy was deeply interested.

Charles muttered something about being happy to explain away any "misunderstanding," and Harold dived among a pile of school books on the table, snatched up a history with a jerk, and hurriedly began tumbling over the leaves, apparently trying to hunt up some of his "mooted points." But he seemed to be floundering about from Preface to Finis quite at random, and the "mooted points" eluded his search. Perhaps he had picked up the wrong history.

"I heard you asking about a dog the other day," he said suddenly, looking up from his history. "Now, Charley, if you want to buy one, a chum of mine has got a splendid pup for sale—awful cheap, too."

"Yes?" said Charles. "Is—is it a good bargain—I mean, a good dog—a pup likely to make a good dog?"

"Guess 'tis!" said Harold enthusiastically.

But Mrs. Marchemont perceived that Charles was not in the humor to accept this desirable pup, even as a gift.

The same housemaid that had delivered Charles's parcel to Judith that morning, now stepped into the room with a scuttle of coal, and set about replenishing the fire in the grate, first courtesying respectfully to gloomy-looking Charles.

"Oh, Susan," said Mrs. Marchemont, with sudden animation, "did you give Miss Judith the parcel you spoke of? You are so careless that I cannot depend on you at all. You said a parcel came last evening, but that you forgot to give it to Miss Judith."

"Yes, ma'am," said Susan meekly; "but I gave it to her all right about ten o'clock this morning. Some other boy brought another little parcel last evening, but Jane says she got it, and delivered it straight. I'm awful sorry about it."

Then Susan, her duty done, slipped out of the room.

"Can't you find it?" Charles asked sharply, strangling a sob.

"No," said Harold, with a look of relief. "Oh, well," tossing the book upon the sofa, "it isn't much difference, anyway."

"Why, Harold!" said his mother, with a look that threatened mischief to the indifferent student.

"Good evening, then," said Charles. "Is this the way out?" opening a door which communicated with the hall. "I see it is; good evening."

And so, measuring five miles an hour, he took his leave of the house—forever.

A minute later Judith came into the room.

"Well, my dear," said Mrs. Marchemont, "that was strategy."

"Well, mamma, Robert has gone, too; mortally offended."

"Robert?" aghast. "How was that?" Then, noticing the open-eyed and open-eared Harold, she said, "See which way they've gone, Harold. But don't let them see you, mind."

Harold jumped up and trotted off briskly.

"Now, Judith."

"Well, he proposed again, and I told him that Charles had proposed the same way. Then he got angry, and asked if I meant the signal for him or for Charles. I told him frankly that I believed I liked Charles best, but that the signal was for him only. But I was cross, and angry about the way you treated Charles, and I suppose I showed it plainly. Then we had a long talk, and he went away in a towering rage at everything and everybody. I tried to reason with him, but it was no use."

"Well, one or both will come back to-morrow, Judith," Mrs. Marchemont said soothingly. "Poor girl! what an ordeal it was for you!"

Soon afterwards Harold bounded into the room, saying breathlessly: "They met not far off, and talked a long time; and then both laughed a little, and hoisted up their shoulders, and lit their cigars, and shook hands real hard, and said Judith was a good girl, but she hadn't much mind, and that wasn't her own, but her mother's; and then they looked up at the electric light, and Charley said,

'Thence we came forth to rebehold the stars,' and Robert—"

"Yes," said Judith, "that is the last line of the 'Inferno,' where their pilgrimage down below is completed."

"Quite complimentary!" said Mrs. Marchemont. "Well, go on, Harold."

"Then they both sighed, and looked pretty solemn, and said nobody seemed to be able to get into the 'Paradisio' worth a cent this evening, and went away smoking like a steamboat when the fireman is coaling her up."

"Never mind, Judith," said Mrs. Marchemont. "I know what young men are; they will be back to-morrow."

She was woefully mistaken. Neither Charles nor Robert ever came back, or ever again proposed to Judith Marchemont. Judith grieved a few days for Charles, whom she sincerely liked. But at Easter a new lover appeared on the scene; she fell in love with him; and said "yes" when he proposed in the orthodox, matter-of-fact way.

It will be some years before either Charles or Robert attains his "Paradisio" here below.

CITY LIFE VS. COUNTRY LIFE.

"MY dear fellow, you don't know anything about it. I have 'been there,' and know whereof I speak."

"Pshaw! Man knows but little here below, and knows that little mighty slow, to paraphrase the poet who lived before railway accidents were introduced or the telephone clerk was patented. Your own experience must convince you that all a man can learn in this world, from suffering, from observation, from dead books, or even from communicative Nature, amounts to but a handful of cobwebs, a bucket of cinders, with here and there a live coal of knowledge—so called. But is it knowledge?"

"So you are in for an argument again, White? Very well, then; we will fight it out, if it takes us till midnight. Please wait till I slip off my boots and fire this necktie into a drawer. Make yourself comfortable in my long-suffering chair, for I am going to lock the door and put the key in my pocket. When I have convinced you that city life is as different from country life as a nightmare is different from a cheering visit from an old friend, then will I sheathe my jack-knife, and unlock the door, and bid you good morning or Happy New Year, as the case may be. Remember, this is August the 6th, and the hour is nine p.m."

"Am I the old friend, or the nightmare, old fellow?"

"My dear White, you are the old friend. I can count on my fingers all the friends I have in the wide world who are worthy of that sacred name. You are one of them; but some of the warmest and noblest live in the country. In fact, my only boast is that I am a countryman myself."

"Your only boast! Oh——!"

"Well, *one* of my only boasts. One of these friends, as I've told you, took holy orders, and is to-day in Buffalo. We seldom correspond, but the old friendship is eternal. One of them is dead to me forever; another ——. But what we want to do is to argue, not talk. Come, open fire."

"What is your line of argument? Do you hold that city life is the *summum bonum*, and that country life is simply existence?"

"By no means. Each has its charms, and you and I love both. What I hold is this: A hermit like myself does far better to shut himself up in a house in the city, for genuine peace and solitude, than in the country. Here one can have perfect freedom, and immunity from care. There is no occasion to go out of doors for anything, because all a man can ask for is brought to him."

"Peace and solitude! Why, the street cars roar and jingle along in your hearing eighteen hours a day, and circus parades pass the door! As for not going out, you simply *must* go out."

"Not a bit of it! When a child comes here and thirsts for a drink of fresh water, what do we have to do? Simply turn a tap, and load the poor innocent up with a water-works mixture of animalcules, diluted sewerage and so on. In the country it is different. There you must go from ten feet to ten rods right out doors, frighten the chickens out of their wits if it is day-time, or mayhap run foul of an erratic polecat if it is midnight. The colder the day or the blacker the night, the more thirsty and persistent that child becomes. My aunt once got an idyllic black eye by running the pump-handle, that was pointing like the needle of a compass at the North Pole, plumb into her optic, one night when I was thirsty. It was months after that before I durst get thirsty again over night, or demur if they teased me with lukewarm water."

"Nonsense, old fellow! They have buckets and pails in the country, and in them they accumulate water, even as they accumulate hens' eggs in a market-basket."

"True; but the thirsty child will have *fresh* water, because he is built that way. Experience and observation both teach this. Fresh water and fresh youth are akin."

"Granted. But the city water, you acknowledge, is more or less impure. Observe that *I* don't say so, or—"

"No; I took that watery argument out of your bucket, or you would have made the most of it, though now you disclaim it."

"Quite so, my great logician. But when your hypothetical thirsty child drinks country water, he imbibes the Simon-pure article."

"I doubt it. Did you never see a well, White, with a bull-frog Masonic Lodge in possession? Did you never hear of a white-haired boy that unloaded the contents of a rat-trap into the ancestral well? Did you never hear my gruesome story of the German who innocently quaffed a goblet of the Simon-pure article, which was richly flavored by a luxuriant willow hard-by, and asked, in mingled astonishment and disgust, 'Have any of your pets died lately?' Did you never see a red-headed hired boy, with a far-away-California look in his big blue eyes and a railway pamphlet in his pocket, dreamily empty the dish-water where it could most easily meander into the well? Lest you should steal a march on me and sing the praises of the spring in the hollow,—which spring, by the way, is as far from the house as the water-works offices are from us here,—let me jog your memory and ask if you never saw the muley cow roil the waters of that crystal spring, or the unwashed hog lave his fevered snout therein?"

"But you claim that you can den up like a hermit in the city, and never have occasion to go out at all. Will you be good enough to give me particulars?"

"I can and will. In the country, if you wish to buy a newspaper or post a letter, you must journey an English mile—perhaps a German mile—to do it, over roads that may be moderately dusty or outrageously muddy. In the city, the postman drops your letters and regular papers in the letter-box, and the smiling newsboy comes and gives you your choice of fifteen papers—half of which you never heard of, and never want to hear of again."

"But the jaunt in the country will be medicine to you."

"Good. But suppose you are unable to go so far, or haven't time? Three miles, to post a letter and get a box of cigars!"

"Nonsense! You can send for your mail."

"Good, again. I knew you would think of these things. My dear White, I once sent for my mail by a boy who wouldn't rob a crow's nest, or throw stones at the glassware on the telegraph poles, or eat onions, or drink sweet cider, or pick up a whet-stone if he found it in the road. What do you suppose became of my mail?"

"I give it up."

"Well, as it turned out, there was a letter and two papers. That boy's sister got it into her head that these were fashion papers (just as if a blasé man like myself would care for fashion papers), and she slipped off the wrappers. I don't think she got much information out of the papers, but on one there was a scrap of news, written in English, and on the other there was ditto in Spanish. She could read the English first-rate; but the other bothered her. However, she copied it off, and her sister-in-law, who had studied French at the joyous age of fourteen, insisted that it was Ollendorffian French, and lost her reason trying to make it out. As for the letter—"

"But how did you find out these things?"

"Such things are sure to come out, White; especially in the country. Two days afterwards the good boy brought me my mail. The wrappers on the papers were *apparently* undisturbed, but the envelope of the letter was so worn and crumpled that the post-marks were indecipherable. That might have proved unfortunate, for it was the third and last of a series of anonymous letters that I had received. But I had long since found out the identity of my fair correspondent, though she was not yet aware of it. But you will agree with me, perhaps, that it may prove a rash experiment to send for your mail. Some things are not well done by proxy, eh?"

"You certainly gleaned a little knowledge—or rather wisdom—that time."

"True. No cobwebs mixed with it, either."

"Well, go on. How can you get the necessaries of life, even in the city, without bestirring yourself to get out?"

"How? My dear White, you must keep your eyes

locked up in your revolver-case, and your ears in your trowsers pockets, lest you should hear and see and so learn something. Let us outline the programme of one day,—say, Wednesday,—for both city and country. In the city, then, at 8 a. m. a gigantic milkman rings you to the door and gives you a good, Scriptural measure of milk. Winter and summer, rain or shine, you can rely on getting it. He will never fail you—except for ten days, when he is away on his bridal trip, and then he sends a deputy, who has learned the 'route' and makes punctual time within three days. But if he should miss you, you can hail any one of a dozen others passing the door. In the country you will get better milk, and generous, neighborly measure, I grant you. But—those stupid cows have to be hunted down, day after day, which is no joke for the tired farmers. Again, they are likely to 'go dry' just when the doctor orders you to drink a quart of milk as a morning recreation. If he orders you to take egg and milk for pastime, why, then will the hens lay off, too. The practical dairyman suffers no such contingencies to bother him."

"Oh, go on; you make me tired."

"Please remember that the key of the door is in my pocket. At 9 a.m. the grocer sends around, in his inquisitive way, to know what your orders are. At 9:15 the coal-oil peddlar turns up with his stone-blind horse and oil-soaked conveyance. He has only fifty cents' worth of clothes on his back, to be sure; but he has thirty dollars in his various pockets, and three thousand more in the savings bank. He will sell you good, marketable oil, at ten cents a gallon cheaper than you can get it in the country—where, many a time, I have seen 'most potent, grave, and reverend seigniors' sauntering along the sidewalk of the township metropolis, with a large, rusty, conspicuous, aggressive coal-oil can in their right hand, which they will shift to their left to shake hands, in a hearty, honest way that wins the admiration even of the ungracious city snob. You will admit that in the country it is coal-oil or candles, while in the city home gas can be used altogether. At 9:30 you will hear a crash outside that may suggest the idea of an alderman capsizing in a fit; but it is only the iceman slinging a lump of ice upon your door-step. It is beneath his dignity to ring door-bells. If it is glad-eyed June, at 10:10 a.m. the strawberry huckster will sell you berries that you will relish if you will only shut your eyes; and at 3 p.m. and at 6 p.m. his rivals will come along and sell you just as good berries at half the price. At 10:11 a.m. your baker will drive up behind him with your bread, and while you are taking in your supplies from them the baker's horse will damage three dollars' worth of strawberries, and the affair will come out in the newspapers. At 12 p.m.—"

"That *would* be pleasant, now, wouldn't it?"

"It would be, for the neighbors, certainly. But how long would you have to live in the country to see such things? At high noon the butcher will call, if you are a sensible man and leave orders for him to do so, and he and the vegetable men will supply you with enough to keep the cook-stove busy for a week. In the midst of your midday meal a good-natured Polish Jew, who speaks five different languages, will pay you a friendly call and offer you eighty cents for the accumulated old clothing of as many years—or in rounder numbers, of one hundred years. In the country you might have converted these into a scare-crow; but the crows would have laughed at it, and the neighbors would have criticised it. At 2 p. m. the city chimney-sweep will come and threateningly show you a mandamus from the City Hall, setting forth that if your chimneys are not swept on next Monday, you will be sent to the penitentiary for ten years for arson and as many more for high treason, the sentences not to run concurrently; whereas in the country you would have had to let your chimneys burn out of themselves, at the risk of wounding the fine sensibilities of the English insurance companies."

"This is not argument; it is balderdash."

"Come, now; if the discourse were yours, *I* should politely call it badinage. But even balderdash may be argument. At 3 p. m. a venerable old man, who may have seen better days, or may see them yet, will come around and naively sell you three packages of envelopes and of note-paper, at ten cents a package. To be sure, there may be better and cheaper down town, but neither better nor cheaper in the country. At——"

"Hold on! I've got you this time! The Government, or Post-office authorities, don't send around colporters with postage-stamps, and it isn't a speculation for private parties. You *must* send out for them!"

"You will not break in on my narrative again in that way, White. Lo! at 10 p.m. a neighbor across the street will come in without hat or cane. He will plead that he must write seven letters for the morning mail, and that he is 'long' on stamps and 'short' on envelopes; can you make a deal? Lo! here is the opportunity to unload some of the dearly-bought envelopes. He leaves you stamps enough to mail five letters, and materially reduces your stock of envelopes. See?"

"But such a thing might happen in the country."

"Eh? Well, yes; I stand rebuked. In fact, it would be much more likely to happen in the country.—At 5 p. m. a sunburnt book-agent will visit you, with forty-seven dollars' worth of literature in his grip. Here you have your choice of all the best works issued by the leading subscription-book publishers in America. What luck!"

"Are you afraid of him, or does he 'unload' on you?"

"My dear White, I used to be much more afraid of a dashing young gossip I knew in the country. Peace be to her ashes! She talked herself to death at the early age of twenty-two. Now, I take the initiative with this young man, and talk him black in the face, and then write him out a charm against hungry dogs, and advise him how I would tackle a man who has just five minutes to catch a train, and how I would lay for the man who had just got out of jail for subscribing in an order-book with his shot-gun. Then I cheerfully subscribe for a book that he says is to be published five years hence, but which I know is already out."

"Well, have you done?"

"No; but I will stop to wind my watch."

"Oh, say! You wouldn't know an argument from a horse-shoe!"

"That reminds me of more arguments. Three or four times a year there is an election going on in the city, and the opposing parties will send around a carriage and insist on giving you a free ride to the polls. Suppose the 'rate-payers' are called upon to vote $700,000.00 to help a new railway build into the city. You ride with the Antis, because they send a more luxurious carriage, and vote for the railway people on principle. If you are sick in bed with sciatica or pneumonia, it doesn't make a bit of difference; they will have your vote, and Death may claim your life, or not. The only thing they draw the line at is this: They hate to go carting around patients who are suffering from diphtheria or yellow fever."

"But what has all this to do with the country?"

"I am coming to that. The city horse will not shy at the circus parade you spoke of, neither will he be led from the narrow line of the street car rails by the seductive music of a three-hundred-dollar hand-organ, which can be heard four blocks away, and which truly causes its owner to earn his bread by the sweat of his brow. But with the country horse it is different, you know. This summer an old friend of mine undertook to drive me along the beautiful roads of our native district. He will not ask me to go again, neither will he pride himself on his Jehuship. All went merry for the first two miles, and then we suddenly came upon a city dude, touring the country on his 'bike'—his shycycle, as my friend jocosely and not inaptly called it. The only mistake the youth made was in setting out before he had mastered his wheel; and the only mistake our horse made was in turning wildly into the same ditch into which the youth had upset himself. Forty beautiful spokes suddenly became worthless wire; while my friend was thrown headlong upon the unfortunate bicyclist. But it didn't interrupt our journey half so much as it did the latter's. This seemed to infatuate our horse, however, and he bowled us along most enjoyably. Anon we heard a noise like a freight-train coming right along the highway. My friend jumped out at once, and led poor Sam, the horse, now trembling like a leaf, to a telegraph pole, and tied him fast with six or seven pieces of strap and a rope. I asked him if his fall had made him crazy, and he said, 'No; I wish I had a logging-chain besides these.' He explained nothing and I asked nothing, for if it was a question of ignorance on my part, I wasn't going to give it away. Presently a steam thresher outfit, drawing three contented-looking men and two wagons, came craunching along, and I began to wish we had had a city horse. The men laughed at us till the tears came, and I'm sure I didn't blame them. But it was no joke to Sam. That telegraph pole is fifteen degrees out of plumb to this day. When the steam thresher monster was a quarter of a mile past us on its journey, my friend led Sam out into the road, climbed into the buggy, and we were off again like a flash. But we were just five minutes too late for our letters to catch the English mail, and we began to feel discouraged. But on our way home we got along famously, and were beginning to congratulate ourselves. We were almost at the top of a big hill. On below in the hollow was my friend's home and our journey's end. Suddenly a piercing scream came from this hollow, and our horse began to plunge violently.

"'What can it mean?' gasped my friend. 'If it comes again, Sam will kill something!'

"It did come, again and again. Sam did not 'kill something'; but he ran away, and threw us both into a bed of nettles on the brow of the hill. I give you my word that neither my friend nor I got a broken neck; but we saw Sam dash on and knock the buggy to pieces, and fetch up at last, with considerable harness still on him, at the stables. The shrieking ceased; but what do you suppose it was?"

"Oh, your ridiculous imagination."

"You are away off. It was my friend's city cousin, a lively girl of fifteen. She was fishing her first fish in the stream in the hollow, and had captured an astonished crab on her fish-hook. Both were frightened to death; but the crab couldn't scream!"

"So you prefer city life to country life?"

"I never said so, White. I am like the boy in the stupid fable; I like both, off and on."

"I agree with you, in part. But what have we been arguing about?"

"I don't know; I have talked for the sake of talking. I am not through yet, but if I get through in time I am going to get my life insured and go back to the country to-morrow."

"Not through yet! Say, give me that key! I give in; I am more than convinced; I am overwhelmed.—That's good; thank you. Say, old fellow, you didn't touch on two things, after all: pure country air, and——"

"True. Now it is my turn to give in to you, White."

"And how you contrive to post your love-letters, whether in city or country. You don't trust them to ordinary mortals to post, and the letter-carrier is not likely to help you. But perhaps you have some jugglery, which——"

"Give me back the key, White, and we will fight it out all over again."

"You go to the mischief! Good night!"

And the door shut with a bang.

COULD I BUT KNOW!

To One Miss Frost.

Could I but know that the dim years
That swift will come, as they have gone,
    Would one day bring
    The cruel sting
From my sad heart, which nothing cheers.
    Could I but know
    Whether or no
In remote time bright days will dawn,
And fierce Despair yield up his fears.

Could I but know, oh silent one!
That you would care were I cut off;
    Would waste one tear
    Over my bier;
Would sad reflect my race was run.
    Could I but know
    If you would go
Still wreathed with smiles, still quick to scoff
At the poor wretch whose work was done.

Could I but know, long-loved sweetheart,
That you would heed gen'rous renown
    Coming to me,
    Glorious, free!
Would you then feel or joy or smart?
    Could I but know
    Whether or no
Fame would bring me your smile or frown,
Or one kind word, wrung from your heart.

Could I but know that, after all,
The old-time love might burst aflame,
    Surge in your heart,
    Wake with a start,
Wake to new life, come at my call!
    Could I but know
    It might be so!
For mistakes past mine be the blame,
Since, to all time, I am your thrall.

LUCY AND THE FORTUNE-TELLER.

"MY dear Hart, I am delighted to see you again."

"I might say the same; but it isn't necessary; you know my nature. What I wish to do, if you will only give me a chance to get in a word, is to congratulate you. I am told you are engaged to a handsome young lady. Now perhaps you will be good enough to invite me to the wedding."

"Your congratulations are a trifle premature, old fellow; I can't quite persuade the young lady to make up her mind. Do you know, one reason why I am so pleased to see you is because I want you to help me out of my difficulties."

"I always did admire your engaging frankness, Jack. But what can *I* do about it?"

"You can suggest ways and means by which I can prevail on the young lady in question to quit coquetting with me. I am even more anxious for this wedding to come about than *you* are. Give me some of your sage advice."

"Well, I could suggest twenty things to you, if—"

"Suggest *one*!"

"One? Give me five minutes to think it over, and I will suggest a hundred!"

"Don't tantalize me in this way!"

"Jack, is your lady-love superstitious—however little?"

"She is inclined that way, for a fact. But what of it?"

"Everything. Take her out for a walk, say, to-morrow afternoon, along the river, and just before you come to the Great Western bridge you will encounter an old gipsy woman fortune-teller. Keep mum, and your sweetheart herself will suggest the idea of having her fortune told. The rest follows naturally."

"You are to personate the fortune-teller?"

"It is most wonderful that you should have guessed it, Jack! Your penetration passes all belief!"

"Oh, come, now, Hart; I *knew* you could hit on something."

"For the fun of the thing, you might come along with quite a party of young people. It will be just as easy to make a dozen matches as one. But you must post me thoroughly as to your sweetheart's idiosyncrasies and history, because I don't want to make any mistakes. I think you may quietly begin your preparations this very day for a brilliant and speedy wedding."

"My dear Hart, how can I thank you enough!"

"Don't mention it. I shall charge the young lady six shillings for telling her fortune, and you will have to pay it, on the spot. Fortune-tellers don't give credit, you know. But I mean to send her a handsome wedding present."

Then the two young men held a long conversation, and when they separated Hart Montague was indeed "thoroughly posted." The lover, Jack Herrick, once ventured on a mild protest that it was taking an unfair and ungentlemanly advantage of his sweetheart, but his friend appeased him by quoting the old saying that "all is fair in love and war."

Lucy Pendleton was indeed somewhat superstitious; but that, in the eyes of her admirers, was only another of her many charms. She was a lovely girl, but capricious. This was not likely to frighten away any suitors, though

Jack Herrick realized that his chances of winning her were altogether dependent on her caprice, not on his solicitations.

Behold the pair, then, strolling along the classic Avon on the next afternoon. With them were three or four young ladies, each with an escort. They had some vague idea of joining a picnic party up the river, but had no suspicion that Jack was directing their movements. For once in a way, Jack was master of himself and of the situation.

"Oh, look!" cried Lucy, as they turned a bend in the river. "There is a ridiculous old gipsy hag! Let us go up and speak to her."

The word *ridiculous* admirably described the creature before them. In fact, Jack had no little difficulty in recognizing his friend Hart, so faithfully did that scamp represent the typical gipsy fortune-teller.

The party drew near, and saluted the gipsy with mock politeness. Jack was all impatience, of course, though not at all apprehensive of the fraud's being discovered. His impatience was soon quieted.

"Can you tell fortunes, mistress?" inquired Lucy.

"I have told the fortunes, sweet lady, of the greatest people in England. The stars are to me an open book. I look into the future as into a looking-glass, and the past is mirrored before me as the full moon upon the broad river."

"Tell me something first of the past. The future doesn't trouble me so much as you may think."

"Give me your left hand, sweet lady; and let the young man give me as a fee the silver in his left hand vest-pocket."

Lucy ungloved a fair hand, and for one brief moment it was attentively examined by the gipsy. Then with a start it was dropped. "The future *will* trouble you, sweet lady, ere many moons. Fate is already knocking at the door of your heart."

"Well," asked Lucy curiously, "what do you read?"

"Time enough to tell you that, sweet lady. First I will tell you something of your past, as you wished me."

"Never mind the past at all. Tell me of the future."

"Not so. On the day you were thirteen years old you were saved from drowning in this very river."

"Yes!" acknowledged Lucy, starting in her turn.

"On the thirteenth of the seventh month, July, 1887, you narrowly missed being hit by a rifle-ball. You thought a little brother had accidentally fired the shot. It was not so. His ball found another billet."

Lucy, as well as the other young ladies, now became thoroughly interested.

"You have noticed how often the numbers thirteen and seven have occurred in your history, sweet lady?"

"Certainly I have, and wondered at it," assented Lucy.

"These numbers will follow you all your life. One is lucky, the other unlucky. There are thirteen letters in your name; you have had six offers of marriage. If you do not accept the seventh, you must wait for the thirteenth. This man will be an outlaw, but this line in your palm shows that the seventh man will propose this evening. If you refuse him he will kill himself, and you will fall to the outlaw, who will poison you in 1913."

Miss Lucy was now becoming alarmed. "How shall I make sure who is the seventh?" she asked.

"There are but four letters in his Christian name, sweet lady, as in yours; though there are seven in his family name. His destiny is illustrious. He will be titled by your Queen ere you are three years married; will fight three battles against the Italians, and fix his name upon the stars forever. He will be so rich that ten horses cannot draw his gold. But if you refuse him, all this glory ends in brimstone; he will shoot himself."

"Is he handsome, too?" asked Lucy, with great interest.

Hart and Jack exchanged amused glances. Hart did not think the prospective bridegroom handsome, so he replied: "See for yourself, sweet lady; his picture is the thirteenth in a book that was given you on your seventeenth birthday."

Lucy remembered perfectly well that Jack's photograph was the thirteenth in her album, and that she had always looked upon this accidental placing of it as ill-omened. Still, if this old witch said he was the man—

"Is there no ill luck in that?" she asked at length.

"Sweet lady, it is destiny. The lucky and the unlucky numbers chase each other all through your life. Link your fate with the great man's, and you will live long and be happy. His star will never wane—unless you refuse him this evening."

Jack now began to look triumphant. He even began to fancy that his friend's wild talk was prophetic.

"What of the person who fired the rifle-ball?" Lucy suddenly asked. "Who was he, and when shall I see him again?"

"Sweet lady, these are dark things. It is not good for you to know everything, but I will tell you that you will be in Rome in July, seven years distant, and that on the thirteenth of the month, at seven minutes to noon, you will meet him face to face. If the man who proposes seventhly is then your husband, his glittering sword will disable your secret enemy; if the bearded outlaw is then your husband, your secret enemy will again attempt your life."

" And kill me ? " gasped Lucy.

" No, sweet lady; you escape sorely wounded, and live for your outlaw husband to poison you in 1913."

" Oh, certainly; I forgot about that," said Lucy.

The look of implicit faith on her innocent face was almost too much for Hart Montague. In fact, his triumphant success caused him to feel remorseful rather than jubilant.

But now other members of the party pressed forward to have their fortunes told. This was a critical test for Hart, as he was not familiar with their history, and he feared that perhaps he had overreached himself, after all, in bidding Jack to bring along chance comers. However, he still had his fancy and the future to draw on, and so predicted for one an alliance with a North American Indian; for another, the equivocal dignity of an elevation to the restored throne of Republican France; for another, the cheerful revelation that she would be wrongfully sentenced to death for murder, and pardoned at last on the scaffold; and for another, the equally cheerful alternative of being the wife of three drunkards, each one a worse sot than the first, or of being " cycloned " into a volcano, and there entombed alive.

The next morning the two young men met again, by appointment.

"Jack, my dear boy," said Hart, "I beg to congratulate you once more. Yesterday I read Miss Lucy's hand; to-day I read your face. She accepted you on the spot, eh?"

"Yes; and I herewith ask you to our wedding, on the 7th of the seventh month—that is, next July."

"You are a rascally lucky fellow, Jack; but you don't deserve your good fortune. Do you know, I've been dreaming about that girl all night. If I had known she was half so pretty, I would not have told her fortune; I would have cut you out. Aren't you afraid of me, even as it is?"

Jack laughed, an easy, good-natured laugh. "I will introduce you," he said, "and she will take you for the 'outlaw,' and be afraid of you. But what's the reason you never married, old fellow? You would be more than a match for the cleverest girl in England; you could win whom you pleased."

"I have helped my friends in their love-affairs, time and again, Jack; but when I am concerned myself I have scruples about these things. However, I never had any heart troubles. I say, Jack; I want you to drop a hint some day to those stupid young gallants. One might woo his sweetheart in the guise of an Indian, and another as a 'mountain-climber,' and so on; and the young ladies would take it all as a good joke, and accept it as a marvelous fulfillment of the gipsy's prophecies."

Hart was introduced to Miss Lucy, and the warmest affection sprang up between them; but, even as Jack said, she looked upon him with a vague, unrestful feeling that in the dim future he would, by some process of evolution, metamorphose himself into the gipsy's outlaw,

Hart would never betray any confidences reposed in him, even to expose deception, so that the secret was safe, so far as he was concerned.

Preparations for the wedding went on gaily. A few days before the date fixed for the great event, Lucy said to Jack, "Do you know, my dear Jack, I am going to try and find our gipsy prophetess again. There are a great many things that I wish to consult with her about."

"You will hardly find her, Lucy. She is probably off on her broomstick among the stars she talked of so glibly."

"Jack! How *can* you speak in that way of that gifted woman! She may be able to overhear you, for all you know, even from the stars. Do be careful."

"Yes, but you know, Lucy, my destiny was fixed the moment you accepted me; so I can say what I please. But if you really want to see the old gipsy, I can present you to that personage in five minutes."

"*You* can! Pray, are you in league with her?"

This was said without any suspicion whatever—perhaps without any meaning whatever. But Jack had long felt it his duty to tell Lucy the whole truth, and he thought this an opportune time to do so.

"Lucy," he said, "I will make no more ado about it. It was all a scheme between Montague and me; your old witch was that rascally dog."

A pale little face quivered for a moment, and then poor Lucy swooned away. Jack ran terrified from her presence, and on returning in the evening was politely informed that Miss Lucy was unable to see him.

It was several days before Lucy was able to leave her room. Her first act on being able to sit up was to write

Jack a frank little note that proved at once she was in full possession of her reasoning faculties, if not very well.

This note gave him to understand that he need never show his cruel, ugly face in her father's house again; that she despised him as being worse than a criminal; that she never loved him; that he might have brought his confession around in a way to win her sympathy; that she always hated him; that his friend was quite free from blame; that she might have married him a year ago, if he had had any energy or decision; again that she despised him; that his plot was not clever, it was childish; that he was a credulous, infatuated fool; that he might have won her without resort to any wicked stratagem; and finally, that she despised him, and would not see him.

Poor little Lucy!

It was Jack's turn to be ill when he received this letter. It drove the faint-hearted fellow to despair, and effectually disabused his mind of any further belief in his friend's dazzling prophecies about battle-fields and martial renown.

Lucy recovered finally on the 13th of July. On that fateful day at 7 p.m. her mind was clear and decided on many points—perhaps on most points.

The reader can easily guess how things shaped themselves. Lucy, as many another young lady would have done, married Hart Montague; and in her that young rascal found a wife whom he does not deserve, but whom he loves dearly.

Lucy still believes that seven and thirteen are her lucky and unlucky numbers, and takes a solemn interest in tracing out how they are alternately chasing each other in the most trivial affairs of her everyday life. She has even persuaded Hart to promise to take her to Rome when the seventh year period shall come.

As for poor Jack, he thought seriously of studying law last Christmas, but has finally decided on entering the army by buying a commission. It is somewhat remarkable how curiously events will come about in this uncertain world.

The moral of this story may or may not be that the swain who cannot manage his own love-affairs without calling in the interference of outsiders, richly deserves to "get left."

HOW HE QUIT SMOKING.*

"'TAIN'T no manner of use to say you can't keep from frettin' about these things," said the old man, in his slow, dogged way. "Lemme tell you how I quit smokin', away back in Eighteen fifty-seven. I hain't tetched it sence, except in the way I'm goin' to tell you, and I wan't no ruggeder then to stand a strain onto my system nor you be. You see, I've kep' on livin' all these years without it, an' I'm able to do as good a day's work, ef the notiont takes me, as ever I was; an' I'm seventy year old.

"It come about in this here way: The doctur says to me one day, 'Jim,' says he, 'Jim, you're a-goin' to kill yourself with that old pipe; it's chuck-full of nikkerteen,'. says he, 'the p'isenist kind of stuff they is. You can't quit smokin' at your age,' says he, 'but you'd orter git nice, clean pipes,' says he, 'fur to smoke out of.' 'Doctur,' says I, 'I'll smoke this pipe out in about ten minutes,' says I, 'and then, be gosh! I'll quit!' 'Don't go fur to do that, Jim,' says he, 'or we'll have to bury you,' says he. 'Not yit!' says I. They wan't nothin' more said about it, an' the doctur reckoned I dassn't try it. But I'd give my word, you see, that I'd do it, an' that 'twouldn't kill me, neither; so I done it.

"Yes, sir, I done it; I quit smokin' that very day. I went out an' bought a bran' new pipe, with a long handle onto it that 'd set into my mouth jest as comfurtable, and then I got some splendid terbakker, better'n I'd been used

---

*Taken from the MS. of my book, "THE GREAT TEN-DOLLAR LAWSUIT."—B.W.M.

ter allowin' myself, an' I took 'em along home, an' I shaved that terbakker up jest as fine, an' put it into that there pipe, an' prodded it down with my little finger, an' lighted a sliver into the stove, an' hilt it about six inches above that pipe, an' purtended I was a-goin' to have a good smoke. But I never done it. I put that pipe up onto the chimbley-piece where my old one used ter set, an' rested the bowl agin the fur aidge of the wall, an' h'isted the stem acrosst my gran'father's old spectickle case, where it could p'int at me, jest as coaxin' an' as natchurl, an' then put some nice, long lighters alongside of it. You know in them days matches was scarce an' poor. They was high, too. Then I takes away my old pipe, an' I says to it, kinder solemn, like, 'The time's come fur us ter part, old feller,' says I ; ' but 'tain't me that's got ter go; it's *you*.' I 'most cried, though, to throw the old pipe into the stove, an' know that was the 'final end' of it, as the sayin' is.

"Jest 's I got the stove-led on agin the old woman come in, an' I ups an' says to her, 'Hanner,' says I, ' I've quit smokin'; so you wun't have no more cause,' says I, ' fur to go jawin' around about me settin' onto the table, smokin', an' a-spittin' onto the floor.' 'Jim,' says she, 'Jim, what fool tricks are you up to now? You know you can't keep from smokin' no more 'n you can from talkin' !' says she. But I took an' showed her the bran' new pipe, an' she allowed I'd got some queer notiont into my head, anyhow; but she let on that she reckoned I couldn't never hold out. This r'iled my grit, an' I was determined not ter tetch terbakker. The old woman used to watch me pretty sharp at first, to see ef I didn't go an' smoke on the sly ; but bimeby she give in I'd quit.

"But sometimes on a frosty mornin', you know, when I'd be a-walkin' behind two fellers smokin', an' the smoke 'd come a-waftin' back ter me, like, I'd feel jest 's ef I wanted to take 'two whiffs an' a spit,' as the sayin' is. All the time I knowed there was a pipe at home a-waitin' fur me, all ready fur a good smoke; an' sometimes when I'd go home feelin' kinder hungry, I'd go an' take aholt of it an' examine that it was all right, an' I'd say to it, sorter boastin', like, 'Well, old boy,' I'd say, 'don't you feel terryble lonesome, a-layin' here all alone?' Then I'd put it back agin, where the stem could keep a-p'intin' at me.

"At first I used to have the awfullist time a-puttin' in the long evenin's; but when I got wore down to it I found I could set an' talk to Hanner an' folks that 'd come in jest as clever 's ever I could. They used to joke me some about it, but they got over that when they see how fearful determined I was. The new pipe used to be smoked now an' agin by the boys that come in, jest to keep up its spirits, like; an' they used to say it 'd draw beautiful. But I never done no more 'n purtend to take a few whiffs at it when I filled it agin. I always kep' it filled an' kernspicuous right there onto the chimbley, an' when the terbakker runned out I got some more.

"Bimeby somebody let it fall plumb onto the coals, an' it got cracked an' sp'ilt. I felt terryble bad ter see it go, though I hadn't never tried it fair, with the terbakker really afire. Hows'ever, I went an' got another pipe,— fashionabler 'n the old one, my, it was a daisy!—an' I filled it an' put it in the old spot, where it could lay a-p'intin' at me an' a-temptin' me. Hanner, she scolded some about me goin' an' buyin' more pipes, jest fur to look at, when I might 'a' got her some liver med'cine; but I told her I couldn't git along nohow without a pipe about the house. It's a terryble comfurt to think that it's there, ready fur me 'at a moment's notice,' as the sayin' is. It's a-waitin' fur me now; all I got to do when I git home is to take an' light a match, an' give a good pull, an' there's my pipe a-smokin' away jest as sosherable. But I ain't a-goin' ter tetch it, except jest ter sorter shake hands an' joke it about feelin' so lonesome.

"There's the old doctur, now! I'll jest go and ask him what's the reason some folks can't quit smokin' a pipe without gittin' theirselves buried fur it! I've joked him about it more'n a hundred times."

But the spry old doctor dodged around the corner and was gone.

"C'EST POUR TOUJOURS, NELLY."

To-day I lifted dry-eyed from their grave
    Such sad mementoes of the wretched past
    As in my bitterness I once had cast
Away from me, as being gifts you gave,
Though which, for mem'ry's sake, awhile I'd save,
    Safe in a limbo, whence I hoped at last
    To give them up unto destruction's blast,
When my poor heart had ceased for you to crave.
I gave no thought to the long, wasted years,
    Which are forever lost, but had no will
    To handle but with awe these souvenirs——
For through my heart there shot the old-time thrill,
    E'en though these mute things seemed instinct with jeers,
    To find, though all is lost, I love you still.

HER STORY AND HIS STORY.

AN acquaintance, recently married, after long years of patient waiting, to an old widower,—sincere, unpretentious, and rough-and-ready, a typical Canadian,—gave her admiring relatives and friends this startling account of her newly-acquired husband's ancestry and former greatness:—

"Yes, girls; Mordecai comes of a very old family. They were the wealthiest and most aristocratic people in Central Ontario, and held vast estates right in the heart of what is to-day the city of Belleville. Mordecai often tells of his wild adventures as a boy in that mountainous region, where he killed the most ferocious bears—just for sport, you know. Once he killed a noble stag, after a terrible struggle. He was so venturesome that he often wandered away alone, without any of his father's retainers, or even a guide. Yes, girls; he killed this stag, when his own life was in deadly peril, and afterwards presented it to the Smithsonian Institute at Washington. If we ever go to the American Capital, we must certainly make it a point to see it. Mordecai is acquainted with two members of the President's cabinet and with a number of senators, besides knowing the Premier of Canada and all his cabinet!"

"Oh, how nice that must be!" sighed a fair listener.

"Yes, girls; I will tell you presently about our visit to the Executive Mansion at Ottawa. Well, as I was about to remark, Mordecai says he once or twice regretted endowing the Smithsonian Institute with his stag, it was such a magnificent specimen of the antlered race. He has one very funny story, too, about a friend of his being once chased by a polecat; but my husband is such a polished man that he can rarely be persuaded to mention such subjects. But if he hadn't been the crack shot he is, his friend would—would have lost an evening's enjoyment at the manor-house, where a grand ball was to be given.

"His father died early in life, and Mordecai was extremely kind to his widowed mother. One day when she was unwell and the servants were away, or refractory, the little fellow actually cooked his own dinner rather than disturb his mother—and, of course, brought up as he was, he was as innocent of the kitchen and of culinary affairs as a young prince.

"In those early days, before his father's death and for some years afterward, the family frequently entertained Provincial and foreign notabilities, and Mordecai received his name from a New England grandee who passed a week with them. They kept 'open house,' and their spacious mansion contained many guest-rooms; but it was often crowded, for all that, and the more guests they could entertain, the better pleased were the genial host and hostess.

"You may know, girls, how courageous a lady Mordecai's mother was. One day it was necessary for a messenger to be sent to Toronto, one hundred miles distant. The family coach was in Kingston, undergoing repairs, and after the death of Mordecai's father there was not so large a retinue of servants kept up, so that, on this particular occasion, there was no trustworthy person about the manor to be despatched on this important mission. That undaunted old lady actually undertook to drive there alone, girls; and she did it. Mordecai tells how when night came on she put up at a lonely wayside inn, near the town of Newcastle, and was so nervous that she remained awake half the night.—Not that she was afraid, you know, for she was very courageous; but the novelty of the situation, as Mordecai says, was so startling. The next day the heroic old lady sighted a bear, and she said if she had had her late husband's rifle with her—it descended to him from the first Duke of Marlborough, girls—she would have felled him.

"But all this was years ago. Now I must tell you of our visit to the Dominion Capital. A mere description of the sights of Ottawa would not be very entertaining, so I will pass on to tell you of our picnic at Rideau Hall. His Excellency's private secretary recognized Mordecai at once as an old friend, and escorted us all over the Hall and the grounds. A sharp shower coming up unexpectedly, we took refuge in a lovely little summer-house, or pagoda, where no one ever thinks of venturing. But I could see that Mordecai felt perfectly at home there.

"While we were in Ottawa he got some lovely slatted honey—such a quantity of it, too—and brought it to our new home. Of course *we* couldn't eat it all; but Mordecai and I gave most of it away—he is so generous, you know. Well, he can afford to be; he is next thing to being a millionaire."

"Oh, my!" said her listeners, in unfeigned surprise.

"Yes, girls. Mordecai was brought up with all the choicest wines and liquors on his father's table, as gentlemen's sons were, of course; but he grew up a thoroughly temperate man, and is a Prohibitionist to-day. I don't suppose he would know a drunken man if he should meet one. From all this you will see what his principles are."

"Yes, indeed."

AT this juncture Mordecai himself came in, and when told by an interested young lady of his wife's charming narrative, he proceeded, in his bland, ingenuous way, to give his own account of the family history and of his early triumphs. At first his auditors fancied he was wandering from his text; but presently it dawned upon them that there might be certain vague coincidences in the two stories.

"Yes," he began good-naturedly, "I've seen some pretty rough experiences in my time, and some amusing ones.

" My parents kep' a little tavern in the wilds of Hastings County, near the Bay of Quinté, and I was raised there and spent half my life there. My father was a smart man, for them days, but awful close; and the way he used to charge his guests was something fearful. I have known members of Parliament and Government officials to stop with him—why, I was named for a Massachusetts big-bug, though I'm no hand to brag about such things. As I was going to say, I've known wealthy Englishmen and poorly-paid preachers to go away from dad's telling him to his face that he was the heartlessest old skin-flint they ever came across; and ordinary travelers used to quarrel so with him that sometimes it came to blows. and once a Justice of the Peace, traveling unbeknownst, had the old man fined for his cantankerous behavior. He was always more careful after that, was father; but that was the way he made his money, because, you see, taverns were scarce and poor in that region in them days. But they kep' a very respectable place, and no one could find any fault, except with the old man's outrageous charges. The tavern was large and comfortable, and was oftentimes chuck-full of travelers. You ought to have seen father then! The more people he could jam into the place, and feed, the better pleased he was.

"But father died when I was very young, and mother kep' things going for a few years. She couldn't carry it on as he had done, and us boys were too small to run things, so when she saw she was losing money, she sold out. One time she ran out of liquor. (I'm a teetotaler myself, and vote for no-whiskey candidates, as long as they are good party men, though I was brought up right in the midst of the poisonest kinds of liquors, though father wouldn't allow us to drink, he was so close. But I have seen so many drunken men that I never want to touch any spirits.)

"As I was saying, mother ran out of liquor one time, just as an election was coming on, and there wasn't a living soul she could send away for supplies. She was never any hand to do business by correspondence, as father was,—"

At this point the new wife made a frenzied attempt to head him off. But Mordecai was a little deaf, and he kept on in the same dogged, ingenuous way.

"——and she thought she'd have a nice little excursion, any way. So she left me and the hostler in charge of the tavern, and went away to Toronto on foot. She had to go on foot, though it was a good hundred miles, because father's two horses and his rigs were in Kingston, sold to a livery-stable man. My mother was a plucky woman, though, even for them days. When night came on she wasn't going to spend any money at taverns, so she just roosted in a tree along the wayside, near the little village of Newcastle. But she was almost sorry for it, because she couldn't sleep, hardly.—Not that she was afraid, you know, but it was a sort of a novel situation, even for a pioneer's daughter. The next day she fell in with an old bear, and she said if she had had dad's old gun along—it used to belong to a York County horse-thief, and dad kep' it in payment of his bill. Well, if she had had this old gun along, she could have got a crack at that bear, for sure. But the old lady got kind of discouraged, and came back in the stage-coach, with a driver that had an old account at the bar.

"Speaking of bears, I used oftentimes to run away from home, where they always kep' us working too hard, and went after bears. The country thereabouts is full of hills and hollows, and used to be full of game. I wasn't like these hunters now-a-days, that must have their guides along; I always went alone, and had more sport, too. The old folks never allowed me no spending money, but one day I killed a splendid buck, after a terrible fight with him, and sold it to a professor that came along—not a music professor, you understand, but one from a college. Well, that stag was put into a museum at Washington! It's there now, and Hester and me mean to try and look it up if we ever go to Washington. I know two members of the President's cabinet down there, and lots of senators, and the Premier of Canada, and dozens of members of Parliament; got acquainted with them when I was a station-master on the old St. Lawrence and Ottawa Railway. But I don't suppose they would remember me now.

"Yes, that was a magnificent old buck; but he nearly killed me, and I was always sorry I didn't ask more, for I'm sure the professor would have given me as much as twenty-five dollars for him.

"But I didn't always have such luck. One day I had a falling-out with mother, and cooked my own dinner—and it was a good one, too! for I was brought up to wash dishes and make myself handy about the kitchen. Yes, we had a few words about something; and as I wasn't feeling real well and wanted to brace up for a party there was to be that evening, I went out into the swamp with my gun. First thing I knew, I had beat up a skunk, and if the story wasn't so long I would give you all the particulars, for it's a funny story enough. Well, if I hadn't been a first-rate shot, I shouldn't have got to that party that night.

"But this was in my childhood. The railways came along and boomed things, and towns grew up all over. Why, if my father had only known it, he could have got all the land where the little city of Belleville now lies! And if dad had once got it, and held onto it after his fashion of holding on, Hester here might be a millionairess to-day, with her diamonds and French cooks, instid of being the one jooel of an old man of fifty-nine, with a poor fifteen thousand.

"Hester and me went down to Ottawa here this summer, on our wedding trip. She wanted to see the Governor-General's place, and as I knew one of the gardeners there, I was sure we should be able to see what there was to be seen; so we went. He showed us all around, and pointed out the Governor's private secretary, and we enjoyed a very pleasant afternoon. But a nasty rain came on, and we had to take shelter in a root-house. As I told the gardener, I felt at home there, because I was brought up right out in the country. But the man seemed mad because I didn't give him fifty cents or a quarter—and there he was an old friend of mine!

"Before we came away from Ottawa I bought fifty pounds of strained honey, thinking it would sell first-rate when we got home. But honey was cheap, and it was no go. When we saw it was getting candied, we gave most of it away. But I often laugh at my little speculation in honey!"

And Mordecai leaned back in his chair and laughed heartily—but his wife had fainted away.

NANCY ANN'S ELOPEMENT.

NANCY ANN BRIGGS was a rustic maiden who lived in the north of Durham County, in Ontario. She had been baptised Nancy Ann, and was religiously called Nancy Ann by her parents and all the neighbors. Poor young woman! her education had been sadly neglected; but she could wash dishes, feed hens and turkeys, ride a pony, rattle off simple airs on the rickety melodeon, and fashion Robinson Crusoe-looking garments for her father and her two brothers, with any girl in the township. She was not handsome, but even her brothers admitted that, in spite of her saffron face and her reddish hair, she was tolerably good-looking, especially when rigged out in gorgeous Sunday attire.

Her venerable father, who bore the high-sounding title of Patriarch Briggs, had an account of some thousands in the bank, besides a large and well-stocked farm. The farm was to fall to the boys, of course; but Nancy Ann's dowry would be a modest fortune for a person of her social position, and the stalwart young gallants of the neighborhood were not slow to find this out. The most favored suitor was a spare, chuckle-headed rustic, with yellow hair and green eyes, who sported a time-worn pipe, and doted on his shaggy mustache and on his huge, lazy, good-natured, good-for-nothing dog, Rollo. About the only inheritance this young man received from his parents was his name—Manfred Wallace Trampkowski. But this romantic name was sufficient inheritance, and it won Nancy Ann's susceptible heart.

When she found that this Manfred was poor, she resolved to marry him or no one. Manfred seemed to be quite as much in love with her, and there is this to prove he was: he was naturally absent-minded, and often when asked his name, would gravely answer, "Nancy Ann Briggs."

But Peter Briggs, Nancy Ann's elder brother, conceived a deadly hatred for Manfred, and persuaded himself that the fellow was a rascal, bent only on securing her money. He tried to poison his father against the swain; but the old man stolidly refused to be so poisoned. Patriarch shifted his quid from one side of his cavernous mouth to the other, a trick of his when about to lay down the law to his boys, and made answer:

"Peter, you jest let 'em alone. I tell you, Manfurd's a bully fellow to work—ask anybody 't ever hired him. He can haul more wood, and split more rails, and break more colts, and haul in more hay, 'n any man I 'most ever seen. Manfurd can always work for me, and Nancy Ann's goin' to marry who she likes, same's her mother did afore her. D' you hear?"

Then good brother Peter appealed to his mother, who sarcastically told him that he would do better to look out a wife for himself. But the good soul promised to remonstrate with Nancy Ann—which she did, to no purpose. The simple result was that Nancy Ann and Manfred Wallace continued their courtship without molestation, and brother Peter was not taken into their counsels.

But Peter was the more firmly convinced of Manfred's unworthiness; and he and Tom Sprague, a personable young farmer, resolved to depose him. The god of love had tampered with Tom's heart; he was dreadfully enamored of Nancy Ann. The persecutions of this pair of schemers soon became so intolerable that Nancy Ann and Manfred determined to elope. Tom got wind of this, and went to report to Peter. When Peter had digested the intelligence it occurred to him that by taking prompt and vigorous measures they might disconcert this scheme. Tom's woebegoneness excited his liveliest compassion, and presently a brilliant idea flashed through his mind.

"Tell you what it is, Tom," he said, "we'll hoodwink 'em! You'll help me, a course?"

"Course I will!" returned Tom, rolling his eyes wildly, and putting on a gorgon look. "What's the game, Pete?"

"You know, I s'pose, that that Trampkowski 's the biggest tomfool of a coward 't ever run away from a tramp?"

"Well, Pete, I reckon I know he is," Tom said heartily.

"Well, you and me 's kindy funny fellows; s'pose we play a trick on the rascal. We must do something to git even with him, anyhow. D' you ever hear tell of highwaymen, Tom, that swoop down onto lonely travellers, and make 'em fork over all their money and valuables? S'pose 't we fix up for highwaymen, and stop 'em as they're goin' off? It wonld serve 'em right, I reckon, for puttin' on style, and tryin' to run off in paw's old coach, eh, Tom?"

Tom darted Peter a look of rapturous delight. "Just the thing, old boy; but how'll you work it?"

"Lemme alone for that! I'll fix up for the highwayman, and swoop down onto 'em, and scare that great noodle into spasms. Jest 's he's so scart he's 'most dead, you come runnin' along to the rescue, like, and frighten me off, and rescue Nancy Ann. I'll have my own clothes on under the highwayman's, and I wun't run far 'fore I'll throw the highwayman's toggery off and come back to help you, and so's to make things look all right. Then we'll take Nancy Ann cryin' back to the house; then, if Manfurd ever dares show his face again, after makin' such a n'idjut of himself, I reckon we'll bundle him out s'm' other way. Then Nancy Ann 'll marry you, sure; women always do marry the fellow 't rescues 'em."

"Jest so; but what about the driver, Pete? They'll have a driver, of course; what if he turns to, and fights?"

"My stars, Tom! that wun't do! They'll have our Bill to drive 'em, sure; might recognize me 'f t'others didn't. Tom, I'll tell you. We'll git my brother Jim to step into Bill's place. Jim's jest the chap for it; Jim's a mighty lively boy; always up to some game."

"Well, will Jim pitch in and fight the highwayman, or what'll he do?"

"I'll have Jim git fearful scart, and unhitch the horses, and beg for mercy, and gallop off for home, leavin' the spooneys in the coach at the mercy of the highwayman. Then I'll scare Manfurd 'most to death. Wun't he just howl! Then you'll come rushin' along, and I'll make off in a jiffy."

"And so everybody 'll git scart, all around!" said Tom jocosely.

"Jes' so. Now, let's be off."

Manfred Wallace Trampkowski and Nancy Ann Briggs made every preparation to elope that very evening. They planned to slip away secretly, drive to the village of Ballyduff, and be married. After they had once been legally joined together, they could defy the petty persecutions of brother Peter and Tom Sprague.

12

Bill, the family Jack-of-all-trades, was to be their Jehu. But when the eventful hour came, he took "mighty sick" (the effect of a nauseous dose slipped into his drink by Peter); and Jim, who thrust himself in the way of the disconsolate lovers, was asked, in sheer desperation, if he should like a drive. Jim, a mercurial and monkeyish hobbledehoy, had been instructed beforehand, and he guessed he was always ready for a drive.

So the three stole out of the house, the dog Rollo at their heels. It was a beautiful starlight night, just such a night as a young couple would choose for an elopement. Manfred and Jim speedily harnessed a shuffling old nag to the "coach"—a family heir-loom, which had been rudely fashioned by Patriarch Briggs' father, half a century before.

"Got everythink you want, Nancy Ann, my dear?" Manfred asked tenderly.

"Yaas, Manfred. What a long and lonesome road it'll be to Mr. Parson York's. But then I'm all right with you to purtect me."

"Yaas, Nancy Ann; I'd fight for you through fire and water," said Manfred earnestly, blinking his heavy eyes prodigiously.

"Bet you wun't, you blatherin' liar!" chuckled Jim. "Bet you'll howl like a tom-cat with his tail froze off! And I'll gallop off a piece on paw's ol' bob-tail, and then sneak back and see the show! Ge dup, there, you old fool! G' 'long, I tell you!" and Jim, perched on the roof of the crazy vehicle, smacked his father's home-made whip, and away they rumbled at a round pace.

A long lane led from the Briggs homestead to the main road, which ran to the village. From the lane, near this main road, a by-road, that went no whither in particular, and was of no apparent use to the Briggses or to the township, took its start. Jim did not drive on to the main road leading to Ballyduff, but, according to instructions received from his brother Peter, turned down this by-road. He went rattling along, keeping up his spirits by whistling, bullying the nag, and calling out cheerily to Manfred's dog.

The lovers in the "coach" supposed, of course, that they were traveling along the direct road to the village, and philandered, as lovers will.

"Halt!" yelled a sepulchral voice. "Stand and deliver!"

A figure armed in Guy Fawkes attire sprang from behind a rail fence that skirted the road, strode towards them, and seized the horse by the bridle.

Jim bellowed a shriek that he had reserved for this occasion; but it savored strongly of a war-whoop of delight. "What's the matter?" he thundered, as though *he* were the highwayman.

"Oh, Manfred! what is that?" gasped Nancy Ann.

"I dunno—o—o," faltered Manfred, his pallor unperceived in the obscurity pervading the "coach," but his mortal fright betraying itself in his voice.

Peter and Tom had not misjudged Manfred; he was an arrant coward.

Then the hideous figure in Guy Fawkes costume presented a pistol and threatened to shoot the driver. But it whispered: "'Member what I told you, you jack—"

"It's robbers!" screamed Jim. "We've took the wrong road, and robbers is all around us! Manfurd! Help me!"

Then Manfred plucked up a grain of courage, thrust his head out at the window, and shrieked, "Drive on! We'll be killed 'f you don't!"

"I can't!" Jim shouted back. "He's caught the horse, and he's going to shoot!"

"Manfred, set on Rollo!" said Nancy Ann.

This was a woman's suggestion, but Manfred hastened to act upon it. "Sic 'em, Rollo! Sic 'em, the villains!" he shouted huskily.

Rollo, thinking there must be a squirrel somewhere about that he was called on to chase, ran snuffling and yelping up and down the road.

"Sic 'em, Rollo!" pleadingly.

But Rollo could not be induced to attack masquerading Peter, whose disguise he had at once penetrated, and he frisked about that worthy as though he had found a friend indeed.

"Stand and deliver!" thundered the highwayman.

"Oh, Manfred, th' dog's fascinated!" Nancy Ann ejaculated faintly. "Robber's bewitched him!"

"Drive on!" gasped Manfred.

"Want yer dog shot?" yelled the highwayman.

But Jim now scrambled down off the "coach," unharnessed the nag, and galloped away, making a tremendous clatter, so that Manfred and Nancy Ann should know, beyond all doubt, that he had deserted them, and that they were at the mercy of the highwayman.

The doughty robber, with fine effect, hallooed an execration after the fleeing driver, then flung open the door of the "coach," and again bellowed, his voice admirably disguised: "Stand and deliver!"

This stereotyped form of words was all, he believed, that the highwayman ever addresses to the unfortunates whom he waylays.

"Oh," groaned Manfred, "let us go! We ain't got nothink!"

"Liar!" screamed the outlaw. "Stand and deliver, or I fire!"

"I hain't a cent," protested Manfred.

The loyal brother cocked his pistol threateningly.

"*I* hain't. But," brightening, "*she* has," indicating Nancy Ann.

"Highwaymen don't take nothin' from ladies," said the robber, with lofty scorn. "But who is she? your sister?"

"She's goin' to be my wife; we was goin' to git married."

"Coward!" was the answer. "Coward! Ask your sweetheart to ransom you! Coward, do you know what highwaymen do with such fellows as you be?"

Then Nancy Ann swooned away. An ordinary young lady would have swooned away at the outset, but Nancy Ann was not an ordinary young lady.

"You've got a watch; I know you have; STAN DAN DELIVER!" bellowed the highwayman, at a loss to know how "chivalrous" brigands would deal with that sort of coward.

"'Tain't paid for yit, or you c'd have 't," Manfred gasped.

"Pretty fellow, t' sport a watch 't ain't paid for!" snorted the highwayman.

At that moment Nancy Ann revived, but Manfred did not perceive it, and goaded to desperation he blurted out that the watch would be paid for as soon as he got married.

At this candid statement the highwayman expressed intense scorn. "Stand an' deliver, or I fire!" he roared.

Unobserved, Jim now stole up in front of the "coach," and listened with all his ears. He had slidden off the horse when well out of sight, and turned it loose, knowing it would immediately pick its way back to the stables at home.

"I—I'll give you a hundred dollars soon 's I git married," said Manfred.

Springing lightly into the "coach," Peter despoiled the trembling coward of his watch, and tucked it away in his own pocket. Poor Manfred fetched a groan of agony, but offered no resistance.

A war-whoop was heard in the rear, and a solitary figure was descried, hurrying towards them at a round pace. It was Tom Sprague, on his way to the "rescue."

The highwayman started, clutched his pistol, and then said faintly, "My gracious! tain't loaded!"

Manfred instantly became as bold as a hero of romance. "Git out, you great villain!" he screamed. "I ain't afraid of you—never was! Here, sic 'em, Rollo!—Whoop, there! Come along!" to the rescuer.

The pretended highwayman flung Manfred his unpaid-for watch, saying, "'Tain't *you* I'm 'fraid of, but this brave young man comin';" and then nimbly took to his heels, chuckling gleefully: "Bigger fool 'n I thought! Coward 's scart 's a sick cat! Guess Nancy Ann 'll hate him, like poison; a course she will; women always do hate cowards. She was braver 'n Manfurd; only fainted;

but women always do faint. What bully fun, any how! Guess there ain't many brothers 'd do 's much for their sisters; and I guess paw and maw 'll give in I was right. Guess I know who 's fit for Nancy Ann to marry."

Hiding behind a tree, Peter stripped off his disguises, and making a detour, came up in his proper person, almost on the heels of Tom Sprague.

"Why, Nancy Ann, what's the matter?" Tom asked, with much concern.

"Oh, dear!" cried Nancy Ann. "Robbers was all around us."

"Why, Nancy Ann," piped up Brother Peter, in his natural voice; "why are *you* here? What has happened?"

"Robbers attackted us, and on'y just left us," explained Manfred.

"Oh, Tom! you drove 'em off! How good you are!" said Nancy Ann.

"Left 'cause we scart 'em off, I guess," Manfred said sulkily.

"And so Tom rescued you!" said Peter. "Well, I always knowed Tom wasn't afraid of nothing; 'bout the bravest fellow I 'most ever seen; no wonder the robber 'd slink away when he seen Tom comin' runnin'.—Well, Manfurd, what 'd you do to scare 'em?"

"I—I got 'em off just afore Tom come along," Manfred faltered.

"Well, Nancy Ann, folks at home 'll be fearful scart, you 'way off here at this time of night. You better go right home, or you'll ketch cold. Come on, Manfurd; you and me'll haul home paw's old hen-house; 't wouldn't do to leave it behind for th' robber.—Nancy

Ann, come dear; you and Tom can walk home jest in front; 'tain't far. Manfurd and me 's goin' to haul th' old wheelickull."

And Nancy Ann and Tom walked on in advance, Tom feeling that he had won the way to her heart at last.

"Nancy Ann," he said, "soon 's I can I'm off t' th' Black Hills, to—to make my fortune. Then I'm comin' back, rich as Vanderbilt. Then, Nan-n-cy—Ann-n—." But here the heroic Tom, the gallant rescuer, broke down, and could not articulate further.

Peter, full of jubilance, and Manfred, his bosom glowing with rage and bitterness, tugged away at the venerable " coach."

Apparently, Rollo did not like to see his master thus degraded, and he barked peevishly.

"Git out, sir," said Manfred snappishly, making a bootless attempt to kick the devoted creature.

Now, " sir," addressed to a dog by his master or any one else, is a term of reproach.

As the party neared the home of Patriarch Briggs, a gaunt and shadowy figure, trussed up in the identical garments in which Peter had arrayed himself when he played the highwayman, darted across the path ahead of them, apparently dodging to keep out of sight.

It was Jim, of course, masquerading for his own amusement in the costume which his big brother had discarded.

Rescued and rescuers saw him, and with an involuntary imprecation Peter betrayed himself.

" Good-for-nothin' noodle !" he muttered to himself. " Might 'a' knowed better 'n to let him help us !"

"Stop!" shouted Manfred, quitting his hold on the shafts of the "coach" and bounding after the boy. "Stop, will you, or I'll heave a stone!"

Jim did not stop, but redoubled his speed. But Manfred soon overhauled him, wound his arms around him, and bore him struggling back to the others.

"Same rig 's th' robber had!" Manfred panted. "What —what--"

Jim—though fast in the clutches of Manfred, though fearing terrible retribution from his brother and Tom Sprague—burst into a derisive laugh.

"Nancy Ann," said Manfred, "we've been fooled! Th' robber was some of these fellers, sure 's guns!—What d' you mean?" shaking Jim. "What 've you t' say for yourself?"

"S'pose I wanted them clothes to git lost?" Jim demanded indignantly. "S'pose I wanted to lose that there mask?"

"So; jes' 's I thought!" said Manfred. "Pack o' knaves!"

"Yes; and a nice coward *you* was, wasn't you!" sneered Peter.

"So you're a thief, are you, Pete Briggs? Or was it you, Tom Sprague?"

"I never stole nothin'!" protested Peter. "I give back your watch."

"Oh, Nancy Ann!"

"Oh, Manfred! Manfred!"

"Sister," said Peter earnestly, "don't go and fall in love with such a coward again. Oh, Nancy Ann, here 's Tom, that loves—"

"Tom? I hate him—and you, too!" flashed back Nancy Ann.

Tom Sprague sold his farm, and took to braking on the Grand Trunk—for Nancy Ann married Manfred Wallace. The good brother Peter did not grace the wedding with his presence, perhaps because he was not invited; but Jim got a goodly hunk of wedding cake—which he did not deserve.

Love-lorn maidens sometimes envy the heroines of romance their paragon husbands; but surely none will be so foolish as to envy Nancy Ann her husband.

A TRIP TO WASHINGTON.

NOT A HONEYMOON TRIP.

THE man who goes on an early morning journey and, with an easy indifference, puts off getting his baggage down to the station till the eleventh hour, is at the mercy of the expressman whom he has engaged to call for it. The fact that this expressman, instead of making a note of his patron's address simply ties a piece of grimy cotton string around his little finger, is apt to bring disquieting dreams to the intending traveler and to prove as effective as an alarm-clock in rousing him up at an unseasonable hour.

But the expressman was on hand an hour before the boat was timed to start—for it was a boat, not a train, that I was to leave on, and the preceding paragraph is in so far misleading.

"That boat starts sharp at seven," he said, half-apologetically, "and it is six now."

But he magnanimously allowed me ten minutes to eat my breakfast and to get the landlady's dog shut up. It was his vigorous assault on the door-bell that had roused the dog and induced it to spring headlong out of the window, at the imminent risk of running foul of the dog-catcher. But he was apparently used to that sort of thing, and did not pause ten minutes on that account. "I always allow fifteen minutes over-time," he said, after we had got off, "because somebody is bound for to hender me." I said I wished he had told me sooner about allowing a fifteen minutes' reprieve, as I should have felt justified in asking for something more substantial for breakfast than a raw omelet and some cold oatmeal.

As we drove along the wharf (for I accompanied him) he uttered an emphatic exclamation of disgust on seeing a brother expressman drawn up alongside the steamer, ahead of him. So, it was evidently his ambition to get down to the boats ahead of all comers. I could have approved of this sort of thing much better if I had had a more staying breakfast.

But at last I was on board, bag and baggage. This consisted of a square-sized trunk (capacity 250 cwt., tare 40 lbs.), that had always proved a favorite with expressmen and railway porters, as it was portable, easy to get a good grip on, and, on account of its square shape, would admit of other trunks being flung on top of it without danger of their rolling off. Besides this I had a "small wheel-chair," as I called it, and an invalid tricycle. The size of the "small wheel-chair" almost assumed large proportions to the astonished porter, when he nonchalantly took it with one hand, only to brace himself and grasp hold with both hands; while the tricycle was 42 inches wide, six feet long, and stood four feet high in its stocking feet. As the classical young man from Smith Crik Bridge observed to me, I had a "not inconsiderable quantity of impedimenta" to look after; and I was mean enough to envy the old lady who was only burdened with an occupied parrot-cage, a pet dog in a blanket suit, six or seven venturesome nephews and nieces (mostly boys and tomboys), scattered about the upper and the lower decks, and a valise, that was not burglar-proof, amidships.

A whole-souled passenger, who seemed to have no

baggage whatever to bother about, except a generous load of stimulants, already aboard him, took a most friendly interest in me—so far even as to agree with me in politics, claiming first to be a Cleveland man, from a chance remark of mine, and then a Harrison man, when I commended the course of a member of the President's cabinet. I then artlessly told him that I was a Canadian, to the twelfth generation; and he promptly ordered me up a glass of iced lemonade, and informed me that the Free Soil party would sweep the country in 1900.

Soon I was joined by an affable young Philadelphia tourist, who had come over on an excursion which allowed him only a night's stop-over at Toronto. He had seen nothing, and was badly in need of being posted, as there was a blank of three pages in his note-book for the city of Toronto, which must be filled, somehow. So I posted him, and he posted his note-book. Bearing in mind the thought that I was likely to run across the Washington liar in my wanderings, I was careful to keep within the truth in my information. But we were interrupted by a fresh young man, who knew me, but whom I had forgotten; and I am sorry to say that he wandered straight away from the beautiful truth in everything he said. But he generously left me his card on parting. It was unique in its way, and not adapted to the ordinary card-case. To be brief, it was a sheet of blotting paper, considerably smaller than a leaf from a minute book, with his name in two-inch capitals, his house and office address, his telephone number, and a pointed intimation of his business. He said schoolchildren often struck him for his cards, and I said that children and the unoffending public generally know a good thing when they see it. He couldn't make out what I meant, but as he turned to go wondering away I saw that his left breast pocket hung heavy, and that it was crammed full of his schoolchildren-alluring cards.

It was a fast boat, and soon brought us all to Niagara, where some of us changed from boat to train. The interval was not a long one, and was profitably spent in listening to a telephone conversation between a customs officer and a railway man about a horse deal and a deferred fishing excursion. Their language was good.

The run from Niagara to Buffalo by the Michigan Central was a remarkably pleasant one, enjoyed by all the passengers except one nervous old gentleman, who insisted that we must all change cars before we could possibly get into Buffalo. The fact that the train kept right on and that the good-humored conductor gave his affidavit that it was all right made no difference to the old gentleman, and it was all they could do to keep him from getting off at every stopping-place. At Falls View all the passengers but this excitable party and myself seemed to get off, helter-skelter, to run down the sidewalk and gaze at the Falls. Suddenly it struck him that this must be the place to change cars, and he turned appealingly to me. "No," I said, "these people have got off to see the Falls."—"Fine sight," he said. "Is—is it—the—Niagara Falls?"—"Yes," I told him, "I expect it is." —"Well, well!" he ejaculated. "I never saw them before!"—I believed him. I also believed that he, too, was from Smith Crik Bridge, and that in his guileless innocence he imagined that before he got into Buffalo the train was likely to run alongside of several cataracts, and that if he should travel for two or three days he would run across no end of falls like Niagara. But I felt sorry when I learned that he was a very sick man, going to a quack doctor's institution in Buffalo.

It was a long wait at the Erie station, from 12.15 till 5.30, so I went about a little, looking at the trains and talking to the train-men, as is my wont. I knew I could not see much of Buffalo, and so did not try to see anything. This was not sensible, but it was restful. I had vague doubts as to how the Erie and the Lehigh baggagemen would receive all my stuff, although I had a written order to show them, and so made haste to interview them. The Lehigh Valley baggageman, I learned, was the only one I had to deal with, and I found him to be the most whole-souled railway man I ever ran across, and the most genial to talk to. He and I had a long chat together, and he informed me that he had been on the road, in his present capacity, for thirteen years, and I informed him that I had never traveled above seven or eight hundred miles in my life. He did not despise me for this, but helped me aboard the train himself, put me in the through car for Philadelphia, on the side to get the best view of Portage Falls; and then got my machine and "small wheel-chair" into the baggage car. I was traveling alone, and, as he must have seen, eager to talk to entire strangers, when opportunity offered, so he came back to me for another chat. He blamed me for not coming down in daylight, so that I could see something of the picturesque Lehigh Valley scenery. "Why," he said, "you won't see anything; you won't see how they climb the mountain; it will be dark before we get to Hornellsville. But you must come back in broad daylight." He left the train at Elmira, and I never saw him again. I explained to no one that it wasn't a question of seeing scenery with me, but of getting into Philadelphia in broad daylight.

I didn't make any special effort to go to sleep, as I did wish to see what there might be to be seen, even if it was only the blank nothingness of midnight. But at all hours of the night, wherever the train stopped, passengers were getting on and off. Once in a while I caught glimpses of the river, when the glare from the head-light was reflected on it, and could always tell when we were crossing a bridge. These things were a great consolation to me--till I raised the window to get the midnight air, and then couldn't get it down again. However, at every station and every switch I could the better see the pretty and effective-looking white caps of the trainmen. Once I accosted a switchman with the intelligence that it was a fine night. He looked up at me in evident astonishment, and said, rather plaintively, but with the characteristic indifference of switchmen: "It's raining." When we got fairly down into the coal region the skies, for miles, seemed all ablaze. It was the reflection from the great furnaces, and I congratulated myself that I knew it without having to ask the conductor. There was nothing to mar my enjoyment of this lonely run except the gurgling noise from a tired boy who was just learning how to snore. I am afraid it will take him three or four years of patient practice to get the art of snoring down fine, but in another six months he will be able to count his enemies, if he travels much by night, as Samson counted his slain Philistines, by thousands.

Morning came when the sun rose, naturally. It was raining, surely enough. But I was now able to amuse myself by looking at the toy engines and cars, as I styled them, of the Lehigh Valley Co. Soon two young men appeared in my car from another car. They were good-natured young fellows, and very talkative. They had traveled a great deal, and considerably farther this trip than I had, and were also a great deal hungrier than I was. We took the Reading road at Bethlehem, and at every stopping-point thereafter the two young men would get off with the determination to get something to eat. But they would barely get on the station platform when the train was off again, and they would come back, hungrier than ever, but always good-humored. "It seems funny," one of them said, "to get into Buffalo and see the horse-cars everywhere." I thought it would seem funnier still to him when he got into the great city of Philadelphia and found the same thing.

As we were getting into the city limits an elderly man in his shirt sleeves of linsey-woolsey dropped down beside me to give me the cheering news that we should soon be there; and finding out that he was a New Jersey farmer, as I had half suspected, I at once, and with a recklessness that disarmed him, brought up the subject of his native mosquito. "Is it true," I asked, "that the mosquitoes are as bad over in Jersey as the funny men in the newspapers make them out to be?"—"Naw;" he said, wiping some P. & R. coal dust off his red, honest face, "naw; we hain't seen any this summer." Then I let him talk, as I found he could talk a good deal more sensibly than I could.

At 7:04, sharp on time, the train drew into the station at 9th and Green Sts., and I haven't the slightest doubt that the hungry young men got something to eat. The imposing array of the trains of the Reading Co., together with the rain, kept me about the depot for some little time. At last the rain compromised with me, that is, it slackened up till I got away up Green-street, and then it began all over again.

It amused me to see two stalwart Philadelphia policemen stop a street-car and an omnibus to enable me to cross a crowded thoroughfare on my machine, for, though the same thing has been done elsewhere, my thoughts always drift back to a bright June day when a COUNCILMAN of a country village stopped his horse and buggy directly over a cross-road on seeing me coming, effectually barring my way. This COUNCILMAN stopped ostensibly to examine a dilapidated bridge. He also stopped to impress me with his authority. I waited a minute while he stalked leisurely about, then said, "Would you kindly drive the horse forward a little, so that I may pass." The COUNCILMAN did nothing, but a *man* who chanced along promptly lead the horse out of the highway, while the aggrieved COUNCILMAN muttered, "If time is precious to you."—"If what?" I asked flippantly, and he repeated his remark, when I replied, "I must get past, that's all." Yes, that was all; but I have always wondered which of us enjoyed that scene most, he, in stopping me, or I, in being stopped.

The next day I went down to the Broad-street station, to get off to Bryn Mawr. Here the "special messenger" of the Pennsylvania fixed things for me, and I had no trouble. The return fare is fifty-one cents. "This is one dollar," said the special messenger, as I handed him a bill. Then he brought me my ticket, with the watchword: "Count your change. Come this way." And he saw me safe up the baggage elevator, on my machine, and pointed out the Bryn Mawr accomodation, when he disappeared like a flash, to waylay some other troubled traveler. The ten-mile run over the Pennsylvania's perfect road-bed was all too short. But it looked like more rain, and I got off the train and hurried away. I was afraid I might not find the humorist at home, after all. But the quick step and the genial, "How are you, Bruce!" re-assured me, for I knew it was the humorist himself.

* * * * *

I had to wait on the platform at Bryn Mawr about ten minutes, when I could get back on the same train I had come out on. I had told the conductor I should "lay for" him again, and he had smiled feebly, whether at the slip-shod slang or at the unparalleled compliment thus paid him I don't know. While waiting, the magnificent "Pennsylvania Limited" flashed past, and a thrill of enthusiasm shot through me. "She hasn't stopped since she left Harrisburg!" I cried, and a by-stander looked at me pityingly and said, "Oh, yes, she has!"—"Isn't that the Limited, from Chicago?" I appealed of a train hand, and he corroborated me. "But it will have stopped at Lancaster," insisted the by-stander.—"Only at divisions," said the train hand; and the by-stander turned huffishly away, outraged that a total stranger on the station platform at Bryn Mawr should know (or pretend to know) more about the Pennsylvania Railroad than a native Philadelphian. And I went back, and still it rained.

The next day found me again at the Broad-street station, bound, at last, for Washington. The "special messenger" was on hand, and again got my ticket and relieved me of all worry, though this time the chair and the trunk were to go, if the Union Transfer Co. could get them down in time—which they did not. So I left on the 11:18 train, with my checks, and the baggage came on later. The conductor on this train was particularly obliging, and lighted up when we came to the long tunnels through Baltimore. I don't suppose he lighted up on my account, however. But he was kind. The train was not a "flier," but at last the Capitol loomed in sight, and soon we got sidewalk glimpses of the Washington Negro, and then rolled into the B. & P. depot, where President Garfield was shot. This noble man will always be remembered and venerated.

The next thing I knew I was inquiring the way, for the obliquely-crossing avenues confused me—the more so, as I didn't know one street from another, anyway. "Better keep on the con'crete, sah, or the officers mightn't like it," advised a colored brother; and I concluded to do so. But what avenues, what streets, and what pavements! Washington is famous for its magnificent thoroughfares and its perfect pavements. Away up Capitol Hill I went, to B. street South East, where I got good accommodation. This was not so much due to newspaper advertisements as to the inquisitive, but thoroughly obliging, small boy, who directed me to such good purpose that I found lodgings with his parents. But I felt at home with them at once, and was very comfortable. Lest I should forget it, I will pause here to speak a good word for the frank and courteous citizens of the American capital, whose democratic simplicity is a reality, not a sham.

The next day I went into Virginia—at least, I went down through Georgetown and crossed the Potomac bridge. I anticipated seeing negro women carrying baskets on their heads, and I was not disappointed. Perhaps I might have been disappointed any other day. And I also saw the venerable old negro of tradition, driving a steer tackled to an equally venerable cart, that was six feet wide. I will say it was six feet, but I could just as easily say it was seven, and not grieve my conscience a bit. I was looking for this old negro—and he must have been looking for me, for he said good day to me and looked pleased to see me.

Just after crossing the bridge a small boy came up to me and said, mysteriously: " Mister, you ain't allowed to go on this sidewalk. Kin you give me a cent ?" I said, "I have nothing but a bill; you wouldn't want that, would you?" Then he took the road and I kept the sidewalk. Georgetown is a quiet place, and most of the inhabitants are content to claim a population of only 20,000. It is, like Washington, under District Government. The old Chesapeake and Ohio Canal, unlike the old negro, had got tired of waiting for me, and had practically given up the ghost.

I lost no time in seeing the editor. He was not so formidable a personage, after all. In fact, I thought his cigar seemed more suggestive of danger than he did; and I am glad to say I had no cause to be afraid of him, and of course he wouldn't acknowledge whether he was afraid of me or not.

How pleasant it was to bowl along Pennsylvania Avenue and to wander about the Capitol grounds! The gleaming white shaft of the Washington monument, seen from almost every point, impresses itself as a landmark upon the memory of every visitor. It is an inspiring object, especially when seen from the Capitol. One day I went up the broken sidewalk to the very base of the monument, and took a good long look at the elevator.

The daily stream of visitors is enormous. They see everything, partly because everything is free, and partly because they must give a satisfactory account of the city when they return home. Washington has public squares and little parks everywhere. In these there are always fountains, and negroes, and locusts. The water is usually "hydrant water," and consequently warm in summer; the negroes are always talkative and in a happy frame of mind; and the locusts are always able to sing their old songs. If there is cosmopolitan life to be found anywhere, it is here, for here are typical representatives of all States and all countries. And they are all good-natured, and proud of the beautiful city, and not a bit restless under the mild rule of Washington's 300 po'licemen.

Yes, everything is free—except house-rent—and all officials are obliging. They take a pardonable pride in showing you through the city's magnificent public buildings, and are determined you shall leave with a good opinion of the "National Capital." As was remarked to me many times: "Every one who comes to Washington likes the city, in spite of himself." The citizens are proud of their institutions, and Uncle Sam's Government is extremely popular. They have no mayor or aldermen to vote for, and no vote at Presidential elections. Consequently, there is no pandering to voters, and the citizens have their time to devote to their business. All the same, the keenest interest is felt in Presidential contests. But here is manifestly a system that would not suit some ambitious cities, whose citizens would relapse into barbarism, if it were not for their annual aldermanic elections.

The White House and grounds are always open to the public, and I frequently turned in at the great gates on Pennsylvania Avenue, which stand wide open. There is one notice only, over the driving stables, which reads, "Private Entrance." Otherwise, some eager visitor from Coal Oil Junction might be determined to find out how the horses are shod, and so get his wisdom teeth knocked where they would be safest—down his throat.

It was no joke for me to climb the steep grade of Capitol Hill, but there was always some one to give me a push up it. I usually halted by the imposing Garfield monument—not to look out for possible assistance, but to admire the monument. At least, I am sure it always had that appearance. A ragged little urchin told me the first day the significance of the allegorical figures at the base of the monument, its cost, and other particulars. I said nothing, but humbly reflected that if my gamin informant had been a Canadian boy, he would have been well posted in the best localities to look for cigar stubs, but would have looked with greater interest upon circus posters and bonfires than he would have given to monuments. In Washington even the street urchin reads the newspapers he sells, and has a sense of genuine patriotism. One day I encountered, midway up the grade, a spick and span little buggy, drawn by a team of well-trained goats. I have seen goat teams before, but I never saw clean and civilized-looking goats before. Everybody admired the turnout, especially a Maryland farmer (all the same, he may have been a Government employee), who halted, and observed to me, "Isn't that a dahling team!" I expect he halted because he reflected that it was not every day he could enjoy the spectacle of such a team as the boy's, and such a rig as mine. But I reflected that the Canadian farmer has not yet been born (though one could wish otherwise) who would cheerfully use such an expression as, "Isn't that a dahling team!"

My first day out I went down to the navy yard, where the young marines kindly insisted on showing me everything. As a matter of fact, there wasn't much for me to see, except a big gun, nearly completed. I always liked to see the marines on the street, in their smart attire, and with their careless, janty air. They always looked to be in fighting trim, too. But once I got badly fooled. Seeing a negro in what seemed to be a *negligé* sailor costume, I asked him if he was a U.S. marine. He grinned all over, and said: "No, sah; but I am often mistaken for one. I don't wear no coat, but these heah shirts are made to ordah." "They cost you a dollah and a half apiece, don't they, Jim?" suggested a companion of his. "Three dollahs a pair," corrected Jim, with a bland smile. On my way back from the navy yard, I paused to rest under a grocery awning, and overheard the grocer and an idler discussing the Behring Sea troubles. For the sake of springing a feeble joke on them, I listened attentively, occasionally putting in my oar. When the question was thoroughly discussed, they became the more interested in me, and I said, as I turned to go, "I am a Canadian, and I have just been down inspecting your navy yard." I had expected to see a look of surprise steal over their faces. I saw a good deal more, but kept right on, without pausing to guess exactly what their looks indicated.

Sunday in Washington I spent indoors, on account of a broken tire. I did enjoy looking out of the window at the church-goers and passers-by. Street cars going all day long, and boys boarding them to sell the papers. Apparently, these boys would sometimes innocently accost a clergyman. The negro church-goers, from my locality, seemed most numerous. The only pathetic sight I saw on this Sunday was a little boy of eight or nine years, with his hair hanging down his back in long, straggling curls, and with a bright red sash about his waist. I had noticed the same boy on Saturday, when his hair was braided and negligently hairpinned to his crown; and then, as now, he bravely ignored the whispered jests of other boys, whose parents had them patronize the æsthetic Washington barbers. It was a spectacle to bring tears to one's eyes—a cheap edition of the little lord.

"Which way are you going now?" cried out a friendly voice to me, and I recognized a gentleman of whom I had previously made inquiries. I replied that I thought of going down into Alexandria. "Oh, don't take such a trip as that, where there is nothing you would care to see. Go along New Hampshire Avenue, and take a look at the extravagant mansions there. It is the most aristocratic part of Washington." Presently I concluded to do so, getting a wayfarer to point out to me Secretary Blaine's splendid house, and the building occupied by the Chinese legation. I also had the good fortune to see the Japanese minister and his suite; and I smiled to think how prone we are to judge foreigners by the worst representatives of their nationality, instead of by the best. Canadians would not like to be judged by their fugitive and outcast classes.

I wandered about the Botanical Gardens (very often in quest of a drink of cold water), and spent a good deal of time at the Smithsonian Institute. "Are you from French Canada, or English Canada?" asked a kindly old guard, to whom I had revealed my nationality, thus demonstrating to me that he knew all about my country.

When Friday came around again, it occurred to me that I was getting homesick; so I put a new label on the trunk, and went down to the ticket office. If I had got up fifteen minutes earlier, I could have 'patronized' the Northern Central, the direct route to Suspension Bridge; but, as it was, I decided to inflict myself upon the B. & O. people to Philadelphia, and thence home as I had come. It was only fair play to give all the railroads a show, anyway. The scalpers had nothing up my way, but they expressed their regret, and never once intimated that they took me for a boodler, fleeing to Canada. I have no reason to suppose they did.

It was a magnificent train that pulled out from the foot of Capitol Hill at 4.20 p.m., and we ran to Baltimore without a halt. But shortly after leaving Baltimore the engine broke down, and we were detained more than an hour. Other trains were flagged, of course, but there was an element of danger in the situation that made the waiting time quite interesting. The passengers got off the train in large numbers, and then would pound vigorously on the vestibule doors for admittance—to the great annoyance of the trainmen. One young man climbed down the steep embankment we were on, and gathered a handful of mayweed. With this he returned to the train, crying, "Marguèrites, marguèrites, only fi' cent a bunch." But even this failed to rouse one indifferent passenger, who showed his contempt for railway accidents by falling asleep in his seat. At last the engine was in a fit condition to back the train up to a siding, where another engine was in waiting, and we were off again. The conductor agreed to telegraph ahead to find out whether the Buffalo train could be held. This was doubtful; and I journeyed on through the rain (for it naturally began to rain as we drew near Philadelphia) with the prospect of a "lay over" of twelve hours in the Quaker City.

We got in an hour and twenty minutes late. Immediately a man boarded my car, saying, in an audible voice: "Passengers *via* Lehigh Valley will please change cars, as there is no through connection to-night;" and I knew the "lay over" was inevitable. So I intrusted him with the secret that I had a machine on board, and he kindly set about getting me off. In a short time he, the conductor, the train porter, the brakeman, a policeman, and the big, good-natured station master had me aboard my machine, and I was glad, because I knew that some one of them would be able to tell me where I could get something to eat. However, I spent some little time perusing the inscriptions on the trains, while good-natured Charley Selby, the colored station porter, went out and got me a substantial supper, as the station restaurant was then closed.

Early next morning I went up to Wayne Junction, from the B. & O. station, and had another wait, of nearly two hours. Of course it was raining. There are trains passing here till you can't rest; and the gigantic, odd-built engines of the Reading company are a treat to look at. I wasn't yet wearied when the baggageman called to me, "Bethlehem train, sir! Come this way!" And I was off, on the morning train, with the opportunity of seeing some of the finest scenery in the world, in spite of fate. I declined the trainboy's exciting romances, and even felt no interest in looking up the daily railroad accidents in the newspapers, because I knew I could at least get an unsatisfactory glimpse of Solomon's Gap, Mauch Chunk, the valley of the Wyoming, and the winding Lehigh.

A young man had kindly given up his seat to me, but I was not comfortably settled for so long a ride, and at Bethlehem the conductors (for there seemed to be no end of them) kindly put me into the smoking compartment of the parlor car. Here there were seats for only six, and never more than four in at once, and there was absolutely nothing to mar one's enjoyment of the journey. All the rest of the way I looked out of the window, and I am sure I saw more than most people on that train. "Now," I argued, "if there are not more than seventeen freight cars on the sidings at Mauch Chunk, I shall be able to see something." I am sorry to say that there must have been more than a hundred, scattered about in the most tantalizing way to cut off the view. But it looked just as bad over on the Jersey Central tracks. We played at hide and seek with this latter railroad all the way up to Wilkesbarre, and it was amusing to watch their trains. At Glen Summit we had climbed the mountain, and there, at an elevation of some 2,000 feet, most of the passengers took dinner, in a spacious frame hotel. This is scarcely an adequate description, so I will add that the situation is delightfully romantic.

At Wilkesbarre the smoking compartment was entered by a distinguished party, in the person of two English noblemen, from the Black Country, who may have known more about the topography of Egypt and Farther India than most of us will ever wish to know, but who were all at sea the moment they had crossed the Atlantic. They were over "doing" the mines, and now on their way to Niagara. We flew past ten or twelve stations before they would converse with any one but themselves; but their reserve was broken at last, and all the rest of the way they proved genial enough to have satisfied even a typical Western plainsman. They picked up a vast deal of information, from one source and another, on that trip, because no absurd fear of displaying their ignorance restrained them from asking pertinent questions; and in all cases of doubt appeal was made to the pullman conductor for corroboration or disproof. "Oh," said one of them, as we were running from Sayre, Pa., to Waverly, N. Y., (a distance of two miles), "Oh, there is New York City and New York State!" Yet no one could laugh at such remarks, because they were made so artlessly. Said another, "When it is five o'clock with you, it is ten o'clock in England."—"Yes; and only two o'clock on the Pacific coast." They were so much impressed with the vastness of the country, just from one day's ride, that they were advised to take a six day's journey across the continent. Such practical suggestions as these give foreigners at least a vague notion of our country.

There was a giant on our train, who got off at Hornellsville for his supper, and frightened the depot policeman into a burst of unprofessional laughter. The giant stood seven feet high, and was perfectly proportioned; and the blinds of the dining-hall had to be lowered to keep the vulgar eye from spoiling the giant's appetite.

There was a lively American from Newark in the smoking compartment, who was determined that the English lords should see everything, and be posted in everything. He got them out on the platform when the train slowed over Portage bridge, where they amused all the passengers by one of them jocosely asking for his friend's accident insurance policy. This refreshing witticism, coming from an Englishman, was the funniest incident of the trip. The story told by the American gentleman about the Switch Back was the best story; but probably it is well known. The English noblemen, however, paid most attention to his instructions to them how to find Main-street, Buffalo, from the Erie depot, and the best place thereon to get a bracing drink of something that would enable them to enjoy a midnight glimpse of Niagara Falls.

It was not a highly satisfactory view of the Falls and surroundings that we got crossing the river. Even the Cantilever did not show up to good advantage. I was alone at this time, and had an enjoyable talk with the through conductor of the Lehigh. His run was completed at Niagara Falls station, on the Canadian side, and here he kindly brought me my machine. Conductors do not usually express regret on parting with me, but I inquired the days on which this gentleman makes his return, or eastern, trips, and proposed to come down with him when I revisit Washington—and he heard me through without flinching. I could not but admire such courage. And so we parted, in the expectation of meeting again. I had looked for my friend the baggageman at Elmira, but saw nothing of him. I neglected to inquire on what trains he makes his runs; but am satisfied he would have come in to see me, had he been on our train. My machine would have given me away, of course.

I got off a few ill-timed jokes (for it was midnight) with the customs officer and the station policeman, and was informed that I could have a choice of staying over at the Bridge or at Hamilton, as the next day being Sunday, there was but one train, in the evening, from Hamilton to Toronto. Another "lay over," this time of about twenty hours, was before me. All this was attributable to the collapse of the engine on the picturesque B. & O. However, as they afterwards gave me to understand, they could not guarantee to run on their own time. As for the delay of twenty hours in getting from the Bridge to Toronto, that is a scheme of Toronto and Montreal philanthropists, to enable belated travelers to do the Falls or Hamilton's Mountain (capital M.) on Sunday, when expenses are lighter.

I at once decided to forego the unique attractions of the Ambitious City (with which I was familiar) for a ramble next day about the Falls, as it seemed my destiny to have an opportunity to see everything. Soon I was greeted by a cheery voice, and recognized the young man with whom I had sat on leaving Wayne Junction. He was far from traveling alone, as I was, for he was one of a party of seven, bound for Minneapolis. They all crowded about me, with the *esprit de corps* of fellow-travelers. Besides, it was my country now that we were all in. "This is the young man who gave up his seat to you, and this is the one whom you asked if the car you were in ran through to Suspension Bridge." And so on. A hand shake, and they were all aboard the through Grand Trunk train for Chicago. The English lords did not cross the Bridge, and expressed no desire to visit Canada. I hope I was in no way responsible for this!

Unwashed, and even *sans* breakfast, I made an early morning start for the Falls. Perhaps I was as clean as (and J hope I was no hungrier than) the few people astir at that early hour. I had bargained on being able to enjoy the sublime spectacle with no one about to dictate to me, or say, "Look from this point, or gaze at that projecting rock;" and I was not disappointed. In a word, the Niagara Falls liar and the impromptu poet were *non est*, and the solitude of the early morning hour was a fitting time to see the Falls. I knew from my sharp appetite that I should *seem* to be getting the worth of my breakfast, when I got back; and again I was not disappointed. I crossed the bridge in the afternoon, and looked about on the American side. A party of Scandanavian emigrants, bound for Minnesota, who came in, were too much worn out even to look at the Falls; and I could sympathize with them. But perhaps they did not know they were in that part of the country, or realize they were enjoying the privilege of being, for a time, on Canadian soil! Some of us go through the world as in a dream.

It was an eventful ride to Hamilton. At least, I thought so; but as I had not been able to get any sleep since awakening Friday morning, I was not in the humor, perhaps, to take in the scenic attractions by the way. I got aboard the train there as soon as it was made up. Two others came in shortly afterwards, and in a friendly spirit I warned them that the train did not pull out for an hour and a half. One of them, an American, answered me that he always made it a rule not to keep railway trains waiting for *him*. And we laughed, and were good friends. The other got off at Burlington; and I marveled that he hadn't walked to save time, for we were half an hour late in starting. Two cowboys who came in made things very lively. They claimed to hail from Leadville; but just why cowboys should claim Leadville as their headquarters was something I couldn't make out; so I gave it up.

At Toronto an obliging brakeman took me, and I took his lantern; and so I wound up my trip. I said to him, "I have come all the way from Washington, and have fared as well at your hands as at any person's." Singularly enough, he didn't ask me to go into particulars, but took the checks for my machine, which he had brought me, and seeing me all aboard, made off with his lantern. Then I started for home, wondering if I was not too tired to get there, and not pausing to inquire of a church-comer, whom I knew, how much Toronto had gained in population in the ten days I had been away.

This last sketch was written at the instigation of a misguided friend, who advised me to write something openly about myself, in a frank, desultory way, without jejune clap-trap or any hidebound feeling about egotism. Said friend has been jailed, and such advice will hardly be given me again—but if it should be, I will promise not to heed it.

THE END.

www.ingramcontent.com/pod-product-compliance
Lightning Source LLC
Chambersburg PA
CBHW032013220426
43664CB00006B/227